HOW THE SPECTER OF COMMUNISM IS RULING OUR WORLD

FIRST EDITION

PUBLISHED BY

THE EPOCH TIMES

229 W 28TH ST, 7TH FLOOR

NEW YORK, NY 10001

PRINTED BY

EPOCH PRESS, INC.

7 HIGHPOINT DRIVE

WAYNE, NJ 07470

ISBN 978-1-947150-10-2

How The

SPECTER OF COMMUNISM IS RULING OUR WORLD

From The
Editorial Board of
"NINE COMMENTARIES ON
THE COMMUNIST PARTY"

VOLUME III

An Epoch Times Special Publication

VOLUME III

Table of Contents

The specter of communism did not disappear with the disintegration of the Communist Party in Eastern Europe

Preface

THOUGH THE COMMUNIST REGIMES of Eastern Europe have disintegrated, the specter of communism has not disappeared. On the contrary, this evil specter is already ruling our world, and humanity must not harbor a mistaken sense of optimism.

Communism is neither a trend of thought, nor a doctrine, nor a failed attempt at a new way of ordering human affairs. Instead, it should be understood as a devil — an evil specter forged by hate, degeneracy, and other elemental forces in the universe.

In another dimension, not visible to us, it took the form of a serpent, then that of a red dragon, and it keeps company with Satan, who hates God. It exploits low-level beings and demons to wreak havoc on humankind. The goal of the specter is to ruin humanity. While the divine offers salvation, communism tells people not to believe in the divine, attacks human morality so as to make people abandon tradition, and causes people to disregard the divine's instruction and, ultimately, to be destroyed.

The communist evil specter, with its countless mutations,

is full of guile. Sometimes it uses slaughter and violence to destroy those who refuse to follow it. Other times, it takes recourse in the language of "science" and "progress," offering a wonderful blueprint of the future in order to deceive people. Sometimes it presents itself as a profound field of learning and makes people believe that it is the future direction of mankind. Other times, it uses the slogans of "democracy," "equality," and "social justice" to infiltrate the fields of education, media, art, and law, bringing people under its banner without their awareness. At yet other times, it calls itself "socialism," "progressivism," "liberalism," "neo-Marxism," and other leftist terms.

Sometimes it holds up seemingly righteous banners such as pacifism, environmentalism, globalism, and political correctness. Other times, it supports vanguard art, sexual liberation, legalization of drugs, homosexuality, and other indulgences in human desires, giving the mistaken impression that it's part of a popular trend.

Extremism and violence aren't its only expressions — sometimes it pretends to care for the welfare of society. Yet its root purpose is to destroy, by whatever means, everything that is traditional, whether it be faith, religion, morality, culture, the institution of the family, art, pedagogy, law — whatever it takes to have man fall into a moral abyss and be damned.

Communism and its various mutations are now found around the world. China and Cuba publicly proclaim themselves to be led by communist regimes. Even the United States — the leader of the free world — has fallen prey to attacks by the evil specter. Europe embraces socialism, and Africa and Latin America are enveloped in communist influence. This is the startling reality humankind now faces: The evil specter's conspiracy to destroy humankind has almost succeeded.

Humans instinctively desire to benefit themselves and flee from danger. Instinct urges them to escape from suffering, to make a name for themselves, to establish prosperous enterprises, or merely to enjoy life. It is human to have these thoughts. However, if humans distance themselves from the divine, the evil specter can latch onto and intensify these thoughts to control people.

The hubris of the specter's revolt against divinity also makes those it controls experience a sense of hubris. These individuals then try to play God through the exercise of power, capital, and knowledge, with the aim of ruling the fates of millions and influencing the course of history through social movements.

Humans are created by the divine and have both good and evil in their nature. If people abandon evil and choose compassion, they can return to the divine. What awaits on the opposite side is evil personified — the devil. The choice resides solely with the individual.

Many fundamentally kindhearted people have unknowingly become the communist specter's agents or the targets of its manipulation — what Vladimir Lenin called "useful idiots." Though society as a whole has ended up on the verge of destruction because of the specter's inducements and temptations, very few people have willingly pledged their souls to the devil and chosen to deliberately corrupt mankind. For most, the kindness innate in human nature remains, giving them an opportunity to rid themselves of the specter's influence.

The purpose of this book is to set out this complex and tangled issue in plain language as truthfully as possible. Then people will be able to see the communist specter's tricks. More importantly, this book seeks to present the moral, cultural, and artistic traditions that the divine laid down for mankind. Individuals may then choose between the divine and the evil specter for themselves.

When a person's kind thoughts emerge, the divine will help free him from the devil's control. But the process of seeing the devil for what it is requires that one think deeply and discern clearly. This book seeks to reexamine the tides of history over the last several centuries and, from a high level and with a broad perspective, assess the multifarious masks and forms the devil has adopted in order to occupy and manipulate our world.

The goal of this effort is not to simply recount history, but to understand how we can stop the devil from ever ruling the world again. This relies on each individual's enlightenment, proactive abandonment of evil, and return to the traditions and way of life that the divine laid down for man.

The divine will triumph over the devil. Which side we stand on will determine our eternal destiny.

Chapter Fifteen

The Communist Roots of Terrorism

1. Terrorism and Communist Revolution

Since the terrorist attacks of September 11, 2001, the Western public has become familiar with the global terrorist movement and its representatives. Less well-known, however, is the close relationship between terrorism and communism.

Communist ideology is rooted in hatred and struggle. It regards all aspects of the "old society," including its laws and morality, as the vestiges of an oppressive ruling class to be overthrown by any means necessary. Thus, the communist movement has made terrorism an important tool in its pursuit of power and in spreading its ideology around the world. The terms "terrorism" and "terrorist" were first recorded in 1795 as a reference to the Reign of Terror during the French Revolution, which laid the foundation for the communist movement (see Chapter Two). [1]

Vladimir Lenin relied on terrorism to bring the communists to victory in Russia. Marxist theorist Karl Kautsky, in his 1919 book *Terrorism and Communism*, gave a comprehensive overview of what would come to pass under the proletarian dictatorship that Lenin sought to establish. Reflecting on the violence of the French Revolution, Kautsky argued that Lenin's Bolsheviks had inherited the terrorist character of the Jacobins. [2]

Felix Dzerzhinsky, head of Lenin's Cheka secret police, said in 1918, "We stand for organizing terror — this frankly should be admitted." [3] The Cheka, short for All-Russian Extraordinary Commission, was active during the Russian Civil War, when the Bolsheviks competed with both the anti-communist White armies and rival socialist factions. It employed kidnappings, torture, assassination, and summary execution of "class enemies" on a large scale as part of Lenin's repressions, which became known as the Red Terror.

The Cheka sought to inflict maximal fear and pain on the enemies of the Bolsheviks. According to records and eyewitness accounts collected in *The Red Terror in Russia*, written in 1924 by Russian emigrant historian Sergei Melgunov, many of the Cheka's victims were selected because they were property owners or nobility. They would be paraded out of their homes at night, forced to disrobe, and then shot. The bodies of those murdered by the Cheka, including women, children, the elderly, and the clergy, often bore evidence of sadistic abuse — mutilation, burning, skinning, rape, decapitation, or even more hair-raising acts.

According to Melgunov, while the Cheka boasted about its slaughter, "the number of names published was a good deal smaller than the reality." [4] During the Red Terror, the Cheka alone is believed to have been responsible for the murder of tens of thousands or even hundreds of thousands of people.

The Soviet communist regime regarded Dzerzhinsky as a revolutionary hero. The Cheka was renamed many times before finally becoming the Committee for State Security (KGB), but its agents were always informally known as "chekists." From Dzerzhinsky's death in 1926 to 1990, the square in front of Lubyanka — the headquarters of the KGB — bore his name. In the 1940s, a statue of him was erected in the square, where it stood until being torn down in 1991. [5]

Following the establishment of the Soviet regime, the same pattern of red terror was repeated by communist revolutionary movements around the world. As discussed in previous chapters of this book, Marxist-Leninist regimes have, without exception, relied on terrifying brutality to seize and maintain power. Violence and murder are but one component of communism's terrorist agenda. Even more destructive is how communism uses political and religious fervor to indoctrinate people with Communist Party culture, planting the seeds of deceit, hatred, and violence to be passed from generation to generation.

Today, terrorism comes primarily in three forms: state terrorism under communist regimes; terrorist activity carried out abroad by agents of communist regimes with the aim of spreading violent revolution; and fundamentalist Islamic extremism, which in fact owes much of its ideology and methods to communism.

2. How Communist Regimes Export Terror

While inflicting mass terror and suffering upon their own people, communist regimes support terrorist organizations abroad for the purpose of fomenting revolution or destabilizing rival states.

During the Cold War, the Soviets actively supported a wide range of terrorist activities on a global scale. The Chinese communist regime also has supported terrorist insurrections abroad, spreading Maoist theories of revolution and crafting

3

alliances with terrorist organizations, as well as rogue regimes that are major sponsors of terrorism.

Stanislav Lunev, a former officer in the Soviet military's Main Intelligence Directorate who defected to the West, said that the directorate was a primary mentor for terrorists around the world. [6] Many extremist groups that have staged anti-US attacks had ties with the Soviet security agency, the KGB. These include organizations like the Popular Front for the Liberation of Palestine (PFLP), the Japanese Red Army, the Red Brigades of Italy, the Red Army Faction in West Germany, or various guerrilla groups in South America.

The most influential form of modern terrorism, however, is the radical Islam nurtured by the Soviet bloc as a means of destabilizing the Muslim world.

In the first half of the twentieth century, the Middle East belonged to the Western colonial sphere. As peoples in the region gained independence, the Soviet Union took the opportunity to boost its influence among them. Today, the Middle East finds itself in a complex and chaotic situation resulting from the contradictions between Muslim denominations, the Arab–Israeli conflict, the Cold War, the politics surrounding oil, and the clash of cultures between the West and Islam.

As mentioned in Chapter Five, Ion Mihai Pacepa, the former lieutenant general and acting chief of communist Romania's foreign intelligence service, became the highest-ranking defector from the Soviet bloc when he escaped to the United States in July 1978. In his article "Russian Footprints," Pacepa revealed substantial knowledge about communist support for terrorism in the Middle East. [7] He quoted Aleksandr Sakharovsky, the head of Soviet foreign intelligence, as saying, "In today's world, when nuclear arms have made military force obsolete, terrorism should become our main weapon." Eighty-two aircraft hijackings were carried out in 1969 alone. Many of them were the work of the Palestine Liberation Organization (PLO) with support from the Soviets and Chinese communists. Pacepa recalled that when he visited Sakharovsky's office, he saw "a sea of red flags" dotting a world map. Each flag represented an aircraft hijacking. Sakharovsky told Pacepa that the tactic of hijacking was his own invention.

The concept of "Islamic socialism" began to take hold during the Cold War, when the Soviet Union supported Arab states against Israel. Representatives included Yasser Arafat, who led the PLO from 1969 until his death in 2004, and Gamal Abdel Nasser, who served as Egypt's second president from 1956 until his death in 1970. The PLO, which was supported by the Soviet Union and the Chinese Communist Party (CCP), engaged in widespread terrorist activities.

Between 1968 and 1978, the Romanian security forces made weekly air deliveries of military supplies to Palestinian terrorists in Lebanon. Archives from the East German government show that in 1983, the East German foreign intelligence agency sent $1,877,600 worth of ammunition for Kalashnikov assault rifles to Lebanon. Czechoslovakia provided Islamic terrorists with 1,000 tons of Semtex-H, an odorless plastic explosive.

In the early 1970s, Yuri Andropov, then-head of the KGB and later general secretary of the Soviet Communist Party, began a covert, meticulously planned propaganda campaign to sow the seeds of anti-Semitic and anti-American hate throughout the Arab and Islamic world. Pacepa and coauthor Ronald Rychlak, in their book *Disinformation*, called Andropov the "father of a new disinformation era." [8]

3. The Communist Origins of Islamic Extremism

While the Soviets and Chinese communists funded many terrorist organizations in the Middle East, actually introducing communism in areas with deeply held religious beliefs proved a steep challenge. The Soviet Union's efforts to directly export socialist revolution to the Muslim world met with mixed and often temporary results.

While there were multiple Soviet-aligned states in the Middle East, only South Yemen and Afghanistan were under communist rule for varying lengths of time during the Cold War. In 1979, the Soviet Union launched an invasion of Afghanistan and occupied the country for ten years in an attempt to prop up the communist regime it had recently helped rise to power. In 1989, the Soviets gave up and withdrew from the country.

However, while communism itself failed to establish control over the Muslim world, it did much to influence the creation and development of contemporary Islamic extremism.

Following the 9/11 attacks, the threat of Islamic extremism gained prominence, with the actions of Osama bin Laden and his al-Qaeda terrorist group becoming front-page news. But the ideological source of bin Laden's Islamic extremism can be traced back to a man who has been described as the Karl Marx of radical Islam. [9]

A. SAYYID QUTB: THE MARX OF ISLAMIC EXTREMISM

At first glance, it may seem far-fetched to suggest a relationship between communism and radical Islam, given that Muslims believe in Allah and the prophet Mohammed, while communism is atheistic and aims to eradicate faith in religions. In fact, the theory and methods of modern Islamic extremism are closely linked to Marxism-Leninism.

The pioneer of radical Islam and modern jihad was Sayyid Qutb, an Egyptian liaison for the local Muslim Brotherhood to the Communist International and the Egyptian communist party. [10][11] Qutb's ideas were steeped in communist logic and rhetoric. Born in 1906, Qutb studied socialism and literature in the 1920s and 1930s. He studied abroad in the United States for two years in the late 1940s and joined the Muslim Brotherhood after his return to Egypt. [12]

Qutbism can be described as the pursuit of violence to destroy the old society dominated by "jahiliyyah." As a religious term, jahiliyyah means ignorance of religious truth, and it originally referred to society before the spread of Islam. Qutb called upon Muslims to lay down their lives in the struggle against jahiliyyah, which would supposedly usher in humanity's liberation. To articulate his ideas on this struggle, Qutb reinterpreted both the meaning of jahiliyyah and the Islamic concept of jihad.

Upon mention of jihad, many immediately think of "holy war," but in Arabic, jihad simply means to struggle or to fight. In mainstream Islam, it can be taken to mean internal conflict (self-perfection) or defensive jihad. [13] Qutb, however, extended this definition to include proactive and unbridled use of violence in the "holy war" of jihad and laid out its theoretical foundations. [14] Qutb's philosophy held that any social system that abided by secular laws or ethics was an anti-Islamic jahiliyyah. He saw jahiliyyah as the greatest obstruction for both Muslims and non-Muslims, preventing them from fulfilling Islamic values and law. Even a society that claimed itself Muslim could still be jahiliyyah. Qutb considered the Egyptian social system in which he lived to be one in which jahiliyyah was dominant, so he believed it must be overthrown. [15]

This interpretation of jihad and jahiliyyah mirrors the Marxist philosophy of struggle along class lines. Qutb claimed that the old society of jahiliyyah had been forced on people and, in the process, had robbed them of their freedom. These enslaved people — analogous to the working class in Marxism — had the right to wage jihad to overthrow the oppression of jahiliyyah. Qutb advocated jihad as the means of liberation for all mankind, Muslim as well as non-Muslim. [16] When Qutb's writings were published, many mainstream Muslim leaders thought he had gone too far and condemned his ideas as heresy. [17]

Qutb had long had contact with Nasser, leader of the socialist-leaning Free Officers Movement and later the long-serving president of Egypt. In 1952, Nasser launched a military coup overthrowing the Muhammad Ali dynasty, Egypt's pro-Western monarchy. It is said that this socialist-revolutionary coup was planned by Qutb and the Muslim Brotherhood together with Nasser. However, while Qutb hoped Nasser would establish an Islamic regime, Nasser instead took the path of secularization and in 1954 began suppressing the Brotherhood.

Qutb and the Brotherhood prepared to assassinate Nasser, but the plot failed, and Qutb was imprisoned. He was severely tortured during his first few years in prison, but as conditions relaxed, he was allowed to write. Qutb wrote his two most important works while in prison — *In the Shade of the Qur'an* and *Milestones*. These two books, covering his views on the Qur'an, Islamic history, Egypt, and Western society, laid out in full his advocacy of anti-secular, anti-Western extremism. At one point, Qutb was released from prison, but stayed in Egypt and was jailed again. In 1966, he was convicted and hanged for his involvement in the conspiracy to assassinate Nasser. Qutb walked proudly up to the gallows and toward becoming a religious martyr.

Ayman al-Zawahiri, the leader of al-Qaeda following the death of bin Laden, believed Qutb's execution was what ignited the fire of jihadi extremism. [18] Islamic extremists often cite Qutb's teachings and regard themselves as his "intellectual descendants," as observed by William McCants, counter-terrorism expert and former fellow at West Point Military Academy's anti-terrorism center. [19] Middle East expert Hassan Hassan, in a 2016 report on the Islamic State, quoted a saying popular among ISIS supporters about how the terrorist group's essential doctrine was formed: "The Islamic State was drafted by Sayyid Qutb, taught by Abdullah Azzam, [and] globalized by Osama bin Laden." [20]

B. THE LENINIST VANGUARD OF JIHAD

Another Marxist concept Qutb borrowed was that of "false consciousness," which refers to the ordinary masses' acceptance of the ruler's ideals and culture. The concept holds that this prevents the masses from perceiving their own oppression and overthrowing capitalism in favor of socialism. According to Qutb, those living under jahiliyyah don't realize they are slaves, which is why they do not engage in jihad to emancipate themselves. [21]

One of Lenin's major works is a pamphlet titled with the question *Chto Delat'?* (or in English, *What Is to Be Done?*) in which he argues that the working class will not become conscious of the need for communism unless led to it by an elite group of revolutionaries. Faced with the same question in his crusade against jahiliyyah, Qutb looked to Lenin for his answer.

Qutb's writings are replete with vocabulary familiar to students of Marxism-Leninism, such as "vanguard," "state," "revolution," and the like. The situation and challenges Lenin faced at the time of writing the pamphlet mirror the circumstances faced by Qutb as he formulated his own radical ideology. Lenin placed all hope for a successful revolution on a proletarian vanguard party — a highly disciplined elite organization charged with overseeing the revolution and guiding the masses — and derided the notion that communism could succeed if its agents merely operated in society at large. Qutb copied this theory and replaced the Leninist political party with Islamic extremist organizations.

Lenin, in his emphasis on the organization and the vanguard concept, identified a clear distinction between spontaneity and consciousness, and introduced the idea of party-building. According to Lenin, with only spontaneous action, workers can only make superficial demands, such as pay raises and eight-hour work days, as they lack the consciousness needed to liberate humankind. Lenin believed that external vanguards (usually comprising bourgeois intellectuals, who have the privilege of education) are needed to incite and indoctrinate the workers, so that the workers come to believe that revolution is their only way out and that only by liberating all of humankind can they themselves be liberated. In order to fully realize the vanguard, a tightly knit political party is needed to arrange their activities and provide them with opportunities for underground work as professional revolutionaries. [22]

Glenn E. Robinson, an associate professor at the Naval Postgraduate School in Monterey, California, and a research fellow at the Center for Middle Eastern Studies, University of California–Berkeley, said of radical Islam: "Modern jihadism is distinctively Leninist. Although for obvious reasons jihadi ideologues do not cite Lenin as an inspiration, their concepts and logic, especially Sayyid Qutb's, betray this influence. Having been educated in Egypt in the 1940s, Qutb would certainly have been exposed to Lenin's writings. Two key concepts from Qutb come straight from Lenin: jama'a (vanguard) and manhaj (program). … Lenin's insistence on the centrality of the vanguard's having a detailed and coherent program for undertaking and then consolidating the revolution was likewise echoed, with an Islamic tone, in Qutb's writings."

Drawing from the essence of Leninism, Qutb advocated for the organization of a Muslim version of the Leninist vanguard party. "Qutb made precisely the same argument for the Muslim world," Robinson wrote. "The vast majority of Muslims were too caught up in and corrupted by the system of unjust and anti-Islamic rule to know how and when to take up arms against the state. A dedicated vanguard of jihadi cadres was needed to organize direct action against the state." [23]

This vanguard, which consists of extremists, or what Qutb called "true Muslims," has the revolutionary mission of liberating all Muslims and the whole of human civilization. The vanguard must strike hard on false Muslims, follow Islamic ideology as determined by Qutb's interpretation, establish a new nation based on this Islamism, and use violence to impose Islam on the rest of the world.

In addition to the Leninist vanguard, Qutb's theory also includes utopian ideas like "social equality" and the elimination of classes. [24] Such points echo the stated aims of communism.

After Qutb's death, his brother Muhammad Qutb continued to publish his writings. The book *Ma'arakat ul-Islam
war-Ra'samaaliyyah*, published in 1993, again highlights
Qutb's communist inspirations. Qutb blatantly states that
Islam is a "unique, constructive, and positivist 'aqidah' [creed],
which has been moulded and shaped from Christianity and
communism together, [with a] blending in the most perfect
of ways and which comprises all of their (i.e., Christianity's
and Communism's) objectives and adds in addition to them
harmony, balance and justice." [25]

C. THE COMMUNIST CORE OF ISLAMIC EXTREMISM

Class struggle is another Marxist idea central to Islamic
extremism. Marx spent his whole life trying to incite conflict
between the proletariat and the bourgeoisie to the point of no
return so as to then "solve" the conflict through revolution.
Islamic extremists operate in much the same way.

Destroying the World Trade Center in Manhattan did not
in itself do anything to help realize the united Muslim world
that Qutb envisioned, but it served as a means of exacerbating
the conflict between the Western and Muslim worlds. Terrorist attacks were meant to incite backlash in the West against
Muslims, which would, in turn, incite Muslims to carry out
more attacks. [26] The extremists' methods mirror Marx and
Lenin's promotion of conflicts between the proletariat and
the bourgeoisie in order to create the conditions needed for
launching revolution.

Qutb's theories bear a far greater resemblance to communism than to traditional Islam. While the Islamic extremists
profess to have a religious opposition to communism, they in
fact absorbed the pure essentials of communist revolutionary doctrine. As journalist Chuck Morse has noted: "The real
enemy confronting the free world remains Communism. ... [R]
adical Islam is nothing more than Communism cloaked in the
traditional garments of Islam. The same Communist enemy

that subverted Europe ... took root in the Islamic world and transformed large segments of the Islamic elite." [27]

Finnish political historian Antero Leitzinger believes that modern terrorism was born during 1967 and 1968, developing in concert with the international communist movement. As radical student movements ran amok in the 1960s, students from Muslim countries who studied in the West were connected to leftist thought and brought concepts such as violent revolution back home with them. [28]

In 1974, Abdallah Schleifer, a Muslim convert who later became a professor in media studies at the American University in Cairo, met Zawahiri, the future leader of al-Qaeda. Zawahiri, who was studying medicine at Cairo University at the time, boasted that Islamic extremist groups had recruited the most members from elite institutions such as medical and engineering schools. Schleifer said that these institutions had high concentrations of young Marxists during the 1960s, and that radical Islam was simply a new trend in student rebellion. Schleifer told Zawahiri: "Listen, Ayman, I'm an ex-Marxist. When you talk, I feel like I'm back in the Party. I don't feel as if I'm with a traditional Muslim.'" [29]

Curiously, many observers associate Islamic extremism with fascism (Islamofascism) and, for various reasons, fail to mention its communist origins. Fascism is a form of national socialism, and socialism is the first stage of communism, as Lenin and others have said. Communism is international in scope, aiming for communist revolutions around the world. When considering Islamic extremism in terms of its overall approach and doctrine, it becomes apparent that it has more in common with communism.

D. QUTB AND THE RISE OF TERRORISM

Qutb's writings influenced many young Arabs, including Palestinian scholar and co-founder of al-Qaeda Abdullah Yusuf Azzam. [30] The 9/11 Commission Report both referred to Azzam as "a disciple of Qutb" and outlined Qutb's influence on bin Laden's worldview. [31]

Muhammad Qutb, Sayyid Qutb's younger brother, was one of the primary transmitters of Qutb's views. Muhammad Qutb became a professor of Islamic studies in Saudi Arabia, and he was responsible for editing, publishing, and promoting his late brother's theories. Bin Laden regularly attended Muhammad Qutb's weekly public lectures and read Qutb's books.

Zawahiri said that when he was a youth, he repeatedly heard from his uncle about how great Qutb was and how he had suffered in prison. [32] In 1966, the year that Qutb was hanged, a fifteen-year-old Zawahiri helped form an underground cell that aimed to overthrow the government and create an Islamist state. Zawahiri wrote in his memoir: "The Nasserite regime thought that the Islamic movement received a deadly blow with the execution of Sayyid Qutb and his comrades. ... But the apparent surface calm concealed an immediate interaction with Sayyid Qutb's ideas and the formation of the nucleus of the modern Islamic jihad movement in Egypt." [33] Later, Zawahiri joined the Egyptian Islamic Jihad group, formed in the 1970s, and became bin Laden's adviser, as well as an important member of al-Qaeda, eventually taking over the leadership after bin Laden's death.

In the Sunni Muslim world, Qutb is the most prominent radical thinker. [34] Virtually all the major concepts and ideological innovations of the Sunni jihadi groups can be found in his works. [35] Although the various jihadi groups may differ in form, they all use violence to realize their political aims under the banner of Islam. [36]

The 1981 assassination of the Egyptian President Anwar Sadat by the Egyptian Islamic Jihad and the attacks by Egyptian terrorist group al-Gamma al-Islamiyah in the 1990s against government officials, secular intellectuals, Egyptian Christians, and tourists were all steps in the campaign to bring about Qutb's vision. [37]

The radical jihadi groups that pursue Qutb's ideology are categorized as Salafi-jihadi terrorists. In 2013, there were nearly fifty Salafi-jihadi groups worldwide, with most based in North Africa and the Levant, according to a report by the US-based Rand Corporation. [38] Robert Manne, author of the book *The Mind of the Islamic State: ISIS and the Ideology of the Caliphate*, called Qutb "the twentieth-century father of the political movement now called Salafi jihadism" and a forerunner of the ISIS terrorist group, adding that while Qutb was not directly responsible for ISIS, "he posted the first milestone on the road that would eventually lead there." [39]

Among the various extremist Islamic organizations in existence, although they lack a united vision and are given to ideological infighting, there is one trait common to the overwhelming majority of them: They have essentially inherited Qutb's aggressive form of jihad — communist revolution in a different form.

E. HOW COMMUNISM HAS VICTIMIZED ORDINARY MUSLIMS

Although extremist groups operate in the name of Islam, the biggest casuality is Muslim society. This is because the true motivation behind terrorism — like that of communism — is a desire for killing and destruction, whatever the superficial excuses.

The 2017 report *Islam and the Patterns in Terrorism and Violent Extremism*, published by the Center for Strategic and International Studies, states that "almost all of the human impact of extremist attacks is Muslims killing or injuring fellow Muslims."

According to the report, a "total of 83% of the [Islamic extremist] attacks and 90% of the deaths occurred in solidly Islamic countries," as did the vast majority of suicide attacks carried out on foot or using vehicles. "If one looks at the five worst perpetrator movements in the world in 2016, four are 'Islamist' extremist. A total of 88% of 2,916 attacks and 99% of

14,017 deaths that resulted from the top five perpetrators were caused by Islamic extremist groups." [40]

The State Department's *Country Reports on Terrorism 2018* records a total of 8,093 terrorist attacks that occurred in the world that year, causing 32,836 total deaths. Attacks were overwhelmingly likely to take place in Muslim-majority countries and areas: "In 2018, terrorist incidents occurred in 84 countries and territories. About 85 percent of all incidents were concentrated in three geographic regions: the Middle East, South Asia, and sub-Saharan Africa. In order, Afghanistan, Syria, Iraq, India, Nigeria, Somalia, Philippines, Pakistan, Yemen, and Cameroon experienced the greatest number of terrorist incidents in 2018. Incidents in these 10 countries accounted for 71 percent of the overall total number of incidents and 81 percent of all fatalities from terrorist incidents." [41]

By contrast, terrorist attacks in Western countries resulted in far fewer deaths. A 2019 report by the Cato Institute stated that foreign-born terrorists in the United States caused 3,037 of the 3,518 murders caused by terrorists in the United States from 1975 through 2017. This number includes the 2,979 people killed by the hijackers who carried out the 9/11 attacks. [42]

4. The Chinese Communist Party's Support of Terrorism

The CCP has long supported terrorist activities abroad, including those of Palestinian terrorist leader Arafat. One of the first to apply the tactic of hijacking commercial airliners, Arafat targeted US forces and later became an inspiration for bin Laden.

A. THE CCP'S SUPPORT OF YASSER ARAFAT'S TERRORIST ACTIVITIES

In 1959, Arafat started the Palestinian National Liberation Movement, also known as Fatah, and in 1988, he declared

Palestine an independent state. Until his death in 2004, Arafat was the leading figure of various Palestinian militant organizations. He was also a favorite of the CCP, having visited China fourteen times and met with many Chinese communist leaders, including Mao Zedong, Zhou Enlai, Deng Xiaoping, and Jiang Zemin.

In 1964, Arafat established al-'Asifah ("The Storm"), the military wing of Fatah, after which he immediately went to Beijing to meet with Chinese Premier Zhou Enlai. Zhou reminded Arafat to pay attention to strategy and not to use counterproductive slogans such as those calling for the complete destruction of Israel. [43]

In addition to providing weapons and financial support, Beijing often guided Palestine on how to wage conflict with the United States and Israel while expanding its influence internationally. The CCP also invited Palestinians to receive training in China.

In January 1965, Arafat declared war on Israel in north Palestine using his guerrilla organization, and the PLO set up an office in Beijing that May. The People's Republic of China (PRC) afforded the PLO office diplomatic treatment and openly supported the PLO in various international arenas.

In November 1988, when Arafat announced the independence of the Palestinian state, Beijing immediately acknowledged it and established diplomatic relations.

Arafat and then-CCP General Secretary Jiang Zemin visited each other in 2000 and 2001, a time in which large-scale bloody conflicts broke out between Palestine and Israel. Israel repeatedly condemned Arafat for his role in the violence. With the CCP's support, Arafat was able to contend with the United States and Israel while further destabilizing the Middle East.

The PLO's member organizations were involved in various open and underground militant terrorist activities. They claimed that violent revolution was the only way to liberate the country, an ideology that follows the same doctrine as communist movements. Arafat was very close to the leadership in communist countries and met with members of the Socialist International. Fatah was an observer in the Party of European Socialists.

In 1970, the PLO carried out an assassination attempt on Jordan's King Hussein bin Talal and a failed coup of the Jordanian government. In September that year, the PLO hijacked five commercial planes — four bound for New York and one for London — in what is known as the Dawson's Field hijackings. One terrorist claimed that hijacking a plane had a greater effect than killing a hundred Israelis in battle.

In 1972, the terrorist group Black September, a militant faction of Fatah, massacred eleven Israeli athletes during the Olympic Games in Munich. One of the terrorists was Ali Hassan Salameh, security chief of Fatah and one of Arafat's most trusted lieutenants. In addition to the Israelis killed in the attack, a West German police officer also died. [44]

The United States and Israel named Arafat as the instigator behind a number of terrorist attacks in the Middle East. In 1987, the White House designated the PLO as a terrorist organization and closed the PLO's Palestine Information Office in Washington.

B. THE CCP'S TIES TO AL-QAEDA

For the vast majority of people around the world, the 9/11 attacks were a shocking tragedy. But in mainland China, from internet forums and chat rooms to university cafeterias, large numbers of people rooted for the terrorists, with comments such as "Good job!" and "We strongly support the acts of justice against the United States." According to a survey of 91,701 people on NetEase, a major Chinese internet company, only 17.8 percent of respondents expressed strong opposition to the terrorist attacks, while a majority of people chose "opposition to the United States" or "the best is yet to come" in regard to the tragedy. [45]

The Chinese who cheered 9/11 had no relation to bin Laden or radical Muslims in terms of ethnicity, religion, or heritage, but the roots of their toxic thinking were the same. Like the Islamic extremists in their "holy war" waged against both the non-Islamic world and "false" Muslims said to be deluded by jahiliyyah, the CCP has spent seventy years poisoning the Chinese people with hatred of "class enemies" and indoctrinating them with twisted Communist Party culture.

For the CCP, the commonalities of Islamic extremism and communism go beyond mere ideological overlap. The CCP maintained close ties with the Taliban and al-Qaeda after the Taliban seized power in Afghanistan, as well as during the time the Taliban provided protection for bin Laden. In 1998, after the United States attacked al-Qaeda bases with cruise missiles, the Chinese regime allegedly paid bin Laden $10 million for any unexploded missiles, presumably to steal the technology. [46] [47]

At the same time, the CCP continued to provide sensitive military technology to state sponsors of terrorism. At the end of 2000, the UN Security Council proposed sanctions on the Taliban to force it to close bin Laden's terrorist training camps located on its territory, but the PRC abstained from the vote. Instead, it sent military personnel to support the Taliban immediately after the United States began airstrikes in Afghanistan.

After 9/11, American intelligence officials reported that ZTE and Huawei, China's two military-linked tech companies, were helping the Taliban military establish a telephone network in Kabul, the capital of Afghanistan. [48] On the day of the 9/11 attacks, Chinese and Taliban officials signed a contract to expand economic and technical cooperation. [49]

In their 1999 book *Unrestricted Warfare*, two Chinese military officers discussed a hypothetical second attack on the World Trade Center in New York, following the 1993 failed bombing attempt, noting that it would open up a complicated dilemma for the United States. The authors also named al-Qaeda as an organization with the ability to carry out such an operation. [50] Whether or not the CCP had knowledge of 9/11 before it happened, the regime's concept of "unrestricted warfare" provided theoretical guidance for bin Laden's future operations. Additionally, in 2004, it was revealed that Chinese intelligence agencies used shell companies in financial markets around the world to help bin Laden raise funds and launder money. [51]

The communist camp faced total collapse with the fall of the Berlin Wall, and the CCP was left to face tremendous pressure from the free world on its own. Just as the United States and the free world began to focus their attention on condemning communist tyranny, 9/11 took place. Priorities changed dramatically, and the War on Terror began instead. This gave the CCP a reprieve and allowed communism to expand once again.

The menace of radical Islamic terrorism compelled the United States to divert its resources and attention away from the continued threat of communism, preventing the free world from confronting the unprecedented abuses of the CCP. While the Western world waged war in the Middle East, a large-scale transfer of wealth quietly took place between China and the United States, allowing another communist superpower to rise where the Soviet Union had fallen.

5. The Convergence of Terrorism and the West's Radical Left

After 9/11, radical Western leftist intellectuals cheered the event and defended the perpetrators. Days after the attacks, an Italian playwright and Nobel laureate in literature said, "The great speculators wallow in an economy that every year kills tens of millions of people with poverty — so what is 20,000 dead in New York?" [52] A professor at the University of Colorado–Boulder characterized those who had died in the World Trade Center as "little Eichmanns" (referring to one of the architects of the Nazi Holocaust), saying the victims were part of the "technocratic corps at the very heart of America's global financial empire" and implying that the attacks were a just punishment. [53]

On February 11, 2003, a month before the United States attacked Iraq, bin Laden released an audio recording through Al-Jazeera Television, saying that "there will be no harm if the interests of Muslims converge with the interests of the socialists in the fight against the crusaders," and calling on people to fight against the US military in the streets. [54]

Hoping to prevent the United States from carrying out military operations in Afghanistan and Iraq, and later to hamper its efforts in the War on Terror, various radical left-wing forces launched a large-scale anti-war protest movement. Most members of the prominent anti-war organization ANSWER (Act Now to Stop War and End Racism), founded in 2001, are socialists, communists, and leftists or progressives. Many of its founders had ties with the International Action Center and the Workers World Party, a communist radical organization aligned with the North Korean regime. ANSWER is thus a front-line force aligned with Stalinist communism. Also participating in the anti-war movement was Not in Our Name, a front organization of the Revolutionary Communist Party, which is a Marxist-Leninist party linked to the Chinese communist regime. [55]

In his 2004 book *Unholy Alliance: Radical Islam and the American Left,* American scholar David Horowitz described the nefarious connection between radical leftists and Islamic extremists. According to his analysis, the radical Left around the world has served to indirectly defend Islamic jihadis. [56]

During a meeting with Hezbollah officials, a prominent leftist professor said that the United States was "one of the leading terrorist states." [57] An assistant professor of anthropology at Columbia University told a crowd of about 3,000 students that he "personally would like to see a million Mogadishus." [58] In the 1993 Battle of Mogadishu, alleged al-Qaeda-trained fighters killed eighteen US special forces soldiers. The professor also expressed hope that American soldiers would kill each other.

Some left-wing figures have aided terrorists directly. In 1995, Omar Abdel-Rahman was convicted for conspiring to carry out the 1993 World Trade Center bombing. One of his defense lawyers, Lynne Stewart, was sentenced to prison in 2006 for helping to smuggle messages from Abdel-Rahman to his followers in the Middle East that told them to continue their terrorist activities. Stewart became a political idol for the Left and was repeatedly invited to lecture at college campuses. [59]

Standing with terrorists against Western democratic society is part of the radical Left's long march to destroy and take over Western society from within. The Left is willing to use any method that helps it achieve this goal. At a deeper level, though Western leftist ideology has no superficial relationship with Islamic extremism, their common roots lie in the hatred and struggle of the communist specter.

6. Ending the Fundamental Cause of Terrorism

From the Paris Commune and Lenin's institutionalization of violence to the ccp's state-sponsored persecutions, communism has always used terrorism to achieve its aims. Terrorists use violence to throw society into disorder, and use fear to bring people under their control. They violate the moral values held universally across humanity in order to achieve their ends.

The roots of communism can be seen in the core ideas and methods of modern terrorist groups, as it is communist ideology that provides a theoretical framework for their evil values.

Moreover, beyond the territory controlled by communist regimes, communism has manipulated a variety of groups and individuals to carry out terrorist acts, sowing chaos around the world and throwing up a diversionary smokescreen to confuse and misdirect its enemies.

Radical Islamic terrorism has taken the spotlight in international conflict since the end of the Cold War. However, as the United States and its allies became embroiled in costly and protracted military campaigns in the Middle East, the Chinese communist regime quietly worked to become a superpower capable of challenging the free world. The chaos that prevailed in the Middle East and elsewhere distracted Western governments and the public from the resurgent threat of communism, as well as the unprecedented crimes against humanity being committed by the CCP despite greater economic and cultural ties with the West.

Founded on hatred and struggle, communism is the fundamental cause of terrorism around the world. While the media focuses its attention on terrorist attacks that target Western society, the vast majority of those killed by Islamic extremists are ordinary Muslims living in Islamic countries. Similarly, the more than 100 million deaths caused by communism were nearly all of the victims living under communist regimes.

Until the toxic roots of communism are dug out, humankind will not enjoy a single day of peace. Only by recognizing the role of communism in the terrorist activities that plague our world, and by standing on the side of traditional moral values and faith, can this menace be defeated and the "global war on terror" be brought to an end.

Chapter Sixteen

The Communism Behind Environmentalism

THE CREATOR PROVIDES THE CONDITIONS for human life and all things on earth. Traditional cultures emphasize the benign, symbiotic relationship between man and nature. As the ancient Chinese philosopher Dong Zhongshu wrote in *Luxuriant Dew of the Spring and Autumn Annals*, "Everything on earth was created for the benefit of man." [1] At the same time, people must maintain respect for nature, following the principles of heaven and earth.

In traditional Chinese philosophy, there is a balance between everything, as well as the imperative to avoid doing harm. The Confucian *Doctrine of the Mean* states: "Moral laws form one system with the laws by which heaven and earth support and contain, overshadow and canopy all things. ... It is this same system of laws by which all created things are produced and develop themselves each in its order and system without injuring one another; that the operations of nature take their course without conflict or confusion." [2] The Chinese ancients thus valued protection of the environment. According to legendary records, during the time of Emperor Yu the Great roughly four millennia ago, "in the three months of the spring, people didn't take axes to the forest so the forest could flourish; in the three months of the summer, people didn't put nets to rivers so fishes could breed." [3] Zeng Zi, a disciple of Confucius, wrote, "Wood should only be cut down in the right seasons and animals only slaughtered at the right time." [4]

Such quotes reflect the traditional ideas, found not just in China but also in ancient cultures around the world, of practicing moderation in all things and of cherishing and protecting the natural environment.

Since the Industrial Revolution, society has become increasingly aware of the severe ecological damage caused by pollution. Starting in the West, this damage has been partially offset by the passage of laws and regulations to protect the environment. In first-world countries, the importance of environmental protection is universally acknowledged.

Less well-understood is how environmentalist narratives dominant in society today have been shaped and manipulated by communism. Though the rationale for environmental protection is legitimate, and many people have a genuine desire to improve the environment and safeguard humanity's future prosperity, communist elements have commandeered much of the environmental movement to advance their own political agendas. Communism's infiltration of environmentalism has been underway virtually since the beginning of the environmental movement.

Environmental science is a complex field of study, with research that remains far from conclusive findings on subjects such as climate change. Yet under the influence of left-wing ideology, many "green" activists and organizations have simplified and turned environmental protection into a highly politicized struggle, often employing extreme methods and radical narratives — sometimes to the point of religious fervor. Rather than following the ancient teachings of moderation and conservation, radical leftist environmentalists eschew morality and tradition in their crusade against everything they deem the "enemy" of environmentalism, from private business to procreation. Mixed with other radical movements, the green cause has come to be defined by misleading propaganda and authoritarian political measures, turning environmentalism into a kind of "communism-lite."

This chapter will focus on how environmentalism as an ideology has come to be wed to communism, and how the environmental movement was hijacked, manipulated, and co-opted into serving communism's aims.

1. Communism and the Environmental Movement

After the collapse of the Soviet Union and the Eastern European communist bloc, communists continued to spread their influence in both Eastern and Western societies, while also seeking to establish a tightly controlled global government.

In order to achieve this, communism must create or use an "enemy" that threatens all of humankind and intimidates the public around the world into handing over both individual liberty and state sovereignty. Creating global panic about looming environmental and ecological disasters is almost a guaranteed route to achieving its goals.

A. THE THREE STAGES OF ENVIRONMENTALISM

The formation and development of the environmental movement has been inextricably linked with communism. Its development can be broken down into three stages.

The First Stage

The first stage was a theoretical "gestation period," which can be traced to the years from the 1848 publication of *The Communist Manifesto* by Karl Marx and Friedrich Engels, through to the first Earth Day in 1970.

Marx and his followers did not regard environmentalism as the focus of their theoretical discourse, but Marxist atheism and materialism were naturally consistent with the main tendency of the modern environmental movement. Marx declared that capitalism is opposed to nature (that is, the environment). Marxists devised the term "ecosystem" and quietly infused environmentalism with various public issues.

In the last decade of this phase, from 1960 to 1970, two best-selling books — *Silent Spring* (1962) and *The Population Bomb* (1968) — brought environmentalism to the public arena. The former raised legitimate concerns about the damage done to the natural environment by chemical pesticides, while the latter advocated immediate and widespread population control, sowing the seeds for the anti-human undercurrents of the communist-influenced environmental movement.

The Second Stage

At the macro level, the counterculture of the 1960s functioned almost like a military parade of communist elements in the West. They took the stage by co-opting the civil rights and anti-war movements, then quickly spread to other forms of battles against the "system," including the feminist movement, the sexual revolution, and environmentalism. This is the root of the upsurge in environmental ideology and agitation.

The first Earth Day, held in 1970, marked the beginning of the second stage. Shortly after, in 1972, the United Nations held its first Conference on the Human Environment, in Stockholm. A battery of organizations and monitoring groups were rapidly formed. In the United States and Europe, these groups pushed governments by using protests, propaganda, activism under the guise of scientific research, and so on.

The Third Stage

The third stage began on the eve of the Cold War's conclusion, when communism was in political collapse in Eastern Europe. Around this time, communists began to change gears by pushing the narrative of "saving the world."

In 1988, the World Meteorological Organization and the United Nations Environment Programme created the Intergovernmental Panel on Climate Change (IPCC), and the concept of global warming began to enter the political realm. In 1990, months before the collapse of the Soviet Union, Moscow hosted an international conference on the environment. In a speech, the general secretary of the Communist Party of the Soviet Union, Mikhail Gorbachev, advocated for the establishment of an international environmental monitoring system and a covenant to protect "unique environmental zones." He also expressed support for UN environmental programs, and a follow-up conference, which was subsequently held in 1992 in Rio de Janeiro, Brazil. [5]

What seemed to be the majority of Western environmentalists accepted these proposals and came to view global, man-made climate change as the primary threat to humankind. Propaganda that used environmental protection as an excuse for heavy-handed policies suddenly escalated, and the number and scale of environmental laws and regulations proliferated rapidly.

Owing to the politicization of environmentalist issues, propaganda and hype have overshadowed sound policy and scientific research, as will be discussed later in this chapter.

B. THE MARXIST ROOTS OF ENVIRONMENTAL MOVEMENTS

Eastern tradition views human beings as the spirit of all matter and one of the Three Talents (heaven, earth, and human beings), while Western religions teach that man was created by God in his own image. Thus, human life is endowed with higher value, purpose, and dignity. Nature exists to nourish humankind, and humans have an obligation to treasure and care for the natural environment.

In the eyes of atheists and materialists, however, human life has no such special quality. Engels wrote in one of his essays, "Life is the mode of existence of protein bodies." [6] In this view, human life is no more than a configuration of proteins, no different in any essential manner from animals or plants — thus, it is only logical that humans may be deprived of freedom, and even their lives, for the supposed cause of protecting nature.

In the update to his 1840s book on organic chemistry, German chemist Justus von Liebig criticized British farmers for using imported guano as a fertilizer. British agriculture had benefited from the bird manure, an efficient fertilizer, and crop yields had significantly increased. By the middle of the nineteenth century, the British had ample high-quality food sources. Von Liebig listed various arguments against overreliance on the imported fertilizer, among which was the impact that collecting the guano had on island bird populations, as well as its long-term unsustainability. He also objected to the longer lifespans and larger families of the well-fed British populace, arguing that more people meant more environmental damage. [7]

Marx carefully studied von Liebig's work when writing *Das Kapital* and used his arguments to attack the capitalist system. Marx praised von Liebig's work for having "developed from the point of view of natural science, the negative, i.e., destructive, side of modern agriculture." [8] Marx regarded any effort to create wealth by using natural resources as a vicious cycle, with the conclusion that "a rational agriculture is incompatible with the capitalist system."

After Vladimir Lenin and his Bolshevik Party launched their 1917 coup in Russia, they quickly promulgated the Decree on Land and the Decree on Forests to nationalize land, forest, water, mineral, animal, and plant resources, and prevent the public from using them without authorization.

American meteorologist and author Brian Sussman wrote in his 2012 book *Eco-Tyranny: How the Left's Green Agenda Will Dismantle America* that Marx and Lenin's ideas form the basis of those of today's environmentalists. In their view, no one has the right to profit from natural resources. "Whether it's saving the forests, whales, snails, or the climate, it all comes back to a deep-rooted belief that the quest for such profit is immoral and will ultimately destroy the planet unless ground to a halt," Sussman wrote. [9]

The global environmental movement has involved a large number of thinkers, politicians, scientists, social activists, and media personalities. This text does not have sufficient space to enumerate their thoughts, speeches, and actions in full, but one figure cannot be ignored: Maurice Strong, the founder and first executive director of the UN Environment Programme. Strong, a Canadian, also organized UN conferences including the 1972 Conference on the Human Environment and the 1992 Conference on Environment and Development. He was deeply influenced by his cousin, Anna Louise Strong, a well-known pro-communist journalist who was buried in China. Strong described himself as "a socialist in ideology, a capitalist in methodology." [10]

Strong came to occupy an important place in the global environmental movement. The views espoused by the UN agency led by Strong appear almost identical to Marxist theory; the preamble to the report of the 1976 World Conference on Human Settlements read: "Private land ownership is a principal instrument of accumulating wealth and therefore contributes to social injustice. Public control of land use is therefore indispensable." [11] Strong lived in Beijing after his retirement, but died in Canada in 2015.

Natalie Grant Wraga, an expert on the Soviet Union's disinformation tactics, wrote in a 1998 article: "Protection of the environment has become the principal tool for attack against the West and all it stands for. Protection of the environment may be used as a pretext to adopt a series of measures designed to undermine the industrial base of developed nations. It may also serve to introduce malaise by lowering their standard of living and implanting communist values." [12]

C. ECOLOGICAL MARXISM

At the juncture of the nineteenth and twentieth centuries, British scientist Arthur Tansley originated the ideas of ecology and the ecosystem. Tansley was the first chairman of the British Ecological Society, and while attending University College, London, he was deeply influenced by Darwinian zoologist Ray Lankester. [13] Both were Fabian socialists. Lankester was a frequent houseguest and friend of Marx; he once wrote to Marx saying that he was studying *Das Kapital* (Marx's 1867 text) "with the greatest pleasure and profit." [14]

The originating links between ecological ideas and Marxism appear to emerge in these connections between Tansley, Lankester, and Marx. While environmentalism is an ideology concerned with protecting the environment against damage to the natural environment generally, ecology concerns the relationship between living things and their environment, and thus provides the theoretical basis for defining the harm done to the environment. Eco-Marxism takes these ideas a step further, adding the concept of ecological crises to augment its arguments about the economic collapse of capitalism. It seeks to expand the supposed conflict between the bourgeoisie and the proletariat by adding an inherent conflict between production and the environment. This is the theory of double crisis or double conflict. In Marxist theory, the primary conflict of capitalism is between productive forces and the relations of production, while the secondary conflict happens between the environment of production (the ecosystem) and the productive forces (capitalism). In a Marxist view, the primary conflict leads to economic crisis, while the secondary conflict leads to ecological crisis. [15]

The last century has proven wrong the Marxist prediction that capitalism would collapse in on itself. On the contrary, it continues to prosper. To keep up the fight against capitalism and private business, communists infused environmentalism with Marxist theory, adopting the new rallying cry of "ecological collapse."

D. ECOLOGICAL SOCIALISM

As its name suggests, ecosocialism is an ideology combining ecology and socialism. Inserting typical socialist demands, such as "social justice," along with ecological concerns is an attempt to advance socialist ideology in new ways.

A good illustration of ecosocialism is *The Ecosocialist Manifesto,* written in 2001 by Joel Kovel and Michael Löwy. Kovel was an anti-Vietnam War activist and later psychiatry professor who ran unsuccessfully for the Green Party presidential nomination in 2000. Löwy, a sociologist, is a member of the Trotskyist Fourth International. In the manifesto, the authors resolve to "build a movement that can replace capitalism with a society in which common ownership of the means of production replaces capitalist ownership, and in which the preservation and restoration of ecosystems will be a fundamental part of all human activity." They did not view ecosocialism as merely a branch of socialism, but rather as the new name of socialism in a new era. [16]

E. MAKING GREEN THE NEW RED

When environmentalism entered politics, green politics, or ecopolitics, was born. Green parties, now established in many countries, are the result of green politics, which typically extends beyond environmental protection to include left-wing programs such as social justice, feminism, anti-war activism, and pacifism. Global Greens, for instance, is an international organization associated with the Green Party, and its 2001 charter is heavily influenced by Marxist ideology. [17] After the fall of communist regimes in Eastern Europe, many former communist party members and remaining communist forces joined or established green parties, strengthening the leftist character of green politics.

Former Soviet leader Gorbachev also tried and failed to re-enter politics. He then switched to environmentalism and established Green Cross International. Gorbachev has often promoted the establishment of a world government to prevent ecological disaster. [18]

Many communist parties in the West are directly involved in environmental-protection movements. Jack Mundey, a union activist and co-founder of Australia's green ban movement, was a member of the Communist Party of Australia. His wife was the national president of the Party from 1979 to 1982. [19]

F. MANIPULATING THE RHETORIC OF ENVIRONMENTALISM

Starting mass movements is one of communism's strategies for spreading its influence across nations and the world. Many environmental organizations mobilize large numbers of people to wage environmental protection campaigns. They have lobbied and hijacked government institutions to formulate and enforce unreasonable agreements and regulations. They have also created violent incidents in order to silence the general public.

As the radical leftist Saul Alinsky stated, it is necessary to hide the true purposes of a movement and mobilize people on a large scale to act in support of local, temporary, plausible, or benign goals. When people become accustomed to these moderate forms of activism, it is relatively easy to get them to act for more radical aims. "Remember: once you organize people around something as commonly agreed upon as pollution, then an organized people is on the move. From there it's a short and natural step to political pollution, to Pentagon pollution," Alinsky wrote. [20]

A variety of leftist groups use environmentalism as ideological packaging to carry out street actions advocating revolution. For example, if a country has a "people's climate movement," you can infer that it is a product of communist parties. In the United States, the organizations involved include the Communist Party USA, Socialist Action, the Maoist Revolutionary Communist Party USA, the Ecological Society of America, the Socialist Workers Party, Socialist Alternative, the Democratic Socialists of America, and so on. Such groups hosted the People's Climate March, parading with a sea of red flags through major American cities, including the nation's capital. Slogans at these events have included "System change, not climate change," "Capitalism is killing us," "Capitalism is destroying the environment," "Capitalism is killing the planet," and "Fight for a socialist future." [21]

With more and more communist and socialist elements to strengthen environmentalism, "green peace" has made a full transition to red revolution.

G. ECOTERRORISM

Due to its leftist influences, environmentalism has been relatively radical from the start. There are many branches, including deep ecology, ecofeminism, social ecology, and bioregionalism, with some being extremely radical. The most well-known include groups such as Earth First! and Earth Liberation Front, which utilize direct action — often destructive acts known as ecoterrorism — to stop activities they consider damaging to the environment.

Earth First! was named in 1979, and its slogan is "No compromise in defense of Mother Earth!" The group targets logging operations, dam construction sites, and other projects using direct action and "creative civil disobedience." One of the group's well-known tactics is called tree sitting, in which members sit under or climb up trees to prevent logging. These operations have attracted many leftists, anarchists, and others seeking to rebel against mainstream society.

In 1992, some of the more radical members started a branch called Earth Liberation Front (ELF), copying the ELF name from the Environmental Life Force group that was disbanded in 1978, as well as adopting its guerrilla tactics, particularly arson. In December 2000, ELF perpetrated a series of crimes on Long Island, New York. The radicals smashed hundreds of windows and spray-painted graffiti in a housing development and at the corporate offices of McDonald's, and set fire to sixteen buildings in a condominium development, as well as at least four luxury homes. The main justification for the arson was that the homes were the "future dens of the wealthy elite" and were being built over forest and wetlands. While committing these direct actions, ELF used the slogan "If you build it, we will burn it." [22]

In 2005, the FBI announced that ELF and other extremist organizations were a serious terrorist threat to the United States, having claimed involvement in more than 1,200 criminal incidents, causing tens of millions of dollars in property damage, since 1990. [23] The organization's actions have long since exceeded the limits of normal political protest or differences in views. Communist ideology has exploited hatred to turn some environmentalists into terrorists.

H. GREENPEACE: NOT A PEACEFUL STORY

Greenpeace was established in 1971 and is the largest environmental organization in the world, with offices in more than fifty countries and annual revenues of more than $350 million. It is also one of the more radical environmental organizations.

Greenpeace co-founder Paul Watson, who left the organization in 1977, said: "The secret to [former chairman] David McTaggart's success is the secret to Greenpeace's success: It doesn't matter what is true, it only matters what people believe is true. ... You are what the media define you to be. [Greenpeace] became a myth, and a myth-generating machine." [24]

Patrick Moore, another co-founder, was committed to environmental protection, but left the organization after 15 years, saying it had taken "a sharp turn to the political left." It had developed into an extremist organization displaying hostility toward all industrial production and reflecting an agenda based more on politics than on sound science. [25]

In 2007, six Greenpeace members broke into a British coal power plant and were subsequently sued for causing damage worth about 30,000 British pounds. They admitted to attempting to shut down the power plant, but claimed that they were doing it to prevent even greater damage (an environmental crisis due to greenhouse gases). The court cleared the six of wrongdoing. Before this, Greenpeace had chalked up several court wins over actions such as damaging a fighter jet and nuclear submarine equipment, and occupying Britain's largest waste incinerator. [26]

The strategy of radical environmental organizations such as Greenpeace is to use any means necessary to achieve their goals. On this point, radical environmentalism is highly consistent with communism. Traditional Marxism-Leninism uses the promise of an eventual utopia to justify killing, arson, and robbery. Similarly, under the banner of environmentalism, communists play up environmental crises to legitimize violent and illegal tactics.

In the above example, lawyers for the six Greenpeace members successfully persuaded the jury to accept their criminal behavior as legitimate, demonstrating that society can be misled into accepting specious and groundless arguments. All of this is part of the abandonment of universal values and is an indication of the moral downslide of society.

2. Climate Change

Climate change is a hot topic in today's society, with celebrities, media personalities, politicians, and members of the general public weighing in. The most frequently heard assertion is that the emission of greenhouse gases by humans has caused global warming that will lead to climate disasters.

Advocates claim that this conclusion is reached through scientific consensus and that the science is settled. To some environmentalists, people who reject this conclusion are not only considered anti-science, but also anti-humanity. The voices of those who oppose the prevailing view are stifled, seldom appearing in the media or academic journals, in order to maintain the image of a consensus.

The aforementioned Greenpeace members who damaged the power plant were acquitted in part because a famous expert and proponent of this alleged consensus testified on their behalf. He claimed that the amount of carbon dioxide emitted by the power plant each day would lead to the extinction of up to four hundred animal species.

However, many members of the scientific community, such as retired Massachusetts Institute of Technology meteorology professor Richard Lindzen and former US Department of Energy Undersecretary Steven Koonin, have written that climate science isn't, in fact, settled and that we lack the knowledge needed to make sound climate policy. [27] [28]

A. THE SUPPRESSION OF OPPOSING VOICES

In one article, Koonin wrote:

> *The public is largely unaware of the intense debates within climate science. At a recent national laboratory meeting, I observed more than 100 active government and university researchers challenge one another as they strove to separate human impacts from the climate's natural variability. At*

issue were not nuances, but fundamental aspects of our understanding, such as the apparent — and unexpected — slowing of global sea-level rise over the past two decades. [29]

The issues hotly debated by scientists include whether environmental warming is caused primarily by human activity or by natural factors; how warm the world will be by the end of the twenty-first century; whether humans even have the ability to predict how the climate will change in the future; and whether there is an impending ecological disaster.

Physicist Michael Griffin, a former NASA administrator, said in an interview with NPR in 2007:

I have no doubt that ... a trend of global warming exists. I am not sure that it is fair to say that it is a problem we must wrestle with. To assume that it is a problem is to assume that the state of earth's climate today is the optimal climate, the best climate that we could have or ever have had and that we need to take steps to make sure that it doesn't change. First of all, I don't think it's within the power of human beings to assure that the climate does not change, as millions of years of history have shown, and second of all, I guess I would ask which human beings — where and when — are to be accorded the privilege of deciding that this particular climate that we have right here today, right now, is the best climate for all other human beings. I think that's a rather arrogant position for people to take. [30]

Although Griffin was expressing the humility that scientists should have, he immediately encountered severe criticism from the media and some climate scientists, who called his remarks ignorant. The following week, in a closed meeting at the Jet Propulsion Laboratory in Pasadena, California, Griffin apologized to NASA employees for causing controversy. [31]

A few months later, in an interview for a NASA publication,

Griffin said: "I personally think people have gone overboard in the discussion of climate change, to the point where it has become almost not legitimate to view it as a technical subject. It has almost acquired religious status, which I find deplorable."

Taking Griffin's observation, the use of all means to stifle scientific debate itself violates the spirit of science, as scientific progress itself is the result of debate. "You develop your theories, publish your data, advance your concept, and others shoot it down, or try to. Scientific consensus evolves in that way," he said. [32]

In a similar experience to Griffin's, Swedish meteorologist Lennart Bengtsson received immediate and intense backlash from his peers around the world when he was asked to join the board for the Global Warming Policy Foundation (GWPF), a think tank that challenges global warming theories. The pressure was so intense that he felt forced to tender his resignation from the foundation within two weeks.

In his resignation letter, Bengtsson wrote:

I have been put under such an enormous group pressure in recent days from all over the world that has become virtually unbearable to me. If this is going to continue I will be unable to conduct my normal work and will even start to worry about my health and safety. I see therefore no other way out therefore than resigning from GWPF. I had not expecting such an enormous world-wide pressure put at me from a community that I have been close to all my active life. Colleagues are withdrawing their support, other colleagues are withdrawing from joint authorship etc.

I see no limit and end to what will happen. It is a situation that reminds me about the time of McCarthy. I would never have expecting anything similar in such an original peaceful community as meteorology. Apparently it has been transformed in recent years. [33]

The transformation that Bengtsson observed was the result of communist ideology and struggle tactics hijacking environmental science.

The alleged scientific consensus regarding climate change has transformed climate-change theory into dogma. Climate change is a crucial tenet of today's environmentalism, one treated as sacrosanct and inviolable. The scientists, media, and environmental activists who accept this tenet work together to spread the belief in an imminent ecological disaster. This has become an important tool used by the environmental movement to frighten the public into accepting leftist political agendas, including tax hikes and takeovers by big government, all in order to "save them" from doom. Through the process of establishing and solidifying this dogma, the techniques of communist-style political struggle are all apparent — including deception, mobbing, public shaming, and open conflict.

B. 'CONSENSUS' IN CLIMATE SCIENCE

In 1988, the UN's IPCC was established to assess and synthesize the science related to climate change. One of its missions is to evaluate existing scientific research on climate change and release an authoritative report every several years. These reports are designed to provide a scientific basis for governments in their policy making. They are authored by hundreds of scientists and reviewed by thousands more. Hence, the reports' conclusions are often described as being the consensus of thousands of the world's top scientists.

In 1992, the UN Framework Convention on Climate Change (UNFCCC) stated that its goal was to stabilize the concentrations of greenhouse gases in the atmosphere at a level that would prevent dangerous anthropogenic (human-induced) interference with the climate system. It began with the assertion that climate change was caused by humans and was dangerous. [34] Therefore, the UNFCCC must operate under the assumption that humans are the culprits behind dangerous climate change, as this is necessary for the organization's existence and survival. This assumption has also restricted the focus and scope of the IPCC's inquiry. [35]

Statements of Uncertainty Removed From IPCC Reports

Before the IPCC released its 1995 Second Assessment Report, world-renowned physicist Frederick Seitz obtained a copy. Seitz later discovered that the final report was not the same version that contributing scientists had approved. All statements expressing uncertainty about the effects of human activity on climate change had been deleted.

Seitz's article in *The Wall Street Journal* stated, "In my more than 60 years as a member of the American scientific community, including service as president of both the National Academy of Sciences and the American Physical Society, I have never witnessed a more disturbing corruption of the peer-review process than the events that led to this IPCC report." [36]

The deleted statements included the following:

"None of the studies cited above has shown clear evidence that we can attribute the observed [climate] changes to the specific cause of increases in greenhouse gases."

"No study to date has positively attributed all or part [of the climate change observed to date] to anthropogenic [man-made] causes."

"Any claims of positive detection of significant climate change are likely to remain controversial until uncertainties in the total natural variability of the climate system are reduced." [37]

The IPCC claimed that all modifications were approved by the authors, but the changes reveal how the IPCC's reporting was influenced by politics. The report mostly summarizes existing studies without adding original research. Because the existing research contains so many different views, achieving a consensus meant the IPCC simply got rid of the views that stood in the way.

In April 2000, a first draft of the IPCC's Third Assessment Report said, "There has been a discernible human influence on global climate." The second draft in October said, "It is likely that increasing concentrations of anthropogenic greenhouse gases have contributed significantly to observed warming over the past 50 years." In the final, official conclusion, the statement was even stronger: "Most of the observed warming over the last 50 years is likely to have been due to the increase in greenhouse gas concentrations."

When the UN Environment Programme's spokesman, Tim Higham, was asked about the scientific basis behind the change, he told *New Scientist*, "There was no new science, but the scientists wanted to present a clear and strong message to policymakers." [38]

Put another way, the UNFCCC gave a homework assignment to the IPCC, making the answer they wanted clear. The IPCC then delivered what was required.

'Disaster Consensus' Overstated in IPCC Report

Paul Reiter, medical entomology professor at the Pasteur Institute in France, is a leading expert on malaria and other insect-borne diseases. He disagreed with the IPCC report and had to threaten legal action against the IPCC to get his name removed from the list of two thousand top scientists who were said to have endorsed it. He said that the IPCC "make[s] it seem that all the top scientists are agreed, but it's not true." [39]

In his testimony during a US Senate hearing on April 26, 2006, Reiter said: "A galling aspect of the debate is that this spurious 'science' is endorsed in the public forum by influential panels of 'experts.' I refer particularly to the Intergovernmental Panel on Climate Change. Every five years, this UN-based organization publishes a 'consensus of the world's top scientists' on all aspects of climate change. Quite apart from the dubious process by which these scientists are selected, such consensus is the stuff of politics, not of science." [40]

For example, environmentalists have been promoting the theory that insect-borne diseases such as malaria will wreak havoc as the climate warms. "Global warming will put millions more people at risk of malaria and dengue fever, according to a United Nations report that calls for an urgent review of the health dangers posed by climate change," a *Bloomberg* article stated on November 27, 2007. [41]

But Reiter does not agree with this simple correlation, pointing out that malaria is not confined to tropical areas. Throughout the Russian Empire and Soviet Union in the late nineteenth and early twentieth centuries, up to five million people died annually from the disease. [42] A 2011 study published in *Biology Letters* found that, contrary to the prevailing assumption, rising temperatures decrease a mosquitoes' infectiousness and malaria transmission slows down. [43]

Another scientist who withdrew from the IPCC accused the organization of using so-called disaster consensus as part of its operational culture. Meteorologist Christopher Landsea, a former hurricane researcher at the National Oceanic and Atmospheric Administration and a lead author of the IPCC's fourth assessment report, withdrew from the IPCC in January 2005. In an open letter, he stated, "I personally cannot in good faith continue to contribute to a process that I view as both being motivated by preconceived agendas and being scientifically unsound." He urged the IPCC to confirm that the report would adhere to science rather than sensationalism. [44]

Landsea criticized the lead author of the IPCC report's chapter on hurricane activity for ignoring the scientific studies that could not prove that increased hurricane activity was related to man-made global warming. Instead, the lead author of the report spoke at a high-profile press conference in which it was asserted that global warming was "likely to continue spurring more outbreaks of intense hurricane activity," and gave several interviews before the report was published presenting the same view.

David Deming, a geologist and geophysicist at the University of Oklahoma, obtained the 150-year historical temperature data for North America by studying ice cores and wrote an article about his research, which was published in *Science*. After publication, Deming said "a major researcher in the area of climate change" sent him an email saying, "We have to get rid of the Medieval Warm Period," according to Deming's testimony at a US Senate hearing in 2006. The Medieval Warm Period refers to a period of unusually warm weather that began around AD 1000 and persisted until a cold period in the fourteenth century known as the "Little Ice Age." More than 780 scientists from 462 institutions in 40 countries had contributed to papers over the course of 20 years saying that the Medieval Warm Period existed, Deming testified. However, erasing this period in the historical curve of climate change strengthens the claim that any warming today is unprecedented. [45]

Though hundreds of scientific papers refute the IPCC's alleged consensus, their assertions have been marginalized in the current academic and media environment.

C. ESTABLISHING DOGMA IN THE SCIENTIFIC COMMUNITY

The hype generated by communist forces around climate change is intended not only to pave the way for a global government, but also to destroy research ethics in the scientific community.

Climatology is a young subject with only a few decades of history. Yet the hypotheses surrounding global warming have been prematurely taken as fact. The media has been keeping global warming in the headlines and covering up the inaccuracies in the underlying science. Governments pour funds into researching the global warming hypothesis while marginalizing other findings. The media and politicians label the prediction of catastrophic climate change as "scientifically proven" and spread it worldwide as unassailable doctrine. Thus, thinking on the matter has been largely unified among the general public, and this has planted convoluted notions of right and wrong in people's minds.

If carried to its conclusion, the natural trajectory is the establishment of a global super-government — that is, communism — for the ostensible purpose of saving the earth and humankind from a fabricated or greatly exaggerated crisis. Destroying the old world by any means is a basic strategy of communism.

No matter the academic reputation of a scientist, once he or she publicly expresses doubts about the consensus dogma, he or she immediately faces tremendous pressure from peers and academic institutions, forcing withdrawal. Some people have even argued that global warming skeptics should be prosecuted or criminalized. Those who have lived in a communist totalitarian society have had similar experiences when questioning communist party dogma.

The late David Bellamy, a well-known British botanist and president of The Wildlife Trusts who wrote dozens of books and papers during his career, publicly stated that he did not believe in the consensus dogma of global warming. The Wildlife Trusts responded with a statement expressing dissatisfaction and ousted him several months later when his term expired. [46] Environmentalists who previously showed him respect began to cast aspersions on his mental capacity. [47]

The late William Gray, a renowned professor, was a pioneer of American hurricane research. After he criticized the consensus dogma about human-induced global warming, his research proposals were repeatedly rejected. [48]

In *Climate of Extremes: Global Warming Science They Don't Want You to Know,* co-author Patrick J. Michaels, former president of the American Association of State Climatologists and a climatologist at the University of Virginia, listed numerous examples of environmentalists suppressing scientific opinion in order to reach their alleged consensus. Because Michaels asserted that changes in the climate would not necessarily lead to disaster — and this stance was inconsistent with the consensus dogma — the governor of Virginia instructed him to stop speaking on global warming as a state climatologist. Michaels ultimately chose to resign. [49]

Washington state assistant climatologist Mark Albright was dismissed from his position following an incident involving misleading statements given by the mayor of Seattle, who had asserted that "the average snow pack in the [Cascade Mountains] has declined 50 percent since 1950." Albright began sending his colleagues data that showed the snow pack in the Cascades had been growing, rather than declining, since the 1970s. The state climatologist at the time demanded that Albright begin submitting his emails for vetting before they were sent, and when Albright refused, he was stripped of his title. [50]

In communist countries, crude political interference in science is common. In Western countries, the politics of environmentalism is being used to interfere with academic freedom. Academic research that casts doubt about the consensus dogma is rarely seen in academic journals, a phenomenon that began in the 1990s. In the 1990 documentary *The Greenhouse Conspiracy,* Michaels said he once asked an editor why one of his papers had been rejected for publication, and was told that his work was subject to a higher evaluation standard than that of others. [51] According to the 1990 IPCC report, the understanding at the time was that the extent of global warming was equivalent to natural changes in climate. Therefore, although Michaels's point of view was different from that of many others, it could not be regarded as heretical. However, the goal of establishing a false consensus had already been set, and everyone had to get on board.

In March 2008, scientists who doubted the consensus dogma on climate issues held a private academic event in New York. Many of these scientists said they had encountered various obstacles when trying to publish their research in academic journals. Meteorologist Joseph D'Aleo, former chairman of the American Meteorological Society's Committee on Weather Analysis and Forecasting, said that some of his colleagues dared not attend the meeting out of fear it might affect their employment. He believed that there was "very likely a silent majority of scientists in climatology, meteorology, and allied sciences who do not endorse what is said to be the 'consensus' position." [52]

Climatologist Judith Curry, former chair of the School of Earth and Atmospheric Sciences at the Georgia Institute of Technology, testified in a 2015 US Senate hearing that she had once received an email from a scientist employed at NASA who said, "I was at a small meeting of NASA-affiliated scientists and was told by our top manager that he was told by his NASA boss that we should not try to publish papers contrary to the current global warming claims, because he (the NASA boss) would then have a headache countering the 'undesirable' publicity."

Curry further said in her testimony:

A climate scientist making a statement about uncertainty or degree of doubt in the climate debate is categorized as a denier or a "merchant of doubt," whose motives are assumed to be ideological or motivated by funding from the fossil fuel industry. My own experience in publicly discussing concerns about how uncertainty is characterized by the IPCC has resulted in my being labeled as a 'climate heretic' that has turned against my colleagues. There is enormous pressure for climate scientists to conform to the so-called consensus. This pressure comes not only from politicians, but from federal funding agencies, universities and professional societies, and scientists themselves who are green activists and advocates. Reinforcing this consensus are strong monetary, reputational, and authority interests. [53]

In January 2017, Curry chose to retire early from her tenured position, writing that she "no longer [knew] what to say to students and postdocs regarding how to navigate the CRAZINESS in the field of climate science." In a 2017 interview, Curry said: "Once you understand the scientific uncertainties, the present policy path that we're on doesn't make a lot of sense. ... We need to open up policy dialogue to a bigger solution space. So I'm just looking to open up the dialogue and to provoke people into thinking." [54]

Roger Pielke Jr., a professor at the University of Colorado, said Curry's experience shows that "having a tenured position isn't a guarantee of academic freedom." [55] Pielke was previously a fellow at his university's Cooperative Institute for Research in the Environmental Sciences. Although he agreed with most of the IPCC "consensus" conclusions, he was subjected to similar pressures because he pointed out that the data do not support the idea that extreme weather events such as hurricanes, tornadoes, and droughts had increased due to greenhouse gas emissions. He eventually moved to the University of Colorado's Sports Governance Center. [56]

It is no wonder that Joanne Simpson, a member of the National Academy of Engineering and an award-winning NASA atmospheric scientist, did not declare her skepticism of the "consensus" until after retirement. "Since I am no longer affiliated with any organization nor receiving any funding, I can speak quite frankly," she said. "As a scientist I remain skeptical. ... The main basis of the claim that man's release of greenhouse gases is the cause of the warming is based almost entirely upon climate models. We all know the frailty of models concerning the air-surface system." [57]

D. PROPAGANDA AND INTIMIDATION

In the book *The Great Global Warming Blunder: How Mother Nature Fooled the World's Top Climate Scientists,* Roy Spencer, a climatologist and former NASA satellite expert, listed fifteen propaganda techniques used by environmentalists, including causing panic, appealing to authority, encouraging a herd mentality, resorting to personal attacks, stereotyping, sensationalism, and falsifying records. [58]

In the 2016 article "A Climate of Censorship," British journalist Brendan O'Neill wrote about the derisive rhetoric faced by people in many countries if they dared to doubt the prevailing theory of climate change. For example, a British diplomat said in a public speech that those who doubt climate change should be treated by the media no differently than terrorists, and they should not be given a platform to speak. The former executive director of a large environmental group warned that the media should think twice before broadcasting the views of climate-change skeptics because "allowing such misinformation to spread would cause harm." [59]

Some have even tried to use legal force to suspend freedom of speech in order to extinguish the voices of opponents of the climate-warming hypothesis. Mainstream columnists in Australia have promoted the idea of prosecuting climate change skeptics on charges of crimes against humanity. At a summit attended by top policymakers in Australia, including the prime minister, a proposal was made to deprive violators of their citizenship. One idea was to re-examine Australian citizens and reissue citizenship only to those who have verified they are "environment-climate friendly." [60] In 2015, twenty academics sent a letter to the US president and the attorney general requesting that the Racketeer Influenced and Corrupt Organizations Act be used to prosecute "corporations and other organizations that have knowingly deceived the American people about the risks of climate change," adding that these organizations' "misdeeds" must be "stopped as soon as possible." [61]

Those skeptical of the theory of climate change have been labeled "deniers." This includes groups and individuals ranging from those who acknowledge climate warming but feel we are able to cope with it, to those who completely deny warming as a scientific phenomenon. The potency of the "denier" label is considerable. Charles Jones, a retired English professor at the University of Edinburgh, said that the term is designed to place skeptics on the same level of moral depravity as Holocaust deniers. According to O'Neill, some people even claim that skeptics of climate change theory are accomplices in a coming eco-Holocaust and may face Nuremberg-style trials in the future. He quoted a green columnist as saying: "I wonder what sentences judges might hand down at future international criminal tribunals on those who will be partially but directly responsible for millions of deaths from starvation, famine, and disease in decades ahead. I put [their climate-change denial] in a similar moral category to Holocaust denial — except that this time the Holocaust is yet to come, and we still have time to avoid it. Those who try to ensure we don't will one day have to answer for their crimes."

O'Neill, in his article, commented: "It is usually only in authoritarian states that thoughts or words are equated with crimes, where dictators talk about 'thought crimes' and their threat to the fabric of society. ... It's a short step from demonising a group of people, and describing their arguments as toxic and dangerous, to demanding more and harsher censorship." [62] This judgment is correct. Restricting the right to think is one of the ways communism divorces people from a concept of good and evil that is based on universal values.

3. Communist Environmentalism

In the past decades, with communist forces in retreat and the political and economic catastrophes of communist regimes exposed, communism has latched onto environmentalism to further its agenda.

A. BLAMING CAPITALISM

One of the objectives of communism is to overthrow capitalism and abolish private property. Environmentalism treats capitalism as the enemy, so it shares a common foe with communism. When communism suffered setbacks in the workers' movements in developed Western countries, it shifted gears and hijacked the environmental cause. Normal activism for environmental protection morphed into activism aimed at vanquishing capitalism.

Communist doctrine originally promoted a utopia, a "heaven on earth," to incite revolt and overthrow the existing social system. Under the cover of environmentalism, communism adopted a similar approach, but the vision it described is the exact opposite: In place of the wonderful workers' utopia is instead a frightening dystopia, a vision of a "hell on earth." According to this scenario, in just decades, humanity's very survival will be at risk due to global warming, landslides, tsunamis, droughts, floods, and heatwaves. The target recruits of this movement are not the poor, but rather the wealthy, who are expected to abandon their current lifestyles.

By the original doctrines of communism, after acquiring power, the first step is to strip the affluent of their wealth with the supposed purpose of redistributing it to the poor. In reality, the poor remain poor while all the wealth ends up in the hands of the corrupt officialdom. The second step entails the establishment of a state-controlled economy and the abolition of private property. This destroys the national economy and brings everyone hardship.

The same equation plays out at the international level. Wealthy countries are expected to give aid to poorer countries — that is, to redistribute wealth on a global scale. In reality, poor countries remain poor, as the money that was intended for their development usually ends up in the hands of the corrupt officials of those countries. Meanwhile, the government's responsibility is expanded and market mechanisms are replaced with command economics, using all sorts of heavy-handed environmental policies to obstruct the normal functioning of capitalism, forcing businesses to close or relocate overseas, thus crippling the country's economy. Through these market-oriented methods, the environmental movement seeks to cripple capitalism. Environmental regulations have become important tools for undermining capitalist economies, and are becoming known for eliminating more jobs than they create.

The focus of modern environmentalism is to spread fear of future disasters and to hold the public and governments hostage to this fear. But among those who actively promote this doomsday panic, many live luxurious lifestyles, using plenty of energy and leaving a large carbon footprint. Clearly, they don't think disaster is imminent.

To make use of a crisis mentality, especially using the "common enemy" of global warming to unite different forces to oppose capitalism, it has become imperative for environmentalists to emphasize and exaggerate the nature of the alleged crisis. The simplest way is to stoke mass fear around using the cheapest sources of energy, that is, fossil fuels — coal, oil, natural gas — and also nuclear energy. Environmentalists succeeded in making people fearful of nuclear energy decades ago, and now, they are trying to make people afraid of using fossil fuels by claiming that fossil fuels lead to catastrophic global warming.

However, in reality, climate science hasn't concluded that global warming is caused by human activity, or that global warming will definitely lead to disaster. If natural causes are behind climate change, then all these government policies only serve to impede economic development while often providing only marginal benefits.

For example, officials raise the bar of emission standards for cars with the justification that it reduces the carbon footprint. However, this naturally leads to higher manufacturing costs and less profit, followed by greater unemployment and outsourcing industry to developing countries where costs are lower. Moreover, increasing the fuel efficiency of all cars from 35.5 miles per gallon in 2016 models to 54.5 miles per gallon by 2025 would at most cut the magnitude of global warming by 0.02 degrees Celsius by 2100. [63] This would do virtually nothing to help reduce global warming. Various restrictions of dubious effectiveness have cost millions of workers their jobs and have dealt a heavy blow to manufacturing industries, research faculties, energy innovations, and international business competitiveness in Western countries.

Proponents of environmental protection enthusiastically promote green energy, especially the solar and wind power industries. Unfortunately, the pollution that comes with the generation of green energy is either underestimated or simply hidden. During solar panel production, the deadly poison silicon tetrachloride is created as a byproduct, causing its own environmental problem. A report by *The Washington Post* quotes Ren Bingyan, a professor at the School of Material Sciences at Hebei University of Technology, as saying: "The land where you dump or bury it [silicon tetrachloride] will be infertile. No grass or trees will grow in the place. ... It is like dynamite — it is poisonous, it is polluting. Human beings can never touch it." [64] The production of solar panels typically also consumes enormous amounts of conventional energy, including coal and petroleum.

According to the Paris climate agreement, by 2025, developed countries must collectively mobilize $100 billion each year to help developing countries reduce emissions and "adapt to climate change." If the United States hadn't withdrawn from the agreement, it would have been required to cut its greenhouse gas emissions by 2025 to between 26 and 28 percent below its 2005 levels. This would have meant that every year, the United States would cut 1.6 billion tons of emissions. As for China, the world's biggest polluter, the accord allows it to continue to increase its carbon emissions until 2030. [65]

In a statement formally announcing the withdrawal from the Accord, President Donald Trump said compliance would have cost 2.7 million American jobs by 2025, citing a study by the National Economic Research Associates.

The president said the study also predicted that compliance would cut production in the following US sectors by 2040: paper, which would be down by 12 percent; cement, by 23 percent; iron and steel, by 38 percent; coal, by 86 percent; and natural gas, by 31 percent.

"The cost to the economy at this time would be close to $3 trillion in lost GDP and 6.5 million industrial jobs, while households would have $7,000 less income and, in many cases, much worse than that," Trump said. "In fact, 14 days of carbon emissions from China alone would wipe out the gains from ... America's expected reductions in the year 2030 — after we have had to spend billions and billions of dollars, lost jobs, closed factories, and suffered much higher energy costs for our businesses and for our homes. [66]

With the rise of the environmental movement, communist countries caught a break in their struggle against the West. Unreasonable regulations and agreements choke industries, economies, and technological development in Western capitalist countries. This has hampered America in its role as the leading superpower and bastion of freedom against communism.

We do not deny that the environment needs protecting. However, the goal of environmental protection should be balanced with the needs of humankind. Environmental protection for its own sake is excessive and forsakes humanity while being co-opted by communism. Today's environmentalism doesn't care about balance and has become an extremist ideology. Doubtlessly, many environmentalists harbor good intentions. But in their quest to mobilize and concentrate the resources of the state for the sake of their cause, they are aligning themselves with communism.

B. THE RELIGIONIZATION OF ENVIRONMENTALISM

Michael Crichton, the author of *Jurassic Park*, once said that environmentalism is one of the most powerful religions in the Western world today. He said it possesses the typical characteristics of a religion: "There's an initial Eden, a paradise, a state of grace and unity with nature; there's a fall from grace into a state of pollution as a result of eating from the tree of knowledge; and as a result of our actions, there is a judgment day coming for us all. We are all energy sinners, doomed to die, unless we seek salvation, which is now called sustainability. Sustainability is salvation in the church of the environment."

Crichton believed that the tenets underlying environmentalism are based on blind faith over facts. "Increasingly it seems facts aren't necessary, because the tenets of environmentalism are all about belief. It's about whether you are going to be a sinner, or [be] saved; whether you are going to be one of the people on the side of salvation, or on the side of doom; whether you are going to be one of us, or one of them." [67]

This view has been recognized by a number of scholars. William Cronon, an influential environmental historian in the United States, believes that environmentalism is a religion because it proposes a complex set of moral requirements with which to judge human behavior. [68] Freeman Dyson, the renowned scientist and quantum mechanist, said in an article in the June 12, 2008, issue of *The New York Review of Books* that environmentalism is "a worldwide secular religion" that has "replaced socialism as the leading secular religion." The religion of environmentalism holds that "despoiling the planet with waste products of our luxurious living is a sin, and that the path of righteousness is to live as frugally as possible." The ethics of this new religion "are being taught to children in kindergartens, schools, and colleges all over the world." [69]

Many environmentalists do not shy away from this subject. A former head of the IPCC who resigned following a sexual harassment scandal intimated in his resignation letter that environmentalism was his religion. [70]

As environmentalism has become more ideological and religious in nature, it also has become increasingly intolerant of different views. Former Czech Republic President Václav Klaus, an economist, believes that the environmental movement is now more driven by ideology than true science, becoming a quasi-religion aimed at destroying existing society. This new religion, like communism, describes a wonderful picture of utopia, one reached by using human wisdom to plan the natural environment and rescue the world. This "salvation" is based on opposition to the existing civilization.

Klaus, who wrote the 2008 book *Blue Planet in Green Shackles*, said in a speech, "If we take the reasoning of the environmentalists seriously, we find that theirs is an anti-human ideology." He agreed with biologist Ivan Brezina that environmentalism is not a rational, scientific answer to ecological crises, but rather boils down to an overall denial of civilization. [71]

In addition to hijacking environmentalism as a political movement, communist influences have given environmentalism characteristics of an anti-humanity cult.

Canadian political critic Mark Steyn says that according to the environmentalists, "we are the pollution, and sterilization is the solution." In their view, "the best way to bequeath a more sustainable environment to our children is not to have any." He gave the example of a British woman who had an abortion and underwent sterilization because she believed having children was bad for the environment. [72]

This thinking places the natural environment as the supreme priority, far beyond the sacred position of human beings, by means of even controlling human fertility and depriving people of their very right to exist. This view, which is in essence an anti-humanist ideology, is no different from that of communism. It also goes hand in hand with the Left's attack on the family and traditional gender roles.

Population control has become a method of choice for dealing with environmental degradation, with environmentalist activists and other socialists promoting abortion and anti-natalist policies, and even praising the brutal one-child policy of the Chinese Communist Party (CCP).

Religious fervor, enforced dogma, anti-capitalist action, and debasing humanity before the environment will not lead to a healthier natural environment, much less a fairer or more just human society. Should radical environmentalism succeed in its aims, we would need only to look at the disasters of communist rule over the previous century to predict the end result.

C. POLITICAL INFILTRATION:
BUILDING A WORLD GOVERNMENT

It is difficult to politically impose communism in the democratic Western world, which values individual rights, private ownership, rule of law, and free markets. The radical environmental movement requires the power of the government to compel people to part with their assets and their lives of comfort and convenience.

From the perspective of radical environmentalists, one nation's government is nowhere near enough to tackle the myriad environmental crises facing the planet. Using the justification of an alleged consensus on issues like man-made climate change, they call for an empowered United Nations or the establishment of some other global authority.

If the movement is unable to take off, the vision of an imminent ecological crisis can be played up further, whipping up the panic and fear necessary to influence the public and governments to accept the forceful implementation of environmental policies, and in so doing, achieve the goal of destroying capitalism and imposing communism.

Traditionally, communist states reallocated wealth through revolution. Over the years, however, this approach became increasingly difficult. Therefore, environmentalists adopted indirect strategies, forcing people to quietly give up their freedom and property in the name of preventing environmental tragedy.

A campaign organizer for the group Friends of the Earth stated at a UN conference, "A climate change response must have at its heart a redistribution of wealth and resources." [73] A leading green thinker at the University of Westminster told a reporter that carbon rationing "has got to be imposed on people whether they like it or not" and that "democracy is a less important goal than is the protection of the planet from the death of life, the end of life on it."

In the "battle" against climate change, the United Kingdom was the first to float the concept of individual carbon-ration coupons. One British scientist regarded this as "the introduction of a second currency with everyone having the same allowance — wealth redistribution by having to buy carbon credits from someone less well off."

Those who have lived in the Soviet Union or communist China can easily see this kind of carbon rationing as another method for constructing a totalitarian system. In China, food coupons were once used for buying essentials such as cooking oil, grain, and fabric. Through food rationing, wealth was redistributed, while the central government was given supreme control over people's assets and freedom.

Environmentalists also use their ideology to curtail individual freedom. In Western countries, creating visions of an impending environmental catastrophe became a convenient means of persuading people to give up their rights. The Australia-based Carbon Sense Coalition proposed a list of new laws that would force people to modify their behavior in the name of solving global warming:

- *Ban open fires and pot bellied stoves*
- *Ban incandescent light bulbs ...*

- *Ban bottled water*
- *Ban private cars from some areas*
- *Ban plasma TVs*
- *Ban new airports*
- *Ban extensions to existing airports*
- *Ban "standby mode" on appliances*
- *Ban coal fired power generation*
- *Ban electric hot water systems*
- *Ban vacationing by car*
- *Ban three day weekends*
- *Tax babies*
- *Tax big cars ...*
- *Tax supermarket parking areas*
- *Tax rubbish*
- *Tax second homes*
- *Tax second cars*
- *Tax holiday plane flights*
- *Tax electricity to subsidise solar [power]*
- *Tax showrooms for big cars*
- *Eco-tax cars entering cities*
- *Require permits to drive your car beyond your city limits*
- *Limit choices in appliances*
- *Issue carbon credits to every person*
- *Dictate fuel efficiency standards*
- *Investigate how to reduce production of methane by Norway's Moose ...*
- *Remove white lines on roads to make motorists drive more carefully ...* [74]

Environmentalism is also used to expand the size and authority of government. Various Western countries not only have huge environmental protection agencies, but also use the environment as an excuse to establish new government agencies and expand the authority of existing agencies. All agencies have the bureaucratic tendency for self-preservation and expansion, and environmental agencies are no exception. They abuse the power in their hands to spread the narrative of environmental catastrophe to the general public in order to obtain more funding and to secure their positions within the government structure. Of course, it is taxpayers who foot the bill.

The city of San Francisco established a position for a climate chief with an annual salary of $160,000. One of the poorest boroughs in London, Tower Hamlets, at one point had fifty-eight official positions related to climate change. [75] The logic is the same as that used by universities and companies for hiring "diversity" officers.

Environmentalism is used to suggest that democracy is outdated and to push for the establishment of a multinational or even a global totalitarian government. Environmentalists claim that democracies cannot handle the coming environmental crisis. Instead, to overcome the challenges ahead, we must adopt totalitarian or authoritarian forms of government, or at least some aspects thereof. [76]

Author Janet Biehl summarized this mindset as "the ecological crisis is resolvable only through totalitarian means" and "an 'ecodictatorship' is needed." [77] It asserts that no free society would do what the green agenda requires.

Paul R. Ehrlich, one of the founders of environmentalism, wrote in the book *How to Be a Survivor: A Plan to Save Spaceship Earth*:

1. *Population control must be introduced to both overdeveloped countries as well as underdeveloped countries;*

2. *The overdeveloped countries must be de-developed;*

3. *The underdeveloped countries must be semi-developed;*

4. *Procedures must be established to monitor and regulate the world system in a continuous effort to maintain an optimum balance between the population, resources, and the environment.* [78]

In practice, except for a global totalitarian government, no government or organization could possibly accumulate this much authority. Ultimately, the programs proposed by environmentalists glorify communist totalitarianism and suggest that the communist system is superior.

Ultimately, the programs proposed by environmentalists suggest that the communist system is superior and glorify communist totalitarianism. Since population growth leads to more resource consumption, more carbon emissions, and more waste products, environmentalists advocate for population control or even population reduction. As mentioned above, this has led many Western environmentalists to promote the population control policies of communist China.

Reuters estimated in a report that because of the one-child policy implemented in the 1980s, the CCP was able to cap China's population at 1.3 billion, 300 million less than the projected 1.6 billion. The author of the report noted that the CCP's policy had the side effect of contributing to a reduction of global carbon emissions, completely ignoring the brutality with which the totalitarian policy was enforced — including forced abortions and sterilizations, and economic persecution — as well as the trauma and suffering it brought to the millions of Chinese women and their families whose fundamental rights and privacy the Party trampled underfoot. [79]

One of the biggest issues affecting the environment is pollution. Despite erasing hundreds of millions of people from China's future generations, the CCP's growth-intensive economic model consumes energy at a prodigious rate, making the People's Republic of China the world's biggest polluter, with the worst big-city air pollution and severe water pollution. The majority of rivers in mainland China are no longer safe to drink; contaminated air from China blows across the sea to Korea and Japan, even crossing the Pacific Ocean to reach the American West Coast.

Logically, genuine environmentalists should make communist China the main target of their criticisms, but curiously, many praise the CCP, even viewing it as the hope for environmental protection. The Communist Party USA news website *People's World* has reported extensively on environmental news. The main theme of its reports is the claim that the Trump administration's environmental policies will destroy the country and even the world, while the CCP is the force for its salvation. [80]

Klaus wrote in his book: "Environmentalism is a movement that intends to radically change the world regardless of the consequences (at the cost of human lives and severe restrictions on individual freedom). It intends to change humankind, human behavior, the structure of society, the system of values — simply everything!" [81]

Klaus believes the environmentalists' attitude toward nature is analogous to the Marxist approach to economics: "The aim in both cases is to replace the free, spontaneous evolution of the world (and humankind) by the would-be optimal, central, or — using today's fashionable adjective — global planning of world development. Much as in the case of communism, this approach is utopian and would lead to results completely different from the intended ones. Like other utopias, this one can never materialize, and efforts to make it materialize can only be carried out through restrictions of freedom, through the dictates of a small, elitist minority over the overwhelming majority." [82]

4. Finding a True Solution
to the Environmental Crisis

Humanity and the beautiful and abundant earth were created by the divine. It is an environment in which human beings can live, prosper, and multiply. People have a right to use the resources of nature, and at the same time, have an obligation to cherish natural resources and care for the environment. For thousands of years, human beings have heeded the warnings left by the divine in ancient times and have lived in harmony with nature.

The emergence of environmental problems is ultimately the result of human moral corruption. In modern times, this moral decay has been further amplified by the power of science and technology. The polluted natural environment is but an external manifestation of humanity's inner moral pollution. To purify the environment, one must start by purifying the heart.

The rise of environmental awareness stems from the human instinct of self-preservation. While this is natural and understandable, it has also become a loophole exploited by the communist specter. Communism has latched on to environmentalism to create large-scale panic, advocate a warped set of values, deprive people of their freedom, attempt to expand government, and even impose a world government. Embracing this alternative form of communism in a bid to save the environment threatens to enslave humanity and facilitate its destruction.

A compulsory political program is not the answer to the environmental problems we face, nor is reliance on modern technology a way out. To resolve the crisis, we must gain a deeper understanding of the universe and nature, as well as the relationship between humans and nature, while maintaining an upright moral state. Humanity must restore its traditions, improve morality, and find its way back to the path set by the divine. In doing so, people will naturally receive divine wisdom and blessings, and the beautiful natural world, full of life, will be restored.

Chapter Seventeen

Globalization and Communism

TODAY, MODERN TRANSPORTATION, telecommunications, and digital networks have shrunk geographies and eliminated boundaries that had stood for thousands of years. The world has become smaller and the number of interactions and exchanges between countries is unprecedented. This strengthening of global collaboration is a natural result of technological development, the expansion of production, and migration. This kind of globalization is the result of a natural historical process.

However, there is another kind of globalization, and it is the result of communist ideologies hijacking the natural process in order to undermine humanity. We will address this second form.

Beginning with the Renaissance, human history entered a period of dramatic change. In the late eighteenth century, the Industrial Revolution greatly increased productivity, which spurred social upheaval as well as profound shifts in philosophy and spirituality. As technology advanced, materialist and atheistic ideas became prominent; increasing numbers of people rejected traditional morality and belief in the divine.

Against this historical backdrop, the specter of communism has turned globalization into a powerful tool for its goal of separating people from their traditional cultures and faith. While globalization provides opportunities for international cooperation and understanding, the breakdown of boundaries between nations and economies allows the specter to combine the worst aspects of both the communist and non-communist systems, pursuing broad political and cultural operations to further its agenda around the world. The globalized economic and financial system facilitates this process, making it even harder for individual communities and nations to resist the communist specter's onslaught.

This book has stressed that communism is not merely a theory, but an evil specter. It is alive, and in pursuing its ultimate goal to destroy humankind, it is capable of nearly any kind of mutation that helps it sustain and expand itself. Since the 1990s, globalization has claimed to be about furthering democracy, the market economy, and free trade, and has therefore met with opposition from a number of left-wing groups and figures. But these individuals don't realize that the communist specter is operating on another plane. Communism's aim isn't to use globalization to create a better world, but to take over the world by imposing an ideology of globalist control on all the world's nations.

Globalism has made astounding progress on a variety of fronts, particularly in the economic, political, and cultural spheres. As an ideological force, globalism has many faces and manifests in diverse, even superficially contradictory forms — often eliciting nebulous feelings of a world free from war, poverty, discrimination, or exploitation. But in practice, the methods proposed to achieve these things are essentially similar to the utopian lies of communist revolution.

Though each nation has its own culture and history, their diverse traditions contain universal moral values common to all of humankind. National sovereignty and the cultural traditions of each ethnic group play an important role in national heritage and self-determination, and offer collective protection in the face of various threats, from natural disasters to military invasions. Additionally, an ethnic group's national legends and religious faith help the entire people maintain a sense of identity, and protect them from falling to the specter's evil designs.

While globalists often claim to stand for the cultures of all ethnicities, in recent years it has become increasingly apparent that this ideology actually serves to strengthen leftist causes. Instead of supporting traditional culture, which is rooted in faith and virtue, globalist talking points tend to mirror the Left's "political correctness," "social justice," "value neutrality," and "absolute egalitarianism."

World government, starting with increased supranational bodies and regulation, is the main end goal of globalism. Once a global super-government is formed, communism will easily achieve its goal of eliminating private property rights, nations, races, and the traditional culture of each nation. Revealing how the communist specter manipulates globalization and the relationship between globalism and communism is a pressing matter.

1. Globalism and Communism

Karl Marx did not use the concept of globalism in his writings, but instead used the term "world history," which has very close connotations. In *The Communist Manifesto,* Marx and co-author Friedrich Engels claimed that the global expansion of capitalism would inevitably produce a huge proletariat (working) class in the industrialized nations, and then a proletarian revolution would sweep the globe, overthrowing capitalism and achieving the "paradise" of communism. Marx and Engels also wrote, "The proletariat can thus only exist world-historically, just as communism, its activity, can only have a 'world-historical' existence." [1] That is to say, the realization of communism depends on the proletariat taking joint action around the world — the communist revolution must be a global movement.

Later, Vladimir Lenin modified Marx's doctrine and proposed that the world revolution could be initiated in Russia, despite the predominantly rural character of its society at the time. In 1919, the Soviet communists established the Communist International in Moscow, with branches spread throughout more than sixty countries. Lenin said that the goal of the Communist International was to establish a World Soviet Republic. [2]

Joseph Stalin, the Soviet leader who succeeded Lenin, was known for the temporary policy of "socialism in one country," but proposed several goals of the communist global revolution in his book *Marxism and the National Question*. American thinker G. Edward Griffin summarized Stalin's points as follows:

1. *Confuse, disorganize, and destroy the forces of capitalism around the world.*

2. *Bring all nations together into a single world system of economy.*

3. *Force the advanced countries to pour prolonged financial aid into the underdeveloped countries.*

4. *Divide the world into regional groups as a transitional stage toward total world government. Populations will more readily abandon their national loyalties to a vague regional loyalty than they will for a world authority. Later, the regionals [such as the present*

NATO, SEATO, and the Organization of American States] can be brought all the way into a single world dictatorship of the proletariat. [3]

William Z. Foster, the former national chairman of the Communist Party USA, wrote: "A Communist world will be a unified, organized world. The economic system will be one great organization, based upon the principle of planning now dawning in the USSR. The American Soviet government will be an important section in this world government." [4]

From Marx, Lenin, Stalin, and Foster, to the "community of human destiny" proposed by the Chinese Communist Party (CCP), we can clearly see that the communist specter is not satisfied with having power in only a few countries. Communist ideology, in all its forms, features the ambition to dominate all of humanity.

The proletarian world revolution failed to take place in the form Marx envisioned. What he thought were desperate and dying capitalist societies were instead prosperous and flourishing with private ownership and rule of law. With the collapse of the Soviet and Eastern European communist camp, and the adoption of market principles by the CCP regime, it appeared that the free world had triumphed over communism. But the communist specter hides behind various doctrines and movements as it corrodes, infiltrates, and expands communist elements into every corner of the world. Socialism — the primary stage of communism — has been gaining currency internationally, piggybacking on the destabilizing aspects brought about by globalization and globalist factors.

After World War II, the left-wing forces in European countries continued to grow. The Socialist International, which advocated democratic socialism, included political parties from more than one hundred countries. These parties were in power in various countries and spread across most of

Europe, driving policies of generous welfare, high taxation, and increased state ownership.

Globalization has hollowed out US industry, shrunk the middle class, caused incomes to stagnate, polarized the rich and the poor, and driven rifts through society. This has greatly aided the growth of the Left and socialism in the United States, shifting the global political spectrum sharply left in the last decade or so. Left-wing forces around the world note that globalization has caused income inequality and polarization between the rich and the poor. Alongside these arguments, anti-globalization sentiment has grown rapidly, pinning the blame for the world's ills on capitalism and advocating socialist policies.

After the Cold War, communist ideas infiltrated economic globalization, with the goal that there would be no pure national economy and that the sovereignty of each country's economic foundations would be undermined. The result was to fully mobilize and internationalize human greed. In the last few decades, Western financial powers shifted wealth — accumulated by society over several hundred years — to quickly rapidly build up the economy of mainland China following the CCP's market reforms. The CCP used these investments to prop up its regime, while binding foreign businesses and leaders to its corrupt system.

As the head of the communist forces in the world today, the CCP aims to build up a socialist economic superpower while fortifying left-wing and communist parties around the world. Its totalitarian system upended the rules of normal trade, and it intends to use the enrichment it gained from democratic free markets to co-opt and subvert them from within.

The CCP's economic strength has also spurred on its political and military ambitions, as it attempts to export its authoritarian communist model throughout the world. Looking at the CCP's globalized strategy from the perspective of Marx, Lenin, and Stalin, today's world has many of the conditions necessary for communist revolution.

2. Economic Globalization

Economic globalization refers to the integration of chains of global capital, production, and trade that began in the 1940s and 1950s, matured in the 1970s and 1980s, and became a global norm in the 1990s. International agencies and corporations were the driving forces, as they demanded the loosening of regulation and controls to allow the free flow of capital and goods.

On the surface, economic globalization was promoted by Western countries to spread capitalism around the world. Unfortunately, however, globalization has become a vehicle for the communist specter. In particular, globalization has resulted in Western countries providing financial support to the Chinese regime, resulting in a mutual dependency between the capitalist market economy and the CCP's socialist totalitarian economy. In exchange for economic benefits, the West sacrifices its conscience and universal values, while the communist regime expands its control by way of economic coercion.

A. DESTABILIZING EFFECTS OF GLOBALIZATION

Large international organizations, treaties, and regulations have been formed in the process of globalization, particularly the globalization of national economies. On the surface, this appears to be about the expansion of capitalism and the free market. But in fact, the trend works toward a unified system of economic control, one that is able to issue orders to determine the fate of enterprises in many countries. After this international financial order was established, the phenomenon of developed countries giving long-term economic aid to developing countries was also formed — in line with Stalin's third goal mentioned previously.

In terms of handing out financial aid, international financial organizations, such as the World Bank, usually implement macroeconomic interventionism, which is not only authoritarian but also undermines the free market. It also ignores the social, cultural, and historical conditions of the recipient country. The result is diminished freedom and national sovereignty, as well as greater centralized economic control. American scholar James Bovard wrote that the World Bank "has greatly promoted the nationalization of Third World economies and has increased political and bureaucratic control over the lives of the poorest of the poor." [5]

Economic globalization has also contributed to the development of a homogeneous global culture, leading to greater similarities in consumer trends and unified mechanisms of production and consumption. Many small businesses and those associated with local ethnic groups have simply been wiped out by the wave of globalization. More and more people have lost the environment or incentives to freely engage in commerce within their own borders.

As the world became more interconnected with the development of communication and transportation technology, it seemed as if globalization would deliver financial prosperity and democratic values to the entire global village. In many cases, the opposite has occurred.

Developing countries become part of a global production chain, which leads to the weakening of their economic sovereignty and to state failure in some cases. Some countries become burdened with debt and the need to meet repayments, fundamentally rupturing the foundation of free capitalist economics in those countries.

Globalization weakens developing countries in other ways as well. In the early 2000s, Jamaica opened its markets and began importing large quantities of cheap milk. This made milk more affordable for more people, but it also led local dairy farmers to go bankrupt, as they couldn't compete amid the flood of cheap imports. Mexico used to have numerous light industrial manufacturing plants, but after Beijing gained admittance to the World Trade Organization (wTO), most of those jobs moved to the People Republic of China (PRC). Mexico suffered because it could not match China's high-output manufacturing capability.

Many developing countries are rich in natural resources, but since foreign investment poured in, the minerals have been mined for export abroad with very little economic gain generated for locals. Foreign investment also corrupts government officials. Globalization claims to bring democracy to developing nations, but in reality it has empowered corrupt dictatorships while the general public has been left to starve.

During the 1997 Asian financial crisis, Thailand opened its weak financial system to international investment, which brought temporary prosperity. But when foreign investment left, Thailand's economy ground to a halt. The neighboring countries were also negatively impacted.

As professor Dani Rodrik of Harvard's John F. Kennedy School of Government stated, globalization presents a "trilemma": "We cannot simultaneously pursue democracy, national determination, and economic globalization." [6] This is the fatal flaw of globalization and something communism has exploited.

The benefits and opportunities brought about by globalization have often been limited to a small number of elites. In many countries, globalization has worsened inequality, with seemingly no long-term solutions available.

B. HOW GLOBALIZATION FACILITATES THE SPREAD OF COMMUNIST IDEOLOGY

The communist ideology of egalitarianism and the ethos of struggle have ridden around the world on the back of globalization. It eroded national sovereignty, exacerbated regional turmoil, and heightened the archetypal Marxist conflicts between "the oppressor" and "the oppressed" that leftists use as ideological weapons to fight against the free market, private property, and other aspects of the "old society."

The polarization of wealth created by globalization generates a self-perpetuating cycle. In Western countries, the enormous outflow of jobs and entire industries turned the lower and middle classes into victims of globalization. In the United States, the massive outflow of capital and technology to the PRC, caused millions of manufacturing job losses, leading to the loss of industries and a rise in unemployment. From 2000 to 2011, sixty-five thousand factories were closed, and 5.7 million, or 33 percent, of manufacturing jobs were lost. [7]

The gap between rich and poor has been widening in the United States for decades. Over the past thirty years, the growth of the average wage (adjusted for inflation) has been slowing, bringing about the emergence of the working poor — those who work or seek jobs for twenty-seven weeks of the year, but whose income is below the official poverty level. In 2016, 7.6 million Americans were counted among the working poor. [8]

The polarization of the rich and the poor is a fertile breeding ground for communist ideology to grow. Economic problems impact every aspect of society, but the demand for a solution based on a perceived unfair distribution of income has led to a surge of socialist ideology and of activism for "social justice." Meanwhile, the expansion of social welfare benefits has in turn created more poor families, generating a vicious cycle of decreased productivity and individual reliance on the state.

Since 2000, leftist ideology has grown increasingly influential in the United States, with youth shifting increasingly to the left on social, economic, and political issues. By the 2016 election, a rising demand for socialism was evident, along with increasing political polarization. To a great extent, the impact of globalization lay behind these shifts. At the same time, the greater the economic and social strife Western democratic societies appeared to be suffering from, the more triumphant the force of communism appeared on the world stage.

Without compunction, the communist specter plays both sides of an issue to achieve its aims. Thus, along with the advance of globalization, came anti-globalization campaigns, marked first by the large-scale violent protests in late 1999 in Seattle against the WTO Ministerial Conference. Three large-scale international conferences in 2001 (the Summit of the Americas meeting in Québec, Canada; the European Union summit in Gothenburg, Sweden; and the Group of Eight economic summit in Genoa, Italy) were also beset by such demonstrations.

Worldwide anti-globalization campaigns have drawn participants from a variety of backgrounds. A vast majority of them have been left-wing opponents of capitalism writ large, including labor unions and environmental organizations (also hijacked and infiltrated by communism), as well as victims of globalization and the underprivileged. As a result, the public, whether supporters or opponents of globalization, have ended up inadvertently serving the goals of communism.

C. WESTERN CAPITALISM: NOURISHING THE CHINESE COMMUNIST PARTY

When assessing the successes or failures of globalization, scholars often cite the PRC, which seemed to have greatly benefited from globalization and rapidly came to the fore as the world's second-largest economy. Many predicted that mainland China would ultimately replace the United States as the world's largest economy.

Whereas Mexico, for example, established low-end manufacturing as its model, the PRC set out to obtain the most cutting-edge technology from the West and then replace its competitors. To that end, companies from developed countries were required to set up joint ventures with Chinese companies in order to sell into the China market, which the CCP then used to extract key technologies. The Party adopted numerous methods, from forcing technology transfers to outright stealing via hacking. After obtaining this advanced technology, the PRC pressed its advantage to dump low-priced products on the world market. With the help of export rebates and subsidies, mainland China defeated competitors with below-market prices and disrupted the order of free markets.

As undeveloped countries opened their domestic markets, the PRC instead created multiple trade barriers. The CCP profited enormously by taking advantage of the WTO's rules upon admission in 2001, while simultaneously taking advantage of the global market to dump products abroad. The Party failed to open key industries — including telecommunications, banking, and energy — which in turn enabled mainland China to take advantage of the global economy while reneging on its commitments.

Bought off by economic profits, the Western world turned a blind eye and a deaf ear to the egregious human rights abuses the CCP was committing, and the international community continued to confer generous favor on the regime. In the midst of globalization, a powerful PRC regime, together with a morally corrupt Chinese society, has struck a blow to the market economy and trade regulations in the West.

The PRC has ignored the rules and reaped all the advantages of globalization. In a sense, globalization has been like a blood transfusion for the Communist Party, allowing a fading communist state to spring back into action. Behind the manipulation of globalization is the hidden purpose of propping up the PRC through the reallocation of wealth.

Globalization has been a process of saving the CCP and legitimizing the regime. While the Party strengthened its socialist muscles with capitalist nutrients, the West fell into relative decline, further giving the CCP confidence in its communist totalitarianism and global ambitions. Mainland China's rise also greatly excited numerous socialists and members of the Left worldwide.

While its economy has grown, the PRC has intensified efforts to infiltrate global economic organizations, including the WTO, the International Monetary Fund, the World Bank, the UN

Industrial Development Organization, and others. When assigned to important positions in these organizations, PRC officials persuade them to cooperate with the regime in order to endorse the Party's schemes and defend its policies.

The CCP regime uses international economic organizations to carry out its own economic agenda and corporatist model. If its ambitions aren't halted, there's little doubt that the regime will bring disaster to global politics and economics.

The above are just some examples of how economic globalization has been used to promote and extend communism. With advances in technology and transportation, economic activities are extended beyond a nation's borders. This is a natural process, but in this case, the process was turned into an opportunity for the CCP to begin the path to global dominance. The time has come for society to be alert to what is taking place and to rid globalization of communist elements. If that happens, there will be a chance for the sovereignty of individual states and the welfare of their people to be realized.

3. Political Globalization

Political aspects of globalization include increased cooperation among states, the emergence of international bodies, and the formulation of international agendas and treaties. Following the emergence of such international institutions, as well as rules and regulations that transcend national borders, these organizations have developed into bases of international power, weakening national sovereignty and eroding the cultural, social, and moral foundations of individual nations. In the name of promoting world peace and international understanding, globalist institutions aim to consolidate power for the gradual advancement of the communist program.

The communist specter promotes and uses international organizations to bolster the strength of leftist factors, promoting the Marxist philosophy of struggle and communist regimes' twisted definitions of human rights and freedom. Globalism promotes socialist ideas on a global scale, including attempts to redistribute wealth and form a world government to eventually bring all of humanity under totalitarian rule.

A. EXPANDING COMMUNIST POLITICAL POWER THROUGH THE UN

The United Nations is the largest international organization and was established after World War II to strengthen cooperation and coordination among countries. As a supranational entity, the UN has been used by communist forces in their goal of weakening and abolishing nation-states. From its establishment, the UN was compromised by the Soviet-led communist bloc and has served as a stage for the Communist Party to promote itself and the communist goal of a world government.

When the UN was founded and its charter drafted, the Soviet Union was one of the sponsoring countries and a permanent member of the Security Council, playing a decisive role. The secretary-general of the UN Charter Conference was Alger Hiss, a US State Department official and important adviser to President Franklin D. Roosevelt. Hiss was convicted of perjury in 1950, in connection with the charge of being a Soviet spy. The UN Charter and conventions contain back doors that are beneficial to communist regimes, which likely have a great deal to do with Hiss's involvement.

The heads of many important UN agencies are communists or fellow travelers. Many UN secretaries-general have been socialists and Marxists. For example, the first, Trygve Lie, was a Norwegian socialist who initially received strong support from the Soviet Union. His most important task was to advocate for bringing the PRC into the United Nations. His successor, Dag Hammarskjöld of Sweden, was a socialist and a sympathizer for a global communist revolution. Hammarskjöld often fawned over high-ranking CCP official Zhou Enlai.

The third secretary-general, U Thant of Burma (also known as Myanmar), was a Marxist who believed that Lenin's ideals were consistent with the UN Charter. The sixth secretary-general, Boutros Boutros-Ghali of Egypt, began his political career in the regime of Gamal Abdel Nasser and was formerly the vice president of the Socialist International. [9]

It is easy to understand why the heads of communist regimes regularly receive the highest courtesy from the United Nations. Many UN conventions have been used to directly or indirectly promote communist ideas and expand communist power.

The highest mission of the UN is to maintain world peace and security and its peacekeeping forces are overseen by the under-secretary-general for political and peacebuilding affairs. Of the fourteen individuals who held this position from 1946 to 1992, thirteen were Soviet citizens. The Soviet communist regime never relinquished its attempt to expand communist power, and it had no interest in contributing to world peace. Though the Soviet Union used "safeguarding world peace" as its slogan, the real aim was to hijack the UN, using it as a pro-socialist organization to advance the communist movement.

Communist influence was so entrenched in the UN that the organization acted as a veritable front group for the Soviet Union. FBI Director J. Edgar Hoover stated in 1963 that communist diplomats assigned to the UN "represent the backbone of Russian intelligence operations in this country." [10]

Even after the collapse of the Soviet bloc, the communist legacy remained widespread in the UN. *The Wall Street Journal* reported in 1991: "Many of those working within the Secretariat, or at missions in its vicinity, argue that communism left a legacy within the UN bureaucracy. ... 'It works like a scorpion's stinger,' says one UN professional. 'The scorpion — East Bloc socialism — dies. But the stinger remains poisonous, and strikes new victims.' ... [Over the years,] Westerners who worked at the UN ... found themselves surrounded by what many have called a communist mafia." [11]

The CCP uses the UN as a propaganda platform. For example, top UN officials, including the secretary-general, have promoted the CCP's One Belt, One Road (OBOR), a global infrastructure and investment initiative, as a way to tackle poverty in the developing world. However, the OBOR initiative is a means for the CCP to expand its international hegemony around the world. The initiative has left many countries in debt crises; Pakistan, for example, requested a $6 billion bailout from the International Monetary Fund because of the country's debts problems resulting from OBOR loans. Others have been forced to cede control of critical infrastructure to the PRC. Sri Lanka had to lease an important port to Beijing for ninety-nine years to pay off its debt.

Moreover, the initiative enables the CCP to exert control over the politics and economies of participating countries, while undermining human rights and democracy in those countries. Consequently, many countries are pulling back. However, due to the CCP's political influence in the UN, the agency's senior officials have touted the project. [12]

B. SUBVERTING THE UN'S HUMANITARIAN IDEALS

One of the United Nations' objectives is to improve human rights and promote freedom; this is a universal principle. But the PRC, together with other corrupt regimes, denies the universality of human rights. The Communist Party claims that human rights are the internal affairs of each country, using this as an excuse for its monstrous repression of religious freedom, ethnic minorities, and dissidents. The CCP even praises itself as a defender of human rights for "lifting" hundreds of millions of PRC citizens out of poverty, taking credit for the hard work and ingenuity of the Chinese people.

The CCP has used the platform of the UN to attack the democratic values of the West, relying on its alliances with developing nations to subvert the efforts of free nations to promote universal values. Due to manipulation by communist factors, the UN has not only done little to improve human rights, but also become a tool used by communist regimes to whitewash their poor human rights records. Dore Gold, former Israeli ambassador to the UN and author of *Tower of Babble: How the United Nations Has Fueled Global Chaos,* asserted: "The UN is not a benign but ineffective world body. It has actually accelerated and spread global chaos." Gold outlined numerous examples, including the UN's "value neutrality" and the immorality of "moral equivalence" and "moral relativism"; the organization's general corruption; the fact that undemocratic countries are allowed to hold the majority of votes; and the degree of control given to communist regimes. [13] He called the UN an "abject failure," writing that it was "dominated by anti-Western forces, dictatorships, state sponsors of terrorism, and America's worst enemies." [14]

For example, countries with poor human rights records are allowed to become member states of the Human Rights Council, utterly compromising the worth of the council's human rights reviews. Furthermore, the PRC has bought off many developing countries, ensuring that any criticism of the communist regime's human rights policies has been shelved. The UN's tyranny of the majority has made it a tool for communist forces in opposing free nations on many issues. This has prompted the United States to withdraw from the Human Rights Council. The West wants to promote freedom and human rights but has been repeatedly blocked by communist countries. The council has been hijacked by thugs, and the so-called international conventions adopted have done nothing to bind totalitarian countries. These countries simply mouth the slogans without implementing them.

The UN Charter is very similar to the Soviet Constitution and in direct opposition to the US Constitution. The charter's purpose is not to protect the rights of people, but to serve the interests of political leaders. Likewise, the Soviet Constitution superficially gave the citizens some rights, but in fact, many specific laws were stipulated as "within the scope of the law," which allowed the Soviet regime to arbitrarily deprive citizens of their rights according to its interpretations of "within the scope of the law." The UN Charter and its various contracts and conventions define people's rights in the same equivocal way. For example, in the International Covenant on Civil and Political Rights, statements like "everyone has the right" are attached to provisions such as "the above-mentioned rights shall not be subject to any restrictions except those which are provided by law." This is not just an arbitrary or coinciden-tal choice of blueprint, but a "back door" that communism purposefully established.

As Griffin wrote: "In fact, every single right outlined in the United Nations Covenant on Human Rights may be legally denied if in the opinion of the politicians it is 'necessary to protect national security, or public order, or public safety, or public health, or public morals, or the rights, freedoms or repu-tations of others.' Most wars and national crimes are commit-ted in the name of one of these [provisions]." [15] It is difficult for free countries to arbitrarily deprive citizens of their freedom, yet communist regimes can openly take advantage of loop-holes in the Universal Declaration of Human Rights.

C. PROMOTING COMMUNIST POLITICAL IDEAS WORLDWIDE

The communist specter, through its agents, repeatedly raises global problems and claims that these problems can be solved only through international collaboration and global power structures. Its true goal is to establish a world government. Consequently, various countries are restricted and regulated more and more by a growing number of international treaties, thus weakening their national sovereignty.

Many groups support international power structures of this sort, and although such groups are not necessarily communist, their claims are consistent with communist goals

— that is, to eventually abolish individual nations and establish a world government.

In Chapter Sixteen, we detailed how communism uses the claim of protecting the environment to advance its agenda. Environmentalism has gone hand in hand with the drive to weaken national sovereignty and promote supranational political power.

A media personality said on Earth Day 1970: "Humanity needs a world order. The fully sovereign nation is incapable of dealing with the poisoning of the environment. ... The management of the planet, therefore, whether we are talking about the need to prevent war or the need to prevent ultimate damage to the conditions of life, requires a world government." [16]

The Humanist Manifesto II of 1973 also declared: "We have reached a turning point in human history where the best option is to transcend the limits of national sovereignty and to move toward the building of a world community. ... Thus we look to the development of a system of world law and a world order based upon transnational federal government." [17]

In fact, the establishment of the UN Environment Programme came about precisely because a group that advocated for a global confederacy in 1972 considered the environmental issue to be a world issue, and therefore called for the development of global solutions and the establishment of a global environmental protection agency. Its first director was Maurice Strong, a Canadian with strong socialist tendencies.

At the UN Earth Summit in Rio de Janeiro in 1992 (also known as the UN Conference on Environment and Development), 178 governments voted to adopt Agenda 21. This eight-hundred-page blueprint includes content on the environment, women's rights, medical care, and so on. An influential environmental researcher who became an official of the UN Environment Programme said: "National sovereignty — the power of a country to control events within its territory — has lost much of its meaning in today's world, where borders are routinely breached by pollution, international trade, financial flows, and refugees. ... Nations are in effect ceding portions of their sovereignty to the international community, and beginning to create a new system of international environmental governance as a means of solving otherwise-unmanageable problems." [18]

Superficially, many arguments for a world government seem reasonable, but their true purpose is to spread communism and dominate the world. Communist regimes often publicly decry interference in other countries' affairs while actively participating in the various international organizations promoting the concept of global governance.

Boutros-Ghali initiated rapid advances in the UN's march toward world government during his term as secretary-general from 1992 to 1996. He called for the formation of a permanent UN army and pressed for the right to collect taxes. [19] The United States opposed allowing him to serve a second term, and one can only imagine how much more powerful the UN would be today if not for that intervention.

In 2002, Secretary-General Kofi Annan said, "In an age of interdependence, global citizenship is a crucial pillar of progress." Robert Chandler, a former US Air Force colonel and White House strategist, believed that Annan's so-called progress threatened national sovereignty and opened the way for a global civil society under the governance of a "massive, faceless international bureaucracy, which would ... relegate individuals to the status of worker ants in a socialist authoritarian universe." UN programs like Teaching Toward a Culture of Peace were actually organized and overseen by ultra-leftists, whom Chandler believed were intent on destroying national sovereignty. [20]

The 1958 book *The Naked Communist* outlined the forty-five goals of communists, one of which states: "Promote the U.N. as the only hope for mankind. If its charter is rewritten, demand that it be set up as one-world government with its own independent armed forces." [21] A world government cannot be established in the short term, thus, communists and globalists use various issues to establish international institutions in various fields, then promote the unity of these institutions, and continue to advocate for dependence on the UN.

D. WORLD GOVERNMENT AND TOTALITARIANISM

There is nothing wrong with envisioning a better world or future. Seeking to establish a world government to solve all of mankind's problems, however, is no different from the misguided "dictatorship of the proletariat" or central planning promoted by communism.

Advocating for a world government, strengthening the role of the UN, portraying the UN as a panacea for solving all problems in today's world — all of this is part of an attempt to play God and arrange the future of humankind. Were such a regime established, it would inevitably descend into communist-style totalitarianism.

To attract countries to join it, a world government would invariably offer tantalizing benefits, promises of welfare, and a blueprint of a global utopia for humankind.

However, an unavoidable issue faced by a world government is how to actually implement its policies — be they political, military, economic, or other. To push through its policies on a global scale, such a government couldn't take the form of a free republic like that of the United States; by necessity, it would be a totalitarian regime, like that of the Soviet Union or the PRC.

This centralization would elevate the power of the government to an unmatched level, and its control over society would be unprecedented. At this stage, such a world government wouldn't bother with achieving consensus among its member countries or heed any commitments made to them; instead, it would solely focus on the forceful implementation of its policies.

In the world today, there exist great differences among countries. Many countries have neither orthodox faiths nor free societies, not to mention respect for human rights or high moral standards. If countries were to combine to form a world government, that government would have to adopt the lowest standard among them, eliminating any requirements relating to faith and belief, morality, and human rights. In other words, countries would be given a free pass on these issues, as the concept of so-called "neutrality" in religion, morality, and human rights would be used to unite them. A world government would inevitably promote a mainstream culture in order to unify the world, despite the fact that each country has its own cultural traditions and religious beliefs.

Of the experts, scholars, and government officials who actively advocate a world government, the majority are atheists or those who hold progressive views on religious faith. Clearly, a world government would have atheism as its core value — an inevitable consequence, given that communism is the force behind a world government. Furthermore, because cultural and linguistic differences between peoples would impede global authority, proponents of world government often oppose concepts like patriotism or localism, which are essential for the well-being of nation-states.

To maintain its rule, this world government would forcibly and violently implement ideological re-education. To prevent fragmentation or independence movements by member countries, a world government would greatly strengthen its military and police forces and tighten its control over freedom of speech and the media.

The government of a country or region whose people do not have a shared faith and culture could rely only on totalitarian rule to stay in power, and the result would be the loss of individual freedom.

In the end, a world government could only be realized as a totalitarian project, featuring the same enslavement, abuse, and degradation of its subjects seen under communist regimes today and throughout history. But instead of being confined to a single country, this totalitarianism would extend to the entire world, leaving the communist specter practically unopposed in its plan to corrupt human traditional culture, eradicate belief in the divine, and finally destroy humanity itself.

4. Cultural Globalization: A Means of Corrupting Humanity

As cultural exchanges and capital flows expand throughout the world, the various deviant cultural forms that communism has established over the past nearly one hundred years — such as modern art, literature, and thought; deviant entertainment and lifestyles; and consumerism — are transmitted globally. During this process, the traditions of various ethnic groups are interrupted and severed from their original meaning, resulting in hollow, degenerate lifestyles geared toward consumption and profit, breaking down morality and society wherever they are spread.

Willi Münzenberg, the German communist activist and one of the founders of the Frankfurt School, said: "[We must] organise the intellectuals and use them to make Western civilization stink. Only then, after they have corrupted all its values and made life impossible, can we impose the dictatorship of the proletariat." [22]

Indeed, as described in previous chapters of this book, the heritage of Western civilization has been replaced by deviated modern pop culture. Globalization and globalism bring this degeneracy to all corners of the earth.

Globally, the United States leads in the political, economic, and military arenas. Its unique position in these fields carries over to American popular culture, which is readily accepted and adopted by other countries and regions. After infiltrating and corrupting the family unit, politics, the economy, law, arts, the media, and popular culture across all aspects of daily life in the United States, communism made use of cultural globalization to export this corrupted culture. Seen as the newest, most desirable trends from America, it spread across the entire world. Through Hollywood movies, inhabitants of China's far-flung conservative inland villages learned that single mothers, extramarital affairs, and sexual liberation are all "normal" aspects of life in the "advanced" West. Rock 'n' roll became extremely popular across the world, from Ecuador in South America, to Malaysia in Southeast Asia, to Fiji in the Pacific Islands. In education, the ideology underpinning the Common Core curriculum created by cultural Marxists was almost instantaneously reflected in Taiwan's secondary-school textbooks. In the blink of an eye, the Occupy Wall Street movement in New York was shown on television screens in the remotest mountain hamlets of India.

Cultural globalization is the hurricane that blows the deviant culture of the West and the Party culture of communist totalitarian regimes throughout the entire world, mercilessly sweeping away the traditional values that have guided humanity for thousands of years.

A. DESTROYING THE WORLD'S CULTURAL TRADITIONS

Every ethnic culture has unique characteristics and carries the deep influences of its own special history. Despite the differences between ethnic cultures, they all observe the same divinely bestowed universal values in their traditions. After the Industrial Revolution, technological development brought about convenience, and simultaneously, tradition was labeled by progressives as backward. Measuring everything based on its modernness, novelty, and "progress" — or whether it has commercial value — is now standard.

Communism promotes values that seem noble, but, in reality, are aimed at having humankind abandon traditional values, replacing them with homogeneous and deteriorated modern values instead. Today's so-called common values formed by cultural exchange in the process of globalization aren't from any particular tradition — they are modern values. The elements and values that are adopted by globalism must, of necessity, deviate from tradition. They include only the crassest elements of existing cultural heritage, as well as the aspects that can be commercialized. Notions about the "common destiny of humankind" and "our common future" are the results of such deviated values.

The lowest standard that is recognized during cultural globalization manifests in consumer culture. Product design and marketing, driven by economic interests, are entirely centered on appealing to consumers' base instincts. The aim is to control humankind by seducing, indulging, and satisfying people's superficial desires.

This global consumerist culture is used to corrupt tradition in multiple ways. First, the unique characteristics and meaning behind a product, as originated from its ethnic culture, are removed. In other words, tradition is taken away from products through deculturalization, or standardization. The more alienated a group of people is from their cultural heritage and faith, the more susceptible they become to such a simplified consumerist culture. Over time, through globalization, this population's customs and identity devolve to only the low level needed to maintain a cheap commercial culture bereft of meaning and morality.

Second, the globalized media industry and its monopolies have enabled communist elements to easily make use of the degenerated ideas behind products. They advertise the superficial cultural aspects of products and introduce Marxist ideology while promoting them. The hybridization of cultures through globalization thus becomes another channel for promoting communist ideology.

Third, a global culture makes consumerism the mainstream culture of society. Commercials, films, television shows, and social media constantly bombard consumers with the idea that they are not living a real life if they don't consume or own certain products, or seek to be entertained in particular ways. Communism uses different means and entertainment to prompt people to pursue the satisfaction of their base desires. As people indulge these desires, they move away from the spiritual plane, causing them to deviate from their long-held divine beliefs and traditional values within a few short generations.

As communism quickly spreads its deteriorated ideology amid the backdrop of globalization, it utilizes the herd mentality. With frequent exposure to news media, social media, commercials, television shows, and films, people are bombarded with various anti-traditional ideologies. This creates an illusion that such deteriorated ideologies represent a global consensus. People gradually become numb to the damage wrought by these ideologies, as twisted behaviors come to be seen as fashionable and people are urged to take pride in them. Substance abuse, sexual liberation, degenerate music, abstract art, and much more all spread in this fashion.

Modern art is degenerate and violates all traditional definitions of aesthetics. Some people may have realized this at first, but after modern artworks are constantly exhibited in major metropolitan areas and sold at high prices, and when the media frequently reports on dark and strange works, normal people begin to believe that they're the ones who've fallen out of touch with fashion and that it's their taste in art that needs to be updated. Gaslighted by this aesthetic trend, people begin to negate their own sense of the beautiful and to favor deteriorated art forms.

All manner of deteriorated culture masked as Western culture is currently being spread to every corner of the world. Hollywood, in particular, has become a major carrier of various ideologies that stem from cultural Marxism. The special characteristics of the movie industry allow it to make people subconsciously accept its values. As described in Chapter Thirteen, film has the power to depict compelling atmospheres, narratives, and personalities, immersing audiences in the director's viewpoint. Hollywood movies play an enormous role in shaping audiences' values and worldview.

In this book, we have also discussed how cultural Marxism has taken over Western education (see Chapter Twelve), and, in turn, exposed foreign students studying in Western countries to various leftist ideologies. When they return to their countries, they spread these ideologies, which are seen as attractive because Western countries are more technologically advanced and economically developed. Thus, these ideologies encounter little resistance as they spread and destroy the local traditional culture.

These modern globalist values have also become ubiquitous and mainstream via the corporate culture of multinational corporations. The promotion of sexual liberation has developed rapidly through globalization, seriously impacting and corroding the moral values of traditional society.

In 2016, a large global chain retailer announced that their store dressing rooms and restrooms would be "friendly to transgender people," meaning that men could enter women's restrooms or locker rooms at will if they self-identified as women. The American Family Association said the policy was harmful to women and children and called on consumers to boycott the company. To date, the association's pledge to boycott the store chain has received more than 1.5 million signatures. [23] Boycotts have become unrealistic, however, as more and more companies across society have adopted such policies. Communism is able to utilize the herd mentality because many people do not have a strong will. Once humankind deviates from divinely imparted traditions, everything becomes relative and changes over time. The situation becomes ripe for exploitation.

Under the conditions of globalization, mutual respect and tolerance of different national cultures have become mainstream. Communism has used this to distort the concept of tolerance and make value neutrality a "global consensus," thereby advocating deviant ideas.

B. THE UN'S ROLE IN SPREADING DEGENERATE VALUES

Article 13 of the UN Convention on the Rights of the Child states, "The child shall have the right to freedom of expression; this right shall include freedom to seek, receive and impart information and ideas of all kinds, regardless of frontiers, either orally, in writing or in print, in the form of art, or through any other media of the child's choice." [24]

Some scholars have asked: If parents do not allow their children to wear T-shirts with Satanic symbolism, does it constitute a violation of children's rights? Do children have the right to choose how they speak to their parents? Children may lack judgment; if they commit acts of violence or violate ethical norms, can parents discipline them? These worries are not unwarranted. In 2017, Ontario, Canada, passed a law that parents should not deny children's wishes of gender expression (i.e., children could select their own genders). Parents who don't accept their child's chosen gender identity may be considered to be engaging in child abuse, and their children could be taken away by the state. [25]

In 1990, the World Health Organization announced that homosexuality was not a mental illness, which greatly elevated and spurred on the LGBT movement worldwide. Under the conditions of globalization, AIDS spread globally, and the most susceptible group, homosexuals, became a focus of social concern and public discussion. Communism has thus promoted the expansion of the LGBT cause. South Africa was the first country to introduce a new convention at the UN Human Rights Council that requires that the recognition of sexual orientation and gender identity be used as an indicator of upholding human rights. The convention, the first that directly targeted sexual orientation and gender identity, was ultimately adopted. In reality, the convention normalizes what used to be considered deviant ideas by attributing to them the same importance as natural rights.

Communism thus uses globalization to mutate and destroy traditional culture and moral values in an all-encompassing fashion. This includes the use of developed countries, global enterprises, and international institutions. People are immersed in the superficial convenience of a globalized lifestyle, but they are not aware of the rapid transformations occurring at the level of ideology and consciousness. In just a few decades, these completely new ideas have engulfed many parts of the world. Wherever these ideas go, the culture changes — even the oldest and most closed countries can't escape. If this trend continues, civilization itself will be lost.

Traditional culture is the root of human existence and an important safeguard for human beings to maintain moral standards. It is the key for people to return to the righteous path and be saved by their Creator. In the process of globalization, traditional culture has been twisted and ruined by the arrangements of the communist specter. The long-term moral crisis human civilization faces is unprecedented.

5. Upholding National Heritage and Universal Values

Different nationalities and countries have existed for millennia. Although they exist in different regions, have different social forms and political systems, use different languages, and have different cultural and psychological qualities, all share common universal values. These universal values are the core of traditional culture for all ethnic groups.

By using globalization in conjunction with other historical

processes over the last few centuries, the communist specter has greatly expanded its power in the human world and
brought tremendous damage to the divinely inspired traditional cultures of mankind.

In the first half of the twentieth century, communists
took power in Russia and China, slaughtering the cultural
elites and destroying the traditional culture of these two vast
nations. After World War II, the communist camp infiltrated
and controlled international organizations such as the UN,
abused democratic procedures to allow the majority to conquer
the minority, and used money to win over small countries in
an attempt to use the UN's supranational power to spread its
political system worldwide.

Around the world, especially after the end of the Cold War,
communism's representatives in both the East and the West
began using international political, economic, and cultural
exchanges and cooperation to expand and control globalization. Globalist institutions promote degenerate values in virtually every country on earth, aiding the communist specter's
systematic destruction of universal values, traditional culture,
and faith in the divine.

In the little more than one hundred years since the emergence of communism on the global stage, these transnational
political and economic forces have come to wield formidable power, imperiling sovereign nations everywhere with the
agenda of world government.

Only with the return of tradition can people restore their
national identity and sovereignty and create a harmonious
international environment governed by upright universal
values. This will allow humankind to banish the communist
specter and live under the protection and grace of the divine.

Chapter Eighteen

The Chinese Communist Party's Global Ambitions

THE SPECTER OF COMMUNISM has spent much of modern history establishing itself in our world, whether through overt totalitarian rule or covert subversion. The violent Bolshevik revolution in Russia at the beginning of the twentieth century paved the way for the specter's primary actor: the Chinese Communist Party (CCP).

The CCP was established in 1921 by agents of the Far Eastern branch of the Soviet-led Communist International. Over the next several decades, the Soviet Union played a major role on the world stage, confronting the Western democratic camp in the Cold War, leading Westerners to believe the Soviet Union and its satellite communist regimes in Eastern Europe were the archetypal communist adversary. The CCP, meanwhile, had ample time to establish and strengthen its regime. In 1949, it defeated the Chinese Nationalist government and founded the People's Republic of China (PRC).

The collapse of the Soviet Union in 1991 left the PRC as the world's major communist power. Faced with the new geopolitical situation, the Party took a new, nonconfrontational approach: It enticed the rest of the world to engage with its reformed market economy while retaining a totalitarian political system. As a result, many Western scholars, entrepreneurs, and politicians have stopped regarding the CCP as a communist regime, believing it to have turned on its founding ideological principles.

This could not be further from the truth. Despite adopting the trappings of a market system, the CCP has brought the essential characteristics of communism — deceit, malice, and struggle — to their apex, creating a regime that employs the most pernicious and insidious methods of political intrigue developed over thousands of years of human history. The CCP seduces people with profits, controls them with force, and deceives them with lies. It has cultivated its demonic technique to the point of mastery.

China is home to five thousand years of history and a splendid traditional heritage, which have earned its people respect and admiration the world over. The CCP capitalized on these positive sentiments; after seizing power and taking the Chinese people captive, it conflated the concepts of the Chinese nation and the CCP regime. It presented its ambitions under the camouflage of China's "peaceful rise," making it difficult for the international community to understand its true motives.

But the essential nature of the CCP has never changed. The Party's strategy of economic engagement is simply to use the "nutrition of the capitalist body" to strengthen its own socialist body, to stabilize its rule, and to realize its ambitions, rather than to enable China to see true prosperity and strength. [1] In practice, its methods disregard basic ethics and universal values.

In order to survive and thrive, human society must follow the standards of conduct laid down by the Creator. Among these are the need to maintain high moral character, adhere to universal values, and protect people's rights to what is theirs. The economic development of a normal society needs to be supported by corresponding moral standards.

But the Chinese communist regime has followed a diametrically opposite path, creating a fast-rising economic abomination that has encouraged severe moral degeneracy. The evil specter's motivation for arranging China's "economic miracle" is simple: Economic strength gives the ccp regime the persuasive influence it needs to dictate its terms to the world. These arrangements are not intended to benefit China or the Chinese people, but rather to play on people's worship of money and wealth so that the world will align with the ccp in economic cooperation and international affairs.

Internally, the Communist Party rules through tyranny and the most ruthless aspects of the capitalist system. It rewards evil and punishes good, turning the worst individuals into society's most successful. Its policies magnify the evil side of human nature, using atheism to create a state of utter degeneracy in which people have no moral qualms.

When operating abroad, the ccp advocates the ideology of "socialism with Chinese characteristics" and offers powerful economic incentives as a lure to have people of the free world let down their guard, abandon moral principles, and turn a blind eye to the ccp's vast abuses of human rights and persecution of religion. Many politicians and corporations in Western countries have betrayed their values and compromised themselves for profit, aligning themselves with the ccp's practices.

Western countries hope they can help the ccp make a peaceful transformation, but while China has indeed undergone a degree of superficial modernization and westernization, the Party never changed its underlying nature. Over the past few decades, the practical result of engagement has seen the ccp successfully and peacefully undermine the moral obligations of the United States and corrupt the public will.

The CCP is the main arm of communism and thus the greatest threat to free societies everywhere. The communist specter's aim in strengthening the global power of the CCP is to spread its poison to all corners of the earth and ultimately to have people betray tradition and the divine. Even if the Party's efforts to establish itself as the world's leading power are not directly successful, it will still have achieved its underlying purpose: to part people from their moral values. It does this by tempting people with economic interests, manipulating them with financial traps, infiltrating their political systems, intimidating them with military force, and confusing them with propaganda.

Faced with such great danger, we must carefully examine the CCP regime's ambition, strategy, and tactics.

1. The Chinese Communist Party's Ambition to Dominate the World

The Chinese communist regime is not satisfied with being a regional power. It wants to control the world. This is determined by the Communist Party's innate characteristic of tyranny. By its very nature, the Party opposes heaven, earth, and tradition; it resorts to violence to smash the "old world" and aims to destroy all states, nations, and classes, with the feigned goal of "liberating all humanity." Its unchanging mission is one of constant expansion until the world is united under communist ideology. Its doctrines and practices are by definition globalist.

But because traditional culture had deep roots in society, at times communism has had to adopt a gradual and roundabout approach to supplant it. In the Soviet Union, Joseph Stalin claimed the need for "socialism in one country," while the CCP has adopted "socialism with Chinese characteristics."

Unlike the political parties that share power or hold power by rotation in Western democracies, the CCP has uncontested authority. It sets strategic goals with a scope of decades or centuries. A few years after seizing power in 1949, it rolled out the slogan "surpass Britain and catch up to America," which prefaced the Great Leap Forward. Later, owing to unfavorable domestic and international situations, the CCP assumed a low profile for decades.

After the 1989 Tiananmen Square massacre, much of the international community boycotted the Chinese regime. In response, the Party evaluated the situation and concluded that it was still unable to compete directly with the United States. So rather than attempting to take the lead on the international stage, it took the path of hiding its strengths and biding its time. This was not because the CCP had changed its goals, but rather because it adopts different strategies based on the circumstances of the time.

It can be said that the communist specter used the ancient Chinese strategic feint of "openly repairing the plank roads while secretly advancing via the hidden route of Chencang." The first communist superpower was the Soviet Union, but its ultimate role was to aid the rise and maturation of the CCP regime.

Since World War I, the United States has been the most powerful country on earth, serving to maintain international order. Any country that wants to overturn this order must bring down the United States, so in terms of the CCP's overall strategic considerations, America is the Party's main enemy. This has been the case for decades, and the CCP has never stopped preparing for an all-out offensive against the United States.

In the book *The Hundred-Year Marathon: China's Secret Strategy to Replace America as the Global Superpower*, national security expert Michael Pillsbury wrote that China has a long-term strategy to subvert the US-led world economic and political order and to replace it with communism by 2049, the one-hundredth anniversary of the Communist Party's rise to power in China. [2] Pillsbury notes the Chinese film *Silent Contest*, produced by the National Defense University of China, which states that the CCP's process of realizing its "great cause" of dominating the world "will inevitably run into constant wear-and-tear and struggle with the US hegemonic system," and "it is a centennial contest, not to be shifted by the human will."

The CCP's global strategy is centered on countering the United States. Arthur Waldron, a professor at the University of Pennsylvania and an expert on China, stated at a 2004 Senate hearing that the Chinese People's Liberation Army (PLA) is the only army in the world that is dedicated to anti-US operations. [3] Aside from the PLA, most of the CCP's diplomatic relations and international activities target the United States directly or indirectly.

A. THE CCP'S MULTI-PRONGED STRATEGY TO SUBVERT AND CONTAIN THE US

The CCP has taken a comprehensive approach in its attempt to gain world dominance. In terms of ideology, it competes with the United States and other democratic and free countries. It uses forced technology transfers and intellectual-property theft to close the tech gap and boost its economic confidence. Militarily, it engages in a silent rivalry with the United States by means of asymmetrical and "unrestricted warfare" in places like the South China Sea. It backs North Korea, Iran, and other rogue regimes to impede the United States and NATO.

In diplomacy, the CCP has promoted its periphery strategy and the One Belt, One Road plan. It has very quickly expanded its international influence with neighboring countries, as well as countries in Europe, Africa, Oceania, and Latin America, in an attempt to build an international coalition, develop a Chinese-led sphere, and isolate the United States.

The CCP is using multiple methods to accomplish these goals. The PRC established the Shanghai Cooperation Organization in 2001, the "16+1" cooperation network (now called "17+1") with Central and Eastern European countries in 2012, and the Asian Infrastructure Investment Bank in 2015. It cooperates keenly as part of the BRICS (Brazil, Russia, India, China, and South Africa) economic bloc and vigorously promotes the internationalization of its currency. It seeks to control the formulation of industrial standards (such as those used for the proposed 5G cellular networks) and to dominate public discourse.

The CCP has taken advantage of press freedom in the United States and other Western countries to carry out united-front operations, spread propaganda, and engage in espionage. This is its attempt to manipulate the United States as much as possible and impose change from within, without engaging in conventional warfare.

CCP agents bribe US government officials, congress members, diplomats, and retired military officers. The Party uses economic interests to guide American business owners to lobby for the Chinese communists and to influence US policy on China. It forces high-tech companies to cooperate with the CCP's internet censorship and Great Firewall; coerces and incentivizes many in overseas Chinese communities to serve as fifth columnists; and infiltrates Western think tanks and academic departments. It manipulates these institutions into exercising self-censorship on sensitive topics, thus effectively adopting the stance of the Communist Party. Chinese companies, which are controlled or influenced by the CCP, have invested heavily in Hollywood and the entertainment industry.

On one hand, the CCP develops its influence in various countries to envelop and contain the United States, while on the other hand, it establishes hidden strongholds on American soil to undermine it from within. It has built an extensive network of agents and has fostered splits in US society, posing a serious internal threat.

B. INCITING ANTI-US HATRED IN PREPARATION FOR WAR

The CCP's ideology runs on hatred. The patriotism it promotes entails hating Japan, hating Taiwan, hating Tibetans, hating the ethnic minorities of Xinjiang, hating religious believers, hating dissidents, and, most importantly, hating the United States. There is a saying among Chinese netizens: "For small problems, blame Japan, and for big ones, blame the United States." By inciting hatred against foreign foes, the Party helps smooth over public outrage during a crisis.

Before the Chinese communists seized power, they repeatedly praised the United States for its friendship with China and for the American democratic system. However, after the CCP set up its regime, it immediately took advantage of the suffering China had experienced in modern history, as well as the people's desire for a strong nation. The CCP painted itself as China's savior by stoking hatred against the United States and other foreign nations.

In fact, the CCP does not care about whether Chinese people live or die, nor does it care about China's territorial integrity or its sustainable long-term development. It is a challenge to describe the true evilness of how the CCP has persecuted its own people, betrayed China's sovereignty, destroyed morality and traditional culture, and sabotaged China's future.

By inciting hatred of foreign countries, the CCP aims, first, to paint itself as a savior to the Chinese people to help legitimize its brutal rule; second, to use nationalist sentiment to divert public attention in times of crisis; third, to build support for the Party's expansionist ambitions and base schemes as a means of "rectifying" the humiliations of modern times; and fourth, to use hatred to create the psychological preparedness needed for future wars.

The CCP has indoctrinated the younger generation with hatred of the United States in preparation for using them as its pawns in the effort to supersede America and dominate the world. When the time comes, the CCP intends to use China's youth to infiltrate the United States and its allied democratic states in various fashions, participate in all-out armed conflict, wage unrestricted warfare, and should the need arise, sacrifice themselves in a nuclear holocaust.

The jubilant reactions expressed by much of the Chinese public following the 9/11 terrorist attacks indicated that the CCP was making significant inroads with its propaganda. Currently, on major Chinese political and military forums, one commonly sees sentiments like "China and the United States must have a war" — yet another indication of the CCP's success in educating people to hate the United States. This is a long-term, gradual mobilization for war, deliberately planned and systematically carried out.

The CCP's hate propaganda is not limited to China's borders. Internationally, it explicitly or overtly supports rogue regimes and terrorist organizations in fighting the United States, providing them with financial assistance, weapons and equipment, theoretical contributions, tactical training, and public support. The Party directs the global forces of anti-Americanism, as the PRC now leads an axis of anti-US states.

C. THE CCP'S OVERT INTENTION TO DEFEAT THE US

In 2008, while the United States was struggling with an economic crisis, Beijing hosted the most expensive Olympic Games in history. Dressed in a costume of prosperity, the regime thrust itself onto the international stage. At the time, the US manufacturing industry was in decline, and the country faced an economic crisis approaching the severity of the Great Depression. In the face of such economic difficulties, the US administration asked China to help by buying US Treasurys. The CCP's media mouthpieces immediately began to run articles that claimed "America is surviving by borrowing money from us Chinese"; "America is going downhill, China is in position to replace it"; and so on. Virtually all of the Party-controlled media in China ran such headlines, and the ideas even became part of popular opinion among Western media and scholars.

After 2008, the United States showed signs of decline in areas such as economic standing, military strength, and political stability. On the economic front, the US administration at the time was pushing universal health care, expanding social benefits, placing climate issues at the center of policy, and placing restrictions on traditional manufacturing. Still, the green-energy industry was defeated by made-in-China products, and US manufacturing continued to be hollowed out. There was no way for these policies to counter and guard against the PRC's illicit trade practices and massive theft of intellectual property.

In the face of these trends, many simply accepted the narrative that China was in ascendance and the United States was in decline. US military spending decreased, and the United States adopted a weak diplomatic stance. On the US political front, socialist ideology was on the rise, democratic politics were becoming a showground for partisan squabbling, and government functions were often handicapped as a result. The CCP compared this chaos unfavorably with the focused totalitarianism of its own system, depicting US democracy as a laughing stock.

In 2010, China surpassed Japan to become the world's second-largest economy. In 2014, according to World Bank statistics, if calculated based on purchasing power parity, China's GDP might have surpassed that of the United States. [4] Seeing that the balance of power between China and the United States appeared to be shifting, and believing that America's decline was irreversible, the CCP ended its old strategy of hiding its strength and biding its time. Instead, the Party openly and directly took aim at the international order led by the United States. The official stance of the CCP, the media, and experts gradually started to speak unabashedly of an expansionist "China dream."

In 2012, during its 18th National Congress, the CCP introduced the notion of building a "community of shared future for mankind." In 2017, at its World Political Parties Dialogue, the CCP evoked the ancient imagery of the myriad kingdoms coming to pay their respects at the Chinese imperial court. The CCP went public with its desire to export the communist "China model" to the rest of the world.

The CCP's ambition in spreading what it calls the "China model," the "Chinese plan," or "Chinese wisdom" is to lead the world and establish a new world order. The CCP has been preparing for this in all respects for decades. If this new world order were established, it would present a formidable new axis of evil, an adversary more threatening to the free world than the Axis alliance during World War II.

2. Communist China's Strategies for World Domination

A. ONE BELT, ONE ROAD INITIATIVE: TERRITORIAL EXPANSION UNDER THE GUISE OF GLOBALIZATION

In 2013, Beijing officially introduced its One Belt, One Road (OBOR) initiative, also known as Belt and Road. The plan is for China to invest trillions of dollars to build critical infrastructure, such as ports, bridges, railroads, and energy facilities, in dozens of countries, with the aim of bringing them under China's influence. It is the biggest investment project in history.

"One Belt" refers to the Silk Road Economic Belt, which consists of three land-based components: from China through Central Asia and Russia to Europe and the Baltic Sea; from northwestern China through Central and West Asia to the

Persian Gulf and the Mediterranean; and from southwestern China through the Indochina Peninsula to the Indian Ocean.

"One Road" refers to the Twenty-First-Century Maritime Silk Road, which is a two-pronged effort: The first route goes from Chinese ports to the South China Sea, through the Strait of Malacca and on to Europe via the Indian Ocean; the second heads to the southern Pacific Ocean.

The land-based One Belt consists of six economic corridors:

- The China–Mongolia–Russia Economic Corridor
- The New Eurasian Land Bridge Corridor
- The China–Central and West Asia Economic Corridor
- The China–Indochina Peninsula Economic Corridor
- The China–Pakistan Economic Corridor
- The Bangladesh–China–India–Myanmar Economic Corridor

The New Eurasian Land Bridge Corridor will be based on rail links between China and Europe, such as Yiwu to Madrid and Wuhan to Hamburg and Lyon. Transportation from China to Europe takes just over ten days by rail, compared to over thirty days by sea. The China Railway Express, which runs along these rail links, began its operations in 2011 and has been an important component of OBOR.

The China–Pakistan Economic Corridor is a joint plan by the two governments. It includes a highway connecting Kashgar in China's Xinjiang Province with Gwadar Port in Pakistan, on the Indian Ocean. The CCP gained the right to operate the port, Pakistan's gateway to the Persian Gulf and Arabian Sea, in 2013. The port occupies a critical strategic location, connecting the Strait of Hormuz, through which 40 percent of the world's crude oil passes, to the Arabian Sea.

The general framework of the sea-based One Road is to build

a number of strategic ports to gain control over global sea transportation. In financially robust countries, Chinese companies enter into equity participation or joint ventures. In financially weaker countries, the PRC invests large amounts of money locally and attempts to obtain the rights to operate the ports.

In 2013, China Merchants Port Holdings Co. Ltd. bought 49 percent equity from Terminal Link SAS in France. With this purchase, it obtained the operating rights to fifteen terminals in eight countries on four continents, including the South Florida Container Terminal in Miami and the Houston Terminal Link (now called the Terminal Link Texas). [5]

Other ports and terminals now under China's control include the ports of Antwerp and Zeebrugge in Belgium; the Suez Canal Container Terminal in Egypt; Kumport (or Ambarli) in Turkey; the Port of Piraeus in Greece; Pasir Panjang Terminal in Singapore; Euromax Terminal Rotterdam, which is called "the gate of Europe," in the Netherlands; the second-phase terminal at Khalifa Port in the United Arab Emirates; the Port of Vado in Italy; Kuantan Port in Malaysia; the Port of Djibouti in East Africa; and the Panama Canal.

In addition to investment, the CCP also uses the debt traps created by OBOR to obtain control of strategic locations. Sri Lanka could not pay its debt to Chinese companies, so in 2017, it signed over the use of its Hambantota Port to a Chinese company for ninety-nine years.

The CCP launched its Digital Silk Road in 2018 with the intention of reshaping the future development of internet infrastructure. The Digital Silk Road is considered an advanced stage in the OBOR project, and it mainly includes building fiber optic infrastructure, digital information services, international telecommunications, and e-commerce.

Many countries involved in OBOR do not have a complete credit system. The CCP aims to introduce its systems of e-commerce and electronic payment services, such as Alipay, to these countries, while totally shutting out Western competition.

The Great Firewall, which filters internet traffic in China, is being exported to OBOR countries, as are the systems of mass surveillance already used within China.

The extent of the CCP's strategic reach can be seen from its investment in global infrastructure. According to a November 2018 report by *The New York Times*, the CCP has constructed or is constructing more than forty pipelines and other oil and gas infrastructure projects; more than two hundred bridges, roads, and railways; almost two hundred power plants for nuclear power, natural gas, coal, and renewables; and a series of major dams. At the time of the report, the CCP had invested in at least 112 countries, most of which belonged to the OBOR initiative. [6]

As OBOR took shape, the CCP regime's efforts to supplant the United States on the world stage grew. It aggressively promoted the yuan as an international currency, as well as its own credit system. Chinese-made telecommunications networks (including 5G) are being pushed as the future in many countries, as are Chinese-built high-speed rail lines. The aim is to eventually establish a set of standards that is controlled by the CCP and independent of the current Western standards.

In the early stages of OBOR, the CCP focused on neighboring countries, reaching as far as Europe. Very quickly, the CCP expanded its reach to Africa, Latin America, and even the Arctic Ocean, covering the entire world. The Maritime Silk Road originally consisted of just two routes. A third route, the Polar Silk Road, was added to connect to Europe via the Arctic Ocean. Prior to OBOR, China had already invested heavily in countries in Africa and Latin America. These countries are now part of the major structure of OBOR, which has enabled the CCP to more rapidly expand its financial and military reach in those continents.

The initial goal of OBOR is to export China's excess capacity by building up basic infrastructure such as railways and highways in other countries. These countries are rich in resources and energy. By building their infrastructure, the CCP accomplishes two secondary goals. One is to open routes to ship domestic products to Europe at low cost; the other is to secure the strategic resources of countries that participate in OBOR. The CCP's intention is to increase mainland Chinese exports, not to help the countries along the Belt and Road to establish their own manufacturing industries — the CCP would not help create competition for its own manufacturing.

The real ambition behind OBOR is to use economic strength as a vanguard to establish control over the financial and political lifelines of other countries, transforming them into colonies of the Chinese regime and pawns on the global stage. A byproduct of participating in OBOR schemes is the importation of all pernicious aspects of communism: corruption, debt, and totalitarian repression. The project is a deceptive trap that will not bring lasting economic prosperity to its participants.

These dangers have elicited alarm from many countries, prompting their governments to halt or reduce their involvement in the OBOR scheme. On occasion, Beijing has conceded that it should be more transparent and make adjustments to the heavily criticized debt traps. Nevertheless, the CCP's plans can't be underestimated. While Western enterprises operate on profit-seeking principles and won't tough it out in unstable host countries for more than a few years, the CCP's calculus extends into the next century. It can tolerate operations in unstable international environments over the long term without regard for immediate losses.

The CCP wants to develop pro-communist governments that will support it in the United Nations and other international organizations. It aims to assume leadership across Asia, Africa, and Latin America in its struggle against the free world, and ultimately replace the United States as the world's number one power. Human costs are no object in pursuing these aims — for instance, the Party can force the Chinese people to pay for investment costs that privately owned Western enterprises could never handle. In this war to conquer the world, it is not about how powerful the CCP is on paper, but that the CCP has at its disposal the resources of hundreds of millions of Chinese people irrespective of their living or dying. They are its sacrificial pawns.

Former White House chief strategist Steve Bannon said that with the OBOR project, the Chinese regime had successfully integrated the Mackinder-Mahan-Spykman theses of world domination. In an article discussing this view, Andrew Sheng of the Asia Global Institute wrote:

> Sir Halford Mackinder was an influential British geographer/ historian who argued in 1904 that "Whoever rules the Heartland (central Asia) commands the World-Island (Eurasia); whoever rules the World-Island commands the World." His American contemporary Alfred Mahan was a naval historian who shaped the US strategy to dominate sea power, extending the British maritime empire logic of controlling the sea lanes, choke points and canals by policing global trade. In contrast, Nicholas John Spykman argued that the Rimland (the coastal lands encircling Asia) is more important tha[n] the Heartland, thus: "Who controls the Rimland rules EuroAsia; who rules EuroAsia controls the destinies of the world." [7]

These insights reflect the Western world's growing vigilance against the CCP's ambitions contained in the OBOR project.

Of course, the CCP's ambition is not limited to the scope of OBOR. The initiative is not merely focused on obtaining the rights to land routes, sea lanes, and major ports. The CCP wants to take advantage of any weaknesses that exist around the world. In recent decades, many countries in Asia, Africa, and Latin America became newly independent states created by decolonization. These regions experienced a power vacuum, inviting the CCP to gain footholds. The newly independent countries that were once part of the Soviet Union and its Eastern European satellites had weak sovereign control and were also easy pickings for the CCP regime. Other unstable countries, which Western investors tend to stay away from, naturally fell into the CCP's trap. Small countries, island nations, and underdeveloped countries in strategic locations are all in the CCP's crosshairs.

Even some states once firmly in the Western democratic camp have drifted into the CCP's orbit after suffering from weak economies and high debt. Geopolitically, the CCP is gradually surrounding the United States by controlling the economies of other countries. The aim is to marginalize and eventually remove American influence from those countries, by which time the CCP will have established a separate world order centered on communist hegemony. This is not a new approach. It has its roots in the Party's original strategy of occupying the countryside to surround the cities, which led it to victory in the Chinese Civil War.

B. THE PERIPHERY DIPLOMACY STRATEGY TO EXCLUDE THE US FROM THE ASIA-PACIFIC REGION

Communist Party think tanks define the regime's "periphery diplomacy" as such: "China neighbors fourteen countries along a lengthy land border and looks across the sea at six other neighboring countries. Beyond that, to the east is the Asia-Pacific region, and to the west is Eurasia. That is, the radial extent of China's extended neighborhood covers two-thirds of international politics, economy, and security. Thus, the framework of periphery diplomacy is more than mere regional strategy. ... It is a true grand strategy." [8]

Australia: The Weak Link of the Western World

In June 2017, Fairfax Media Ltd. and the Australian Broadcasting Corp. released the results of a five-month investigation in the documentary *Power and Influence: The Hard Edge of China's Soft Power.* The documentary, which raised concern around the world, described the CCP's widespread infiltration and control over Australian society. [9] Six months later, Sam Dastyari, a member of the Australian Labor Party, announced his resignation from the Senate. Dastyari's resignation followed accusations that he had accepted money from CCP-linked Chinese merchants for making statements in support of Beijing regarding South China Sea territorial disputes. His statements on this critical issue clashed with the views of his own party. [10]

In June 2017, Australia's ABC News updated a report revealing political donations by Chinese-linked entities, ostensibly intended to influence Australia–China trade policies. The report revealed more than $5.5 million in donations from Chinese-linked companies and individual donors to Liberal and Labor party war chests between 2013 and 2015. [11] Furthermore, in recent years, Australian media outlets have signed contracts with Chinese state-run media outlets, agreeing to broadcast propaganda provided by Chinese media to Australian audiences. [12]

In 2017, the book *Silent Invasion: China's Influence in Australia*, by author Clive Hamilton, was rejected three times by Australian publishers due to fear of Chinese repercussions. After much deliberation, a publisher agreed to print it. The censorship elicited widespread concern among Australians about China's influence in their country. [13]

In 2015, Australia allowed a Chinese company with close ties to the PLA to secure a ninety-nine-year lease over Darwin Port — a strategic seaport and military location for guarding against attacks from the north. Former US Deputy Secretary of State Richard Armitage, expressed shock at the deal, and said the United States was concerned about the development. [14]

What is the strategic value of CCP infiltration into Australia? The key aim is to weaken the US–Australia alliance. [15] In its 2017 Foreign Policy White Paper, the Australian government said: "The United States has been the dominant power in our region throughout Australia's post-Second World War history. Today, China is challenging America's position." [16] Malcolm Davis, senior analyst at the Australian Strategic Policy Institute, also said that Beijing was trying to gain a strategic advantage in the region for the purpose of ending Australia's alliance with the United States. [17]

Australia is the CCP's testing ground for soft-power operations in its strategy of periphery diplomacy. [18] The recent history of Chinese communist infiltration in Australia dates back to 2005, when Zhou Wenzhong, then-vice minister of foreign affairs, arrived in Canberra and informed senior officials at the Chinese Embassy of the CCP's new diplomatic approach. He said that the first goal of including Australia in China's greater periphery was to ensure that Australia would serve as a trustworthy and stable supply base for China's economic growth in the next twenty years. The mission of those present at the meeting was to understand how the CCP could broadly exert influence over Australia in the spheres of economics, politics, and culture. [19]

The CCP uses China's economic strength to force Australia to make concessions on military and human rights issues. The standard approach adopted by the CCP to coerce others into cooperation is to cultivate personal relationships via economic interests and simultaneously create the implicit threat of blackmail. [20]

After years of investigation, Hamilton reported the following: "Australian institutions — from our schools, universities and professional associations to our media; from industries like mining, agriculture and tourism to strategic assets like ports and electricity grids; from our local councils and state governments to our political parties in Canberra — are being penetrated and shaped by a complex system of influence and control overseen by agencies serving the Chinese Communist Party." [21]

Since the 2008 economic crisis, in practice, Australia has proven willing to serve as the PRC's supply base, due to the common belief that China rescued Australia from recession. Hamilton says that the reason the CCP's infiltration and influence is so effective is because Australians have been "allowing it to happen under our noses because we are mesmerised by the belief that only China can guarantee our economic prosperity and because we are afraid to stand up to Beijing's bullying." [22]

Despite awareness of the CCP's infiltration and influence on Western society, and particularly its infiltration and control of overseas Chinese communities, most well-meaning Westerners naively thought that the main purpose of the Party's strategies was "negative" — that is, to silence the voices of critics and those with different political opinions. However, Hamilton says that behind the "negative" operations are the CCP's "positive" ambitions: to use ethnic Chinese immigrants to change the framework of Australian society, and to have Westerners sympathize with the PRC so as to allow Beijing to build up influence. In this way, Australia would be transformed into the Communist Party's helper in the regime's goal of becoming an Asian superpower and then a global one. [23]

Similarly, the CCP is deepening its influence over Australia's close neighbor and ally, New Zealand. Anne-Marie Brady, an expert in Chinese politics at the University of Canterbury, wrote in the 2017 report *Magic Weapons: China's Political Influence Activities Under Xi Jinping* that several Chinese-born members of New Zealand's Parliament had close links with mainland China, and that many politicians had been bribed by massive political donations from rich Chinese merchants and CCP united-front organizations, such as Chinese trade associations in New Zealand. [24] Shortly after her report was published, Brady's office was broken into. Before the break-in, she had received an anonymous threatening letter saying, "You are the next." [25]

The PRC is actively roping in New Zealand's local politicians. For example, members of New Zealand political parties are treated lavishly on trips to China. Retired politicians are offered high-paying positions in Chinese enterprises, as well as other benefits to have them follow Party's directives. [26]

Targeting Pacific Island Nations for Strategic Value

Despite their size, tiny Pacific island nations can have the critical strategic value of serving as maritime bases. Though their total land area is just 53,000 square kilometers (20,463 square miles), their exclusive economic zones over parts of the ocean total 19,000,000 square kilometers (7,335,941 square miles) — an area over six times the size of China's exclusive economic zones. Developing greater ties with Pacific island nations is a publicly acknowledged component of the CCP's military strategy. [27] Currently, the Pacific area can be divided into five spheres of influence: American, Japanese, Australian, New Zealander, and French.

To develop its maritime capabilities in the Pacific Ocean, the CCP must first build good relations with island nations, and then slowly push out the US presence. The CCP has been outstripping American activity in the area by investing immense amounts of money in infrastructure projects in Melanesia, Micronesia, and Polynesia, as well as promoting local tourism and making e-business platforms available. [28]

Following large-scale mainland Chinese financial assistance and investment, the arrogant behavior exhibited by CCP officials reflects the regime's mentality when it feels emboldened — it attempts to treat the people of weaker nations the way it treats the Chinese people under its totalitarian control. Naturally, the CCP cannot be expected to respect international regulations and protocol.

At the APEC summit held in late 2018 in Papua New Guinea, the rude and uncivilized behavior of Chinese officials shocked those in attendance. A high-ranking US official described the CCP officials' behavior as "tantrum diplomacy." Chinese officials resorted to shouting as they accused other countries of plotting against China. They bluntly stopped journalists from interviewing attendees at a forum held between Chinese leader Xi Jinping and leaders of the Pacific Island nations, demanding that all journalists refer to the news release by the *Xinhua News Agency*. To prevent statements condemning the CCP regime's unfair trade behavior from being written into a joint communiqué, the officials demanded a meeting with Papua New Guinea's foreign minister. The minister turned down the request on the basis of remaining impartial. [29]

Using Debt Traps to Seize Control of Central Asia's Resources

Following the dissolution of the Soviet Union, the CCP has taken great efforts to develop and cement its relationships with Central Asian countries such as Kazakhstan, Kyrgyzstan, Tajikistan, Turkmenistan, and Uzbekistan. The goal of the CCP's strategy in Central Asia can be viewed from several angles: For one, Central Asia is an unavoidable land route in China's westward expansion. Further, when China constructs infrastructure to transport goods in and out of China, it can also expand its commercial interests in Central Asia. Second, China aims to seize the natural resources, including coal, oil, gas, and precious metals, that are abundant in these countries. Additionally, by controlling Central Asian countries that are geographically and culturally close to China's Xinjiang Province, the regime can tighten its control over the ethnic minorities there.

The CCP has become the most influential actor in Central Asia. The International Crisis Group, a Brussels-based think tank, released a report in 2013 saying that China has been rapidly growing into an economically dominant power in this region by taking advantage of social unrest in Central Asia. Beijing sees Central Asia as a supply base for raw materials and resources and as a market for its low-priced, low-quality products. [30] Meanwhile, the CCP has also poured millions of US dollars into investment and aid in Central Asia in the name of maintaining stability in Xinjiang.

A huge network of highways, railways, airways, communications, and oil pipelines has closely connected China with Central Asia. The China Road and Bridge Corporation and its contractors have been responsible for the construction of highways, railways, and electricity transmission lines in Central Asia. They pave roads on some of the most dangerous and complex terrain and construct new roads to transport China's goods to Europe and the Middle East, as well as to ports in Pakistan and Iran. From 1992 to 2012, in the two decades of diplomatic relations between China and the five Central Asian countries, the total volume of trade between China and Central Asia grew a hundredfold, according to Chinese state-run media. [31]

In Central Asia, the CCP has promoted investments in large state-run, credit-financed infrastructure projects. Some scholars have realized that such investments could form the basis of a new international order in which China would play a dominant role. Seen from this perspective, Central Asia, like Australia, is another testing ground for the CCP's conceptual revolution in diplomatic strategy. [32]

Beijing tends to support corrupt authoritarian leaders in Central Asian countries, and its opaque investment projects are considered beneficial primarily for the local elites. The International Crisis Group's report noted that each of the Central Asian governments is weak and corrupt, and the countries they rule fraught with social and economic unrest. [33] The large infrastructure projects promoted by Beijing are not only linked to massive loans, but also involve official approvals and permits, which are based on vested interests. This gives rise to and worsens the corruption in these regimes.

In Uzbekistan, Islam Karimov, the former first secretary of the Communist Party of the Uzbek Soviet Socialist Republic in the USSR, served as the country's president from the time of independence in 1991 to his death in 2016. In 2005, government forces clashed with protesters in the eastern city of Andijan, resulting in hundreds of deaths. The CCP placed itself as an ally of Karimov, rendering firm support to the regimes in Uzbekistan and other countries in the region in their efforts to safeguard the status quo. [34]

The fragile economic structures of Central Asian countries, in combination with massive PRC infrastructure loans, leave these countries especially prone to falling into China's debt trap. Turkmenistan has suffered from a severe economic crisis, with an estimated annual inflation rate in 2018 of 300 percent, estimated unemployment at more than 50 percent, severe food shortages, and rampant corruption. In 2018, China was the only major buyer of Turkmen gas, and also the largest creditor of its foreign debt, which stood at $9 billion (estimated at 30 percent of GDP in 2018). [35] [36] Eventually, Turkmenistan may have no choice but to hand over its natural gas fields — which generate 70 percent of the country's revenue — to the PRC to pay off its debt. [37]

In 2018, Tajikistan borrowed more than $300 million from China to build a power plant. In return, it transferred the operating license to a gold mine to PRC control for the length of time the mine produces enough gold to repay the debt. [38]

The Kyrgyzstan economy is also in danger, as large-scale infrastructure projects run by the PRC also caused it to fall into the debt trap. The country will likely have to cede part of its natural resources to pay the debt. Kyrgyzstan also cooperated with Chinese communications companies Huawei and ZTE to build digital communication tools in order to tighten governmental control over people, while also leaving the CCP regime a backdoor to extend its surveillance into these countries. [39]

Beijing took advantage of the power vacuum in the aftermath of the dissolution of the Soviet Union to enter the Kazakh energy sector. The Kazakh economy depends on its crude oil production, and its oil revenue is used to buy cheap Chinese products. Apart from oil drilling, this nation's industrial foundation is fragile. With the flow of cheap Chinese products into its market, the Kazakh manufacturing industry collapsed. [40]

Another motive for the CCP's expansion in Central Asia is to crack down on Uyghur dissidents living in the region. The Shanghai Cooperation Organization, a regional alliance driven by China and Russia, allows for extradition between the six member countries. A member country can even send its own officials to another member country to conduct an investigation. In this way, the CCP can extend its suppression of Uyghurs abroad and arrest Uyghur dissidents who have taken refuge in nearby countries. [41]

Using Pivotal States to Secure Strategic Resources

The Communist Party's peripheral strategy involves creating economic indebtedness in pivotal countries, which are then used as a base for achieving strategic goals in the entire region. According to the Party's think tanks, pivotal states are countries that have considerable regional power that Beijing has the capability and resources to guide; they have no direct conflicts with the CCP in terms of strategic interests, and most don't share close interests with the United States. [42] In addition to the aforementioned Australia, Kazakhstan, and others, examples of target countries for the Chinese regime include Iran and Burma (also known as Myanmar).

In the Middle East, Iran receives the greatest amount of Chinese investment. Iran is an important oil producer in the region and has been in ideological opposition to the West since the late 1970s, making it a natural economic and military partner for the PRC. Beijing has maintained close economic and military relations with Iran since the 1980s.

In 1991, the International Atomic Energy Agency discovered that mainland China had exported uranium to Iran and that the PRC and Iran had signed a secret nuclear agreement in

1990. [43] In 2002, when Iran's uranium enrichment project was revealed, Western oil companies withdrew from the country, giving the CCP an opportunity to capitalize on the situation and cultivate closer relations with Iran. [44]

Bilateral trade volume between the PRC and Iran grew by more than one hundred times in the seventeen years between 1992 and 2011, despite international sanctions on the Iranian regime. [45] Due to Chinese assistance, Iran was able to weather the international isolation imposed on it and develop a broad arsenal of short- to medium-range ballistic missiles, as well as anti-ship cruise missiles. The Chinese also provided anti-ship mines and fast-attack boats, and helped Iran establish a covert chemical weapons project. [46]

Another pivotal neighbor favored by the CCP is Burma, which boasts a long coastline providing strategic access to the Indian Ocean. The CCP regards the opening of a China–Burma channel as a strategic step to minimizing reliance on the Strait of Malacca. [47] The Burmese military government's poor human rights record has caused it to be isolated by the international community. The 1988 democracy movement in Burma was ultimately crushed with military force. The following year, in Beijing's Tiananmen Square, army tanks opened fire on pro-democracy demonstrators.

The two authoritarian governments, both condemned by the international community, found a degree of solace in their diplomatic company and have since enjoyed close relations. In October 1989, Burma's Than Shwe visited China, and the two sides signed a $1.4 billion arms deal. In the 1990s, there were again many arms deals signed between the two sides. Equipment the CCP has sold to Burma includes fighter planes, patrol ships, tanks and armored personnel carriers, anti-aircraft guns, and rockets. The CCP's military, political, and economic support thus became the Burmese military junta's lifeline in its struggle for continued survival. [48]

In 2013, the Chinese invested $5 billion into the China–

Burma crude oil and gas pipeline, said to be China's fourth-largest strategic oil-and-gas import conduit. Although it met with strong popular opposition, in 2017, it went into operation with the backing of the CCP. [49] Similar investments include the Myitsone Dam (currently placed on hold due to local opposition) and the Letpadaung Copper Mine. In 2017, bilateral trade between China and Burma totaled $13.54 billion. The CCP is currently planning to create a China–Burma economic corridor with 70 percent of the share held by the Chinese side. This includes a deep-water port for trade access to the Indian Ocean, and the Kyaukpyu Special Economic Zone industrial park. [50] [51]

C. STRATEGY IN EUROPE: 'DIVIDE AND CONQUER'

Europe was at the center of the confrontation between the free world and the communist camp during the Cold War. The United States and Western European nations maintained a close alliance via NATO. To drive a wedge between Europe and the United States, the CCP adopted a strategy of dividing and conquering European countries. Accordingly, the Party adapted its strategy to suit local conditions as it gradually penetrated and developed influence in Europe. In recent years, the differences between Europe and the United States on many major issues have become increasingly apparent. The CCP has had a hand in this.

During the 2008 financial crisis, the CCP exploited weaker European economies that were in urgent need of foreign investment. The Party injected large sums of money into these countries in exchange for compromises on issues such as international rule of law and human rights. It used this method to create and expand the divisions among European countries and then reaped the benefits. Countries targeted by the CCP include Greece, Spain, Italy, and Hungary.

The CCP invested heavily in Greece during the sovereign debt crisis, exchanging money for political influence, and using

Greece as an opening for building more influence in Europe. Within a few years, the CCP obtained a thirty-five-year concession for the second and third container terminals of Piraeus Port, Greece's largest port, and took over the main transshipment hub at the port.

In May 2017, China and Greece signed a three-year action plan covering railways, ports, airport network construction, power-energy networks, and power-plant investments. [52] The CCP's investment has already seen political returns. Since 2016, Greece, a member of the European Union, has repeatedly opposed EU proposals that would criticize the Chinese regime's policies and human rights record. In August 2017, a commentary published by *The New York Times* said, "Greece has embraced the advances of China, its most ardent and geopolitically ambitious suitor." [53]

In 2012, when the CCP initiated what would become the "17+1" cooperation framework, Hungary was the first country to join the initiative. It was also the first European country to sign an OBOR agreement with China. In 2017, bilateral trade volume between China and Hungary exceeded $10 billion. Like Greece, Hungary has repeatedly opposed EU criticism of the CCP's human rights abuses. The president of the Czech Republic hired a wealthy Chinese businessman to be his personal adviser and has kept his distance from the Dalai Lama. [54]

Among the sixteen countries included in the framework, eleven are EU countries, and five are non-EU. Additionally, many have a history of communist rule and have preserved ideological and organizational traces of those regimes. To some extent, conforming to the CCP's demands comes naturally to the post-communist elites.

Europe consists of many small countries, and it's difficult for any one country to compete with the CCP. The Party has used this to handle each government individually, intimidating them into staying silent on China's human rights abuses and pernicious foreign policy.

The most typical example is Norway. In 2010, the Norwegian Nobel Prize Committee awarded the Peace Prize to an incarcerated Chinese dissident. The CCP swiftly punished Norway by preventing it from exporting salmon to China, among other difficulties. Six years later, relations between the two countries were "normalized," but Norway has remained silent on human rights issues in the PRC. [55]

The traditional Western European powers have also felt the growing influence of the CCP. Direct Chinese investment in Germany has grown substantially since 2010. In 2019, the PRC was Germany's largest trading partner for the fourth consecutive year. In 2016, mainland Chinese and Hong Kong investors acquired fifty-six German companies, with investment reaching a high of 11 billion euros. These mergers and acquisitions allowed Chinese companies to quickly enter the market and acquire advanced Western technology, brands, and other assets. [56] The Hoover Institution, a US think tank, labeled these tactics as "weaponized" investment. [57]

The industrial city of Duisburg in western Germany has become the European transit hub for OBOR. Eighty-percent of trains from China transit through Duisburg before heading to other European countries. The city has also inked a deal with Huawei to become a "smart city." The mayor of Duisburg has called the city Germany's "China City." [58]

In dealing with France, the CCP has long used a strategy of "transaction diplomacy." For example, when then-Party leader Jiang Zemin visited France in 1999, he purchased nearly thirty Airbus aircraft, worth a combined fifteen billion francs. This massive sale led the French government to support China's admission to the World Trade Organization.

Following the Tiananmen Square massacre, France became the first Western country to establish a comprehensive strategic partnership with mainland China. The French president at the time was the first in the West to oppose criticism of the PRC at the annual conference of the UN Commission on

Human Rights in Geneva, the first to advocate strongly for the lifting of the EU arms embargo on China, and the first head of a Western government to praise the CCP. [59] In addition, in the late 1990s and early 2000s, the CCP established large-scale Chinese Culture Years in France to promote communist ideology under the guise of cultural exchange. [60]

The United Kingdom, traditionally a powerful European nation and an important ally of the United States, is also one of the CCP's most prized targets. On September 15, 2016, the British government officially approved the construction of the Hinkley Point C unit nuclear power plant in Somerset, England. The government is paying for the plant through a joint venture with China and a French consortium. [61]

The project was severely criticized by experts, including engineers, physicists, environmentalists, China experts, and business analysts, who especially referred to the huge hidden dangers to British national security. Nick Timothy, the ex-chief of staff to Prime Minister Theresa May, pointed out that security experts were "worried that the Chinese could use their role to build weaknesses into computer systems which will allow them to shut down Britain's energy production at will." [62]

As in other parts of the world, the methods the Chinese regime uses to expand its influence in Europe are pervasive and legion. They include acquiring European high-tech companies; controlling the shares of important ports; bribing retired politicians to praise the CCP's platform; coaxing sinologists to sing the praises of the CCP; penetrating universities, think tanks, and research institutes, and so on. [63] For years, the long-established British newspaper *The Daily Telegraph* carried a monthly insert, *China Watch*, produced by the English-language edition of the CCP-controlled *China Daily*. Beijing paid the British newspaper up to 750,000 pounds a year to run the inserts, which featured articles glorifying the Chinese regime. [64]

The CCP's activities in Europe have caused great misgivings among researchers. The Global Public Policy Institute and the Mercator Institute for China Studies published a research report in 2018 exposing the CCP's infiltration activities in Europe. It states:

> China commands a comprehensive and flexible influencing toolset, ranging from the overt to the covert, primarily deployed across three arenas: political and economic elites, media and public opinion, and civil society and academia. In expanding its political influence, China takes advantage of the one-sided openness of Europe. Europe's gates are wide open whereas China seeks to tightly restrict access of foreign ideas, actors and capital.
>
> The effects of this asymmetric political relationship are beginning to show within Europe. European states increasingly tend to adjust their policies in fits of "preemptive obedience" to curry favor with the Chinese side. Political elites within the European Union (EU) and in the European neighborhood have started to embrace Chinese rhetoric and interests, including where they contradict national and/or European interests. EU unity has suffered from Chinese divide and rule tactics, especially where the protection and projection of liberal values and human rights are concerned. Beijing also benefits from the "services" of willing enablers among European political and professional classes who are happy to promote Chinese values and interests. Rather than only China trying to actively build up political capital, there is also much influence courting on the part of those political elites in EU member states who seek to attract Chinese money or to attain greater recognition on the global plane. [65]

In addition to political, economic, and cultural infiltration in Europe, the CCP has also engaged in various forms of espionage. On October 22, 2018, the French newspaper *Le Figaro* carried an exclusive series of special reports that revealed the CCP's various espionage activities in France. This included using business social-networking websites, especially Linke-dIn, to recruit French people to provide information to the CCP for the purpose of infiltrating France's political, economic, and strategic realms, and for gaining extensive insider knowledge in specific situations. The report also said that such cases were only the tip of the iceberg of the CCP's espionage operations in France. [66] The CCP's purpose is the large-scale plunder of sensitive information regarding the French state and its economic assets. Similar espionage activities have also taken place in Germany. [67]

D. 'COLONIZING' AFRICA WITH THE 'CHINESE MODEL'

After World War II, many African countries underwent decol-onization and gained independence. The region gradually lost the West's attention and technology and capital were trans-ferred to China. Strengthened by these resources, the CCP encroached on African countries, infiltrating their politics, economies, and societies and steadily replacing what Western sovereign powers had set up.

On one hand, the CCP has wooed African states under the banner of aiding those countries' development, creating a united front against the United States and other free countries in the United Nations. On the other hand, through economic bribery and military aid, the CCP has relentlessly manipulated African governments and opposition groups, controlling the affairs of African countries while imposing the communist Chinese model and its values on them.

The CCP-controlled Export-Import Bank of China loaned $67.2 billion to African countries from 2001 to 2010. Superfi-cially, the loans did not appear to come with political condi-tions, and the interest rates were relatively low. [69] However, because the loan agreements used natural resources as collat-eral, the CCP effectively obtained the rights to extract massive amounts of resources from those countries.

In 2003, the loan provided by the Export-Import Bank of

China to Angola used crude oil as collateral. The following situation developed, as outlined in Serge Michel and Michel Beuret's book *China Safari: On the Trail of Beijing's Expansion in Africa*:

> *There are Chinese to drill the oil and then pump it into the Chinese pipeline guarded by a Chinese strongman on his way to a port built by the Chinese, where it is loaded onto Chinese tankers headed for China. Chinese laborers to build the roads and bridges and the gigantic dam that has displaced tends of thousands of small [land]holders; Chinese to grow Chinese food so other Chinese need eat only Chinese vegetables with their imported Chinese staples; Chinese to arm a government committing crimes against humanity; and Chinese to protect that government and stick up for it in the UN Security Council.* [68]

In 2016, China became Africa's biggest trading partner and foreign direct investor. [69] In Africa, the CCP's management model has been roundly criticized for its many ills: low wages, poor working conditions, shoddy products, "tofu-dreg engineering" (a term referring to the poor workmanship of buildings in China's Sichuan Province, which led to many deaths following the 2008 earthquake), environmental pollution, bribery of government officials, and other corrupt practices. China's mining operations in Africa also frequently meet with protests from locals.

Michael Sata, former president of Zambia, said during his presidential campaign in 2007: "We want the Chinese to leave and the old colonial rulers to return. They exploited our natural resources, too, but at least they took good care of us. They built schools, taught us their language, and brought us the British civilization. ... At least Western capitalism has a human face; the Chinese are only out to exploit us." [70] In Zambia, Chinese influence can be seen everywhere. Sata was faced with no choice but to make deals with the CCP. Upon taking office, he immediately met with the PRC ambassador, and in 2013, he visited China.

Sudan was one of the earliest bases that the CCP established in Africa, and over the past twenty years, the CCP's investment in this northeastern nation has grown exponentially. In addition to Sudan's abundant oil reserves, its strategic port at the Red Sea was vital to the CCP's plans. In the 1990s, when the international community isolated Sudan because of its support for terrorism and radical Islam, the CCP took advantage and rapidly became Sudan's largest trading partner, purchasing most of its oil exports. [71] The investment by the CCP helped Omar Hassan Ahmad al-Bashir's totalitarian regime survive and develop despite sanctions. The PLA even exported weapons to Sudan during this period, indirectly facilitating the Darfur genocide in Sudan beginning in 2003.

In the international community, the CCP played a two-faced role: While China sent out a peacekeeping team to the UN to mediate the conflict in Sudan, Beijing also openly invited Bashir to China, although he was wanted by the International Criminal Court for crimes against humanity. The CCP declared that no matter how the world changed, no matter what the situation was in Sudan, that China would always be Sudan's friend. [72]

The CCP expends considerable effort on wooing developing nations. The Forum on China–Africa Cooperation (FOCAC) was established in 2000, with its first ministerial conference held in Beijing. During this inaugural meeting, then-CCP head Jiang announced debt relief of 10 billion yuan for poor countries in Africa. In 2006, when Beijing hosted the FOCAC summit, the CCP not only announced debt waivers for forty-four countries, but also pledged $10 billion in funding, credit, scholarships, and various aid projects. [73] During the 2015 summit in Johannesburg, South Africa, the PRC announced that it would provide $60 billion to work with African countries to carry out ten major cooperation plans. [74] On August

28, 2018, the PRC vice minister of commerce noted that "97 percent of products from thirty-three of the least-developed African countries have zero tariffs." [75] On September 3, 2018, during the 2018 summit, the CCP again pledged that it would provide Africa with $60 billion of no-strings-attached aid, interest-free loans, and project-specific capital and investment. At the same time, the CCP promised that for African countries with diplomatic relations with mainland China, it would cancel their inter-government debts that matured at the end of 2018. [76]

When he was prime minister of Ethiopia, Meles Zanawi established a Five-Year Plan for Ethiopia following China's example. The organization and structure of the country's ruling party at the time, the Ethiopian People's Revolutionary Democratic Front (EPRDF), also bore a striking resemblance to the CCP. An anonymous source within the Chinese Foreign Ministry said that many high-level officials in the EPRDF had traveled to China to study and undergo training, and that the children of many important officials also went to China for their education. It was even more apparent at the ministerial level, where virtually every official was reading *The Selected Writings of Mao Zedong.* [77]

In March 2013, at the BRICS summit, the Ethiopian prime minister stated that China was both a trading partner and a development model for Ethiopia. Today, Ethiopia is called Africa's "New China." Its internet monitoring and censorship, the totalitarian nature of its government, its media control, and the like are all cast from the same communist mold as China's. [78] The PRC has also held training sessions targeted at leaders and government officials from other African nations.

Yun Sun, co-director of the China Program at the Washington-based Stimson Center, said:

They organized this kind of political training with three objectives in mind. First, that the CCP's regime is legitimate —

it is attempting to tell the world how the CCP has successfully managed China and how this success could be replicated for developing countries. Second, the CCP seeks to promote the experience China had in its development, during the so-called "exchange of ideas on how to govern the country." Although the CCP is not explicitly "exporting revolution," it is certainly exporting its ideological approach. The third objective is to strengthen exchanges between China and Africa. [79]

After several decades of painstaking effort, through commerce and trade, the CCP gained a strong foothold in Africa's economy. By using economic incentives, it has bought off a number of African governments, such that officials in those countries follow Beijing's every instruction. A scholar in the PRC establishment declared: "China's progress over the past forty years has proven that it doesn't need to do what the West did to achieve success. ... The impact of this on Africa is beyond what you can imagine." [80]

E. ADVANCING INTO LATIN AMERICA

Being geographically close to the United States, Latin America has historically been within the United States' sphere of influence. Although a number of socialist regimes appeared in Latin America when the tide of communism swept over the world during the mid-twentieth century, those influences ultimately did not amount to a significant threat to the United States' role in the region.

After the collapse of the Soviet Union, the CCP began to target Latin America. Under the banner of "South to South cooperation," it started to infiltrate all areas of society in the region, penetrating areas like economy, trade, military, diplomacy, culture, and the like. The governments of many Latin American countries, such as Venezuela, Cuba, Ecuador, and Bolivia, were already hostile toward the United States, and the CCP made full use of this when it extended its influence across the Pacific, further aggravating the tensions these nations had with the United States and heightening their anti-American stance.

The CCP could now freely operate in America's backyard, support the socialist regimes in Latin America, and thus lay the groundwork for long-term confrontation with the United States. It is no exaggeration to say that the CCP's infiltration and influence in Latin America have far exceeded what the Soviet Union had achieved.

First, the CCP used foreign trade and investment to expand its influence in Latin America. According to a report from the US-based think tank Brookings Institution, in 2000, mainland Chinese trade with Latin America was $12 billion, but by 2013, it had ballooned to more than $260 billion, an increase of more than twenty times. Prior to 2008, Chinese loan commitments didn't exceed $1 billion, but in 2010, they had increased to $37 billion. [81] From 2005 to 2016, the PRC pledged to loan $141 billion to Latin American countries. Today, Chinese loans have exceeded those from the World Bank and the Inter-American Development Bank combined. The CCP also promised in 2015 that it would provide Latin America with $250 billion in direct investment by 2025 and that bilateral trade between China and Latin America would reach $500 billion.

Latin America is currently the PRC's second-largest investment target, after Asia. [82] China is the top trading partner to the three largest economies in Latin America — Brazil, Chile, and Peru — and the second-largest for Argentina, Costa Rica, and Cuba. With highway construction in Ecuador, port projects in Panama, and a planned fiber-optic cable running from China to Chile, the CCP's influence throughout Latin America is clear. [83]

All the while, the CCP has deployed its state companies to turn Latin America into its resource base, including Baosteel's vast investment in Brazil and Shougang's control over iron mines in Peru. The CCP also has shown great interest in Ecuador's oil and Venezuela's oil and gold mines.

In the military domain, the CCP has been stepping up its infiltration of Latin America in both scope and depth. Jordan Wilson, a researcher with the US–China Economic and Security Review Commission, found that since the mid-2000s, the CCP had progressed from low-level military sales to high-end military sales, reaching nearly $100 million in exports by 2010. Starting in the 2000s, the CCP substantially increased its military exports to Latin American countries. The recipients of these arms sales were anti-US regimes, most notably Venezuela. At the same time, there has been an increase in military training exchanges and joint military exercises. [84]

The CCP is rapidly developing ties with Latin America across diplomatic, economic, cultural, and military dimensions. In 2015, new requirements outlined in a defense white paper by the CCP "specifically assign the PLA to 'actively participate in both regional and international security cooperation and effectively secure China's overseas interests.'"

On the diplomatic front, due to the CCP's incentives and threats, a number of countries have chosen to sever diplomatic ties with the Republic of China (Taiwan) and instead embrace the communist PRC. In June 2017, Panama announced that it had ended diplomatic relations with Taiwan and now recognized "only one China." Three years earlier, the CCP had started actively planning to invest in Panama's infrastructure, such as ports, railways, and highways, with the total amount of investment reaching about $24 billion. [85] China has already acquired control over both ends of the Panama Canal, which is of great international strategic importance.

The CCP has also invested close to $30 billion in El Salvador's La Union port. In July 2018, the US Ambassador to El Salvador warned in El Salvador's *El Diario De Hoy* newspaper that Chinese investment in the port had a military objective and deserved close attention. [86]

On the cultural front, by the beginning of 2018, the CCP

had established thirty-nine Confucius Institutes and eleven Confucius Classrooms in Latin America and the Caribbean, with total enrollment exceeding 50,000. [87] Confucius Institutes have been identified as institutions used by the CCP for spying, as well as transmitting Communist Party culture and ideology under the guise of traditional Chinese culture.

The CCP's expansion and infiltration into Latin America is a serious threat to the United States. By using access to the Chinese market and dependence on economic investment and military aid to sway the policies of Latin American governments, China is able to pull them into its own sphere of influence and pit them against the United States. The canals, ports, railways, and communications facilities the CCP builds are all important tools that will be used to expand and establish its global hegemony.

F. THE CCP'S GROWING MILITARY CAPABILITIES

As China's military power has developed, it has become more aggressive in areas such as the South China Sea. In 2009, Chinese vessels followed and harassed a US surveillance ship (the USNS Impeccable) while the latter was conducting routine operations in international waters there. [88] A similar incident took place in international waters in the Yellow Sea when Chinese vessels repeatedly came within thirty yards of the USNS Victorious, forcing it to make a dangerous sudden stop. [89] In September 2018, a Chinese warship conducted aggressive maneuvers warning the USS Decatur to depart the area. The Chinese ship approached within forty-five yards of the bow of the Decatur, forcing the American vessel to maneuver to prevent a collision. [90]

The CCP revealed its military ambitions long ago. Its strategy is to move from being a land power to being a maritime superpower and eventually establishing hegemony over both. In 1980, Beijing's strategy was to perform active defense, and its focus was mainly on defending its own borders. At the time, its main adversary was the Soviet Army. In 2013, Beijing's frontline defense turned into active offense for the purpose of expanding its frontline. It proposed "strategic offense as an important type of active defense." [91]

The US Department of Defense stated in an annual report to Congress in 2018:

> *China's maritime emphasis and attention to missions guarding its overseas interests have increasingly propelled the PLA beyond China's borders and its immediate periphery. The PLAN's [the Chinese navy's] evolving focus — from "offshore waters defense" to a mix of "offshore waters defense" and "open seas protection" — reflects the high command's expanding interest in a wider operational reach. China's military strategy and ongoing PLA reform reflect the abandonment of its historically land-centric mentality. Similarly, doctrinal references to "forward edge defense" that would move potential conflicts far from China's territory suggest PLA strategists envision an increasingly global role.* [92]

The PRC has built islands and militarized reef islets in the South China Sea, equipping them with airports, shore-based aircraft, and missiles. It fortified three strategically important islets, namely Fiery Cross Reef, Subi Reef, and Mischief Reef, with anti-ship cruise missiles, surface-to-air missiles, and airfields. The islands essentially serve as stationary aircraft carriers that can be used in the event of military conflict. At the strategic level, the PLA navy is capable of breaking through the boundaries of the island chain that stretches from the Kuril Islands in the north to the islands of Taiwan and Borneo in the south, giving it the capability to fight in the open ocean.

Lawrence Sellin, retired US Army colonel and military commentator, wrote in 2018: "China is now attempting to extend its international influence beyond the South China Sea by linking to a similar framework for dominance in the northern Indian Ocean. If permitted to complete the link,

China could be in an unassailable position to exert authority over roughly one-half of the global GDP." [93]

The dominance of the South China Sea isn't an issue of territory, but of global strategy. Each year, close to $5 trillion in merchandise moves through the South China Sea. [94] For China, its Maritime Silk Road begins with the South China Sea, and an estimated 80 percent of its oil imports will travel by sea. [95] Peacekeeping in the South China Sea following World War II fell to the United States and its allies, which poses a big threat to the Chinese regime.

M. Taylor Fravel, associate professor of political science at the Massachusetts Institute of Technology, wrote that since 1949, China has engaged in twenty-three territorial disputes with its neighbors. It settled seventeen of these disputes. In fifteen of these settlements, Beijing offered substantial compromises on the allocation of disputed territory. But when it comes to issues in the South China Sea, since the 1950s, even when the Chinese navy was militarily insignificant, it has taken an uncompromising approach and has claimed indisputable sovereignty over the region. China has never used such absolute language in other territorial disputes.

Fravel listed several reasons for China's strong stance on South China Sea issues. "China views offshore islands such as the [Spratly Islands] as strategic. From these islands, China can claim jurisdiction over adjacent waters that might contain significant natural resources and even jurisdiction over some activities of foreign naval vessels," he said. "South China Sea outcrops can also be developed into forward outposts for projecting military power. ... They might also aid China's submarine force by preventing other states from tracking Chinese submarines that seek to enter the Western Pacific from the South China Sea." [96]

The Chinese regime's aggressive and expansionary actions in the South China Sea, especially the steps it has taken in recent years to change the status quo, have heightened military tensions in the greater region. In reaction, "Japan, of course, has reversed a decade of declining military outlays, while India has revived stalled naval modernization," wrote author and geostrategist Brahma Chellaney in 2018. [97] Masking its efforts with the excuse of safe passage for energy and freight, China's active expansion in the South China Sea has tipped the balance of power in the region and increases the possibility of military conflict. Geoscientist Scott Montgomery of the University of Washington pointed out that "Chinese perception of the [South China Sea] as a security concern has led to an erosion of security in the region." [98] Western scholars believe that Chinese military officials are looking at how to project power ever farther abroad. In 2017, the PLA established its first overseas military base in Djibouti, on the Horn of Africa. [99]

The CCP regime maintains the largest army in the world, with two million active personnel, according to a 2019 International Institute for Strategic Studies report. [100] The PLA also has the largest ground force in the world, the largest number of warships, the third-most naval tonnage, and a massive air force. It has a nuclear strike capability consisting of intercontinental ballistic missiles, ballistic-missile submarines, and strategic bombers.

Communist China's military expansion is not limited to the traditional divisions of land, sea, and air; it is also making advances in the realms of space and electromagnetic warfare.

The Chinese regime also has 1.7 million personnel in the People's Armed Police, a paramilitary organization primarily tasked with maintaining internal order. Like the PLA, the organization is under the unified leadership of the CCP Central Military Commission; in addition to this the CCP also maintains a large number of reserve and militia units. The Party's military doctrine has always stressed the importance of "people's war." Under the CCP's totalitarian system, it can quickly redirect all available resources for military use in the event of war. This means that the CCP has a pool of over a billion people from which it can draft huge numbers of people. Even overseas Chinese factor into the CCP's military and intelligence strategy; in 2017, the PRC passed a "national intelligence law" demanding all Chinese citizens assist the Communist Party, no matter where they reside.

China's GDP increased rapidly between 1997 and 2007. The PLA ground forces now have thousands of modern main battle tanks. The PLA Navy has two aircraft carriers in its fleet and is building more. Ninety percent of PLA Air Force fighters are of the fourth generation, and the CCP has begun to introduce fifth-generation fighters.

In early 2017, China announced a 6.5 percent inflation-adjusted increase in its annual military budget to $154.3 billion. Analysis of data from 2008 through 2017 indicates China's official military budget grew at an annual average of 8 percent in inflation-adjusted terms over that period. [101] Observers estimate that the CCP's actual military spending is twice as much as what is officially acknowledged. Aside from this, the military strength of the regime is not fully reflected in military spending because its actual military expenditure is higher than the public figures, and the CCP can requisition many civilian resources and manpower at its discretion. The entire industrial system can serve the needs of war, which means its true military capabilities far exceed official data and the usual estimates.

The CCP uses a broad range of espionage to catch up with the United States in technology. According to some estimates, more than 90 percent of espionage against the United States conducted via hacking comes from the PRC, and the CCP's networks infiltrate large American companies and the military, stealing technology and knowledge that the Chinese cannot develop independently. [102]

The CCP has built a global system consisting of more than thirty Beidou (Big Dipper) navigation satellites, with global GPS military positioning capabilities. In conjunction with this, the PLA is fielding increasingly advanced combat-capable drones. At the 2018 Zhuhai Airshow in China, the debut of the CH-7 Rainbow drone caught the attention of military experts. The Rainbow series signifies that China has caught up in the technology for developing armed drones. A large number of the earlier CH-4 Rainbows have taken over the military markets of Jordan, Iraq, Turkmenistan, and Pakistan, countries that were restricted from purchasing armed drones from the United States. [103] The latest CH-7 Rainbow, in some ways, is as well-equipped as the X-47B, the best drone the United States has to offer. [104] A video played at the airshow simulated the drones combating the enemy, which was clearly the US military. [105] The drones' small size allows them to be deployed from a variety of platforms, including civilian vessels, which could give the CCP an advantage over Taiwan in a potential conflict. [106] A large number of aerial drones can form clusters under the control of satellites and artificial intelligence, making them useful in regional and asymmetrical conflicts.

The stealth fighter Chinese J-20, also unveiled at the Zhuhai Air Show, resembles the American F-22, while the Chinese J-31 appears modeled on the F-35. Though still lagging behind the US military in many respects, the PRC defense industry is closing the gap with the United States in developing modern jet fighters.

In terms of tactics, the PLA focuses on asymmetric capabilities: asymmetric warfare, asymmetric strategy, and asymmetric weapons. [107] Adm. Philip Davidson, commander of the US Indo-Pacific Command, described China as a "peer competitor." He said that China is not trying to match America's firepower one-to-one; rather, it is trying to catch up with the United States by building critical asymmetric capabilities, including the use of anti-ship missiles and capabilities in submarine warfare. Because of this, he warned that "there is no guarantee that the United States would win a future conflict with China." [108]

One such asymmetrical weapon is the Dongfeng 21D anti-ship ballistic missile. Traditionally, ballistic missiles are used for delivering nuclear warheads to stationary targets such as cities and military bases, but the Dongfeng 21D is a unique weapon intended for use against US aircraft carrier battle groups at sea. The CCP has also followed the Soviet Cold War-era strategy of deploying large numbers of cruise missiles in an effort to offset US naval supremacy. In 2018, the PLA revealed its land-based YJ-12B supersonic anti-ship cruise missile, known as the "aircraft carrier killer." It has drawn a 550-kilometer "death zone" in the western Pacific, in which American carrier battle groups will be susceptible to ultra low-altitude saturation strikes.

Armed with missiles like the Dongfeng 21D and the YJ-12, the PLA does not have to match the US Navy in one-to-one strength — such as the number of deployable aircraft carriers — to be able to deny it regional access to the Western Pacific.

Following the rapid expansion of its military power, the PRC has become a huge weapons exporter to the world's authoritarian regimes, such as North Korea and Iran. On the one hand, the goal is to expand its military alliances, and on the other hand, to disperse and counter US military power. To this end, the CCP regime encourages hatred against the United States, finding common cause with other anti-American regimes.

At the same time, the CCP leadership has adopted terrorist military theories such as unrestricted warfare. It advocates the necessity of war by saying that "war is not far from us; it is the birthplace of the 'Chinese century.'" It legitimizes violence and terror with sayings such as "death is the driving force for the advancement of history." It justifies aggression with the sayings "there is no right to development without the right to war" and "the development of one country poses a threat to another — this is the general rule of world history." [109]

Zhu Chenghu, a major general and the dean of the PRC's National Defense University, publicly stated in 2005 that if the United States intervened in a war in the Taiwan Strait, China would preemptively use nuclear weapons to raze hundreds of cities in the United States, even if all of China to the east of Xi'an (a city located at the western edge of China's traditional boundaries) were destroyed as a consequence. [110] Zhu's statements were made largely to probe the reactions of the international community.

It is important to be aware that the CCP's military strategies are always subordinate to its political needs, and that the regime's military ambitions form only one dimension of its broader scheme to establish communist hegemony over the entire globe. [111]

3. Unrestricted Warfare With Chinese Communist Characteristics

In the process of realizing its global ambitions, the CCP recognizes no moral limitations and obeys no laws. As discussed in *Nine Commentaries on the Communist Party*, the history of the CCP's founding and rise to power was a process of gradually perfecting the evilness found through history, both in China and around the world, including the Party's nine inherited traits: "evil, deceit, incitement, unleashing the scum of society, espionage, robbery, fighting, elimination, and control." [112] These traits are seen everywhere through the CCP's global expansion, and the Party has continually enhanced and strengthened its techniques and their malignancy. The CCP's unrestricted warfare is the concentrated expression of these evil traits and an important part of its success.

The idea of unrestricted warfare has always run through the CCP's military practices, but the term was first used officially in the 1999 book *Unrestricted Warfare*, written by two Chinese colonels. As the name implies, unrestricted warfare has these characteristics: "[It is] a war beyond all boundaries and limits, ... forcing the enemy to accept one's own interests by all means, including methods of force and non-force, military and non-military, killing and non-killing. ... The means are all-inclusive, information is omnipresent, the battlefield is everywhere ... beyond all political, historical, cultural, and moral restraints."

Unrestricted warfare means that "all weapons and technologies can be used at will; it means that all boundaries between the worlds of war and non-war, military and non-military, are broken." It utilizes methods that span nations and spheres of activity. Finance, trade, the media, international law, outer space, and more are all potential battlefields. Weapons include hacking, terrorism, biochemical warfare, ecological warfare, atomic warfare, electronic warfare, drug trafficking, intelligence, smuggling, psychological warfare, ideological warfare, sanctions, and so on. [113]

The authors of *Unrestricted Warfare* believe that "the generalization of war" is the inevitable future direction and that every field must be militarized. They believe that utilizing a large number of nonmilitary personnel is the key to unrestricted warfare, and that the government must quickly prepare for combat in all invisible fields of war. [114]

Many people refer to various professional or social environments as "battlefields" by way of metaphor, but the CCP takes this literally. All fields are battlefields because the CCP is in a state of war at all times, and everyone is a combatant. All conflicts are regarded as struggles of life and death. Slight problems are magnified to be questions of principle or ideology, and the whole country is mobilized, as if in a state of active war, to meet the CCP's goals.

In the 1940s, during the Chinese Civil War, the CCP used economic warfare to harm the economy of the Nationalist government (Kuomintang, or KMT) of the Republic of China and cause it to collapse. The Party used espionage to obtain the Kuomintang's military plans even before the KMT's own troops received them. The CCP continues to use unrestricted means of warfare today, on a yet larger and broader scale. Unrestricted warfare, which breaks all conventional rules and moral restraints, leaves most Westerners, Western governments, and Western companies unable to understand the CCP, much less contend with it.

The CCP implements many seemingly mundane means, in numerous fields, to achieve its goals:

- Exporting Party culture and lies to the world through foreign propaganda

- Controlling global media and carrying out ideological warfare

- Using fame, honey traps (sexual entrapment), interpersonal relationships, bribery, and despotic power to gain leverage over the leaders of global organizations, important political figures, experts in think tanks and academic circles, business tycoons, and influentials from all walks of life

- Supporting, inciting, and allying with rogue regimes to distract the United States and Western governments

- Using trade diplomacy to make free countries compete against one another, using the market of more than one billion Chinese consumers as bait

- Deepening economic integration and interdependency to tie up other countries

- Violating World Trade Organization trade rules

- Making false reform commitments to accumulate trade surplus and foreign exchange reserves

- Using the market, foreign exchange, and financial

resources as weapons to suppress human rights through economic unrestricted warfare and to force other countries to abandon moral responsibility and universal values

- Forcing Chinese working in private enterprises abroad to steal information from them

- Making hostages of China's citizens and those of other countries

A. THE CCP'S GLOBAL PROPAGANDA OPERATIONS

In 2018, when the PRC's state-run broadcaster established a branch in London, the outlet encountered an enviable problem: receiving too many job applications. Nearly six thousand people applied for the ninety positions available. [115] People's eagerness to work for the CCP's mouthpiece — the jobs required reporting news from the PRC's perspective — reflects the decline of the Western media industry and the threat that the CCP's foreign propaganda poses to the world.

The World's Largest Propaganda Machine

Mao Zedong once demanded that the *Xinhua News Agency* "take charge of the earth and let the whole world hear our voice." [116]

After the 2008 financial crisis, Western media outlets faced their own financial and business crises. The CCP seized the opportunity to deploy its "external propaganda" campaign. *The People's Daily, China Daily, Xinhua*, China Central Television (CCTV), China Radio International, and other Communist Party mouthpieces set up newspaper distribution, radio stations, and television stations around the world.

Chang Ping, former news director of the major Chinese newspaper *Southern Weekend*, said that between 2009 and 2015, the Chinese regime allocated 45 billion yuan ($6.52 billion) to the "national strategy for external propaganda in public relations and publicity." According to Chinese media sources, the 45 billion yuan was only a small part of the total expenditure. [117] The CCP spends between an estimated $7 billion and $10 billion per year on media targeted at non-Chinese foreigners, according to a 2015 report published by The Wilson Center. [118]

In March 2018, the Propaganda Department of the Central Committee of the Communist Party of China led the integration of CCTV, China Radio International, and China National Radio to establish the China Media Group, also called Voice of China. It has become the largest propaganda machine in the world.

The CCP's foreign propaganda apparatus attempts to blend in by recruiting mainly local reporters and presenters. A video call between Xi Jinping and the Washington, DC, bureau of CCTV America in February 2016 showed that the majority of the journalists employed there were not Chinese. [119] But the CCP's propaganda department drives the content they report. China's state-run media thus produces local packaging in the target country, using local faces and voices to spout the Communist Party's thinking and conflate the regime with the Chinese people. It uses locals abroad to spread the CCP's stories and the CCP's voice — not China's true stories and not the voices of the Chinese people.

The Party also provides scholarships to young foreign journalists, including in the areas of food and education, so that they can study or be trained in mainland China and, at the same time, be instilled with the CCP's views on journalism.

In many situations, the CCP's propaganda appears unsuccessful due to its crude narratives, which damage its credibility. However, it uses a raft of tactics, including using foreign media as its mouthpiece, ruthlessly attacking any media and individuals that criticize the CCP, and forcing support for the CCP.

Aligning the World's Media With the CCP

In 2015, the foreign ministers of ten countries condemned the CCP for building artificial islands in the contested waters of the South China Sea. At the same time, a radio station in Washington, DC, claimed that external forces had attempted to fabricate the facts and aggravate tensions in the South China Sea. It failed to mention the CCP's takeover efforts. The station, WCRW, repeats a great deal of content favoring the position of the CCP — and curiously, it runs no advertising. Its only customer is a Los Angeles company, G&E Studio Inc., itself 60 percent controlled by China Radio International (CRI) in Beijing. G&E broadcasts its programs in Chinese and English on at least fifteen US stations, covering Salt Lake City, Philadelphia, Houston, Honolulu, and Portland, among others. [120] The biggest benefit of this operation is to conceal the role of the CCP and listeners are made to feel that Americans themselves are expressing their support for the CCP.

Globally, CRI operated thirty-three such stations in at least fourteen countries in 2015. By 2018, it had fifty-eight stations in thirty-five countries. [121] The control and operations are carried out via local Chinese companies, making it legal, although many people are unhappy about the Party hiding its propaganda. Under the banner of democracy, the CCP advocates for communism and attempts to manipulate its audience into adopting its views by exploiting loopholes in the laws of free societies. It uses democracy to destroy democracy.

The *China Daily*'s inserts are another important part of the CCP's external propaganda campaign. *China Daily* publishes pro-CCP news inserts in *The Washington Post* using a layout style that can give readers the impression that it's *The Washington Post*'s content, as the text indicating the insert is an advertisement is placed in an inconspicuous location. [122] The CCP struck similar deals with more than thirty other newspapers, including *The New York Times*, *The Wall Street Journal*, *The Daily Telegraph*, and *Le Figaro*.

On September 23, 2018, *China Daily* also inserted a four-page supplement that looked like ordinary news and commentary in the local Iowa newspaper *Des Moines Register*. The material attacked the US president and the pending trade deal, in what some called an attempt to influence the upcoming midterm elections. [123]

When it comes to information warfare, the CCP's totalitarian regime has several advantages over other countries. The Party blocks media from all democratic countries, but is able to insert its state-run media in democratic societies. The CCP prevents media inserts from free countries being added to its own media, but the CCP can insert its content into the media from free societies. CCP media serve the Party first and foremost, and Western journalists will never hold executive roles in their Party mouthpieces. The CCP can, however, send its own undercover people into Western media or train foreigners into being mouthpiece reporters for the Party's media.

As long as the West still regards the CCP media as legitimate, the West will continue to lose in the information war. In 2018, the US Department of Justice ordered *Xinhua* and China Global Television Network to register as foreign agents in the United States. It was a step in the right direction but far from sufficient, the problem being the lack of reciprocity in the first place. More recently, the US government has taken stronger action to counteract the CCP's propaganda narratives. Starting in March 2020, the US State Department began placing restrictions on PRC-controlled media outlets operating in the United States, such as naming them foreign missions and limiting the number of staff they can hire. Trump administration officials such as Secretary of State Mike Pompeo have been especially vocal in their criticism of the Communist Party's attempts to win the propaganda war.

The Communist Party also excels in controlling overseas Chinese-language media. Through coercion and enticement, the CCP has recruited a large number of Chinese-language media, including some Taiwanese-founded media that previously had a strong tradition of anti-communism. The CCP-sponsored World Chinese Media Forum is used as a platform to communicate the Party's instructions to Chinese media around the world. More than four hundred and sixty overseas Chinese media executives from more than sixty countries and regions attended the 9th World Chinese Media Forum held in Fuzhou on September 10, 2017.

An example of the impact of this media-control work can be found in the reporting of *The China Press* (called *Qiao Bao* in Mandarin), a California-based Chinese-language media outlet that carries CCP propaganda in the United States. *The China Press*'s lengthy reports during the CCP's 19th National Congress in 2017 were almost identical to those published by official Party media. [124]

The CCP-controlled Overseas Chinese Media Association, with more than one hundred and sixty media members, swung into action during the 2014 Umbrella Movement's pro-democracy protests in Hong Kong. The group urgently rallied one hundred and forty-two pro-PRC media outlets in Asia, Europe, Africa, the United States, and Australia to publish its "Safeguarding Hong Kong" declaration supporting the CCP's perspective. [125]

Alongside the PRC's economic "colonization" of Africa, CCP media has also reached all corners of the continent. The China-based television and media group StarTimes is now operating in thirty African countries and claims to be "the fastest growing and most influential digital TV operator in Africa." [126] The regime has been relentless in its penetration of overseas media.

Suppressing opposing voices is another aspect of CCP overseas propaganda operations. The Party threatens journalists who expose it with visa denials and other forms of harassment, leading to self-censorship. The result is that there are few global media corporations that take a completely independent stance on the CCP without regard to consequences imposed by the regime.

There are several ways for a tyrannical regime like the CCP to improve its public image. The first and most direct way is to implement genuine reform and transition to a form of government that respects human rights, universal values, and the rule of law. The second way is for the regime to cover up its crimes through censorship. The third way is to actively convince the outside world to side with the regime. The third method offers the most effective form of cover for tyranny.

The CCP has used both the second and third methods simultaneously over decades. It employs a variety of large-scale propaganda activities to target foreigners, changing the minds of people to make them think positively about communist China, or at least not criticize its fundamental flaws. In some cases, CCP propaganda is even able to pull them into the mire, turning them into active allies. Through extensive investments and shrewd operations, the Party has established a worldwide system for creating alliances, isolating enemies, and turning neutral entities into sympathizers or scoundrels.

Manipulating Cultural Exchange to Indoctrinate the World in CCP Culture

Ideological and political indoctrination is an essential tool in the CCP's destruction of traditional Chinese culture. But in recent years, the Party has advertised its commitment to restoring traditional culture, seeking to frame itself as the legitimate representative of the Chinese nation and its identity. As discussed in previous chapters of this book, this wave of supposed restoration has left out the soul of the traditions, replacing it with a fake version infused with deviant Communist Party culture. This has not only deceived the world, but also further undermined China's ancient heritage. Typical examples of this effort are Confucius Institutes, which are set up on college and high school campuses around the world.

Confucius Institutes subvert important academic principles of autonomy and freedom of inquiry, aim to promote the

CCP's version of historical events, distort the history of China, and omit the CCP's appalling human rights record. In some Confucius Institute classrooms, quotes from Mao are hung on the wall. On the surface, Confucius Institutes claim to teach Chinese culture, while, in fact, they promote communist doctrine and transmit Party culture.

According to incomplete statistics, as of the end of 2017, the PRC had established at least 525 Confucius Institutes (targeting colleges and universities) and opened 1,113 Confucius Classrooms (targeting elementary and secondary schools) in more than 145 countries. [127] Confucius Institute funding is provided by Hanban, an organization affiliated with the CCP's United Front Work Department (UFWD). The use of funds is supervised by personnel from the PRC's embassies and consulates.

In addition to offering cultural and language courses, Confucius Institutes also distort history and even organize protests against activities the CCP believes threaten its dominance. For example, pro-Beijing speakers invited to Confucius Institute-sponsored events have repeated the CCP's lies about Tibet, while others have claimed the United States drew China into the Korean War by bombing Chinese villages, according to a 2018 report by the congressional US–China Economic and Security Review Commission (USCC). [128]

The US National Defense Authorization Act for the 2019 fiscal year condemned the CCP's attempts to influence US public opinion, especially "media, cultural institutions, businesses, and academic and political groups." The act explicitly prohibits any national defense funds from being given to Chinese-language departments in US universities where a Confucius Institute exists. [129]

The CCP's foreign propaganda campaign is a major project aimed at globally reshaping the public's views on the regime. The CCP spreads its noxious ideology through this propaganda work, which has severely misled people about the regime, its

mode of operations, its human rights abuses, and communism in general.

B. THE AIM OF UNITED-FRONT WORK:
DISINTEGRATING THE FREE WORLD FROM WITHIN

On December 18, 2018, the CCP celebrated the fortieth anniversary of its so-called reform and opening up. It awarded the
China Reform Friendship Medal to ten influential foreigners to "thank the international community for supporting
China's reform." [130] These ten foreigners included Juan Anto-
nio Samaranch, former president of the International Olympic Committee, which had selected China to host the 2008
Olympics Games; and Robert Lawrence Kuhn, an American
businessman who lent his name as author of a fawning biog-
raphy of former CCP head Jiang. Over the past few decades,
countless politicians and celebrities have acted as accomplices
to the CCP's united-front tactics.

Mao labeled the united front as one of the CCP's "three
magic treasures." Western governments have been deceived
and suffered losses by these tactics, but some are beginning
to wake up, and a number of investigative reports about the
united front have been published.

The USCC's 2018 report *China's Overseas United Front Work*
outlines the CCP's overseas united-front work structure and
operations, including how the CCP uses various types of governmental and non-governmental organizations for its united-front work and the implications for the United States and
other Western countries. The report states, "This elevation of the
importance of United Front work has resulted in an increased
number of UFWD officials assigned to top CCP and government posts, adding roughly 40,000 new UFWD cadres." [131]

The think tank Global Public Policy Institute published
a report in 2018 detailing the activities of CCP's united front
in Europe. [132] The Hoover Institution at Stanford University
released a detailed report on the same topic on Nov. 29, 2018.

The report states: "China's influence activities have moved beyond their traditional United Front focus on diaspora communities to target a far broader range of sectors in Western societies, ranging from think tanks, universities, and media to state, local, and national government institutions. China seeks to promote views sympathetic to the Chinese Government, policies, society, and culture; suppress alternative views; and co-opt key American players to support China's foreign policy goals and economic interests." [133]

The CCP's united front primarily targets the following actors in the West: politicians and businesspeople; academicians and members of think tanks; overseas Chinese leaders, businessmen, and students; the movie and entertainment industries; and overseas dissidents.

Politicians and Businesspeople

The USCC report says the CCP regards its united-front work as an important tool to strengthen domestic and international support for the Party. This includes buying off Western politicians. Through persuasion, temptation, and relationship-building, the CCP maintains close ties with many high-level officials in Western governments. The Party treats these politicians as its "state treasures," giving them lavish gifts and conferring upon them titles such as "old friends of China." Among them are current and former United Nations secretaries general, heads of state, high-ranking government officials, senior government advisers, heads of international organizations, famous academics and think-tank scholars, and media consortium tycoons. All these people in the united-front network are expected to voice their support for the CCP at crucial moments.

Patrick Ho Chi-ping, a former Hong Kong secretary for home affairs, was convicted in the United States for bribery in December 2018. Ho had close ties to the CCP, and bribed high-ranking officials in two African nations on behalf of

China Energy Co. Ltd., a CCP-linked energy corporation in order to obtain mining rights. [134]

US court papers also document the corruption and espionage carried out by Chinese telecommunications giant ZTE. Two high-ranking telecom officials in Liberia testified that between 2005 and 2007, ZTE bribed numerous officials — including the president, government officials, and judges — with paper bags full of thousands of dollars in cash. [135]

The CCP uses money and women to entrap political leaders and then use them as pawns for the regime's ends. In a memorandum following the November 2014 midterm US elections, CEFC China Energy outlined a plan to establish relationships and friendships with politicians. Ye Jianming, the now-disgraced chairman of the company, has strong ties to European political leaders. He once asked a security adviser to a US president to persuade the US army not to bomb Syria because he wanted to buy up oil fields there. Ye also boasted connections to senior officials at the Federal Reserve and the United Nations, as well as family members of US government officials. [136]

When deemed necessary, the CCP can form various temporary united fronts to isolate its enemies. For instance, the CCP has used the votes of developing nations whose officials it previously suborned to pass or block motions at the United Nations. Via proxies, it has disrupted US efforts to stabilize the Middle East. In the meantime, it has been able to forge new economic alliances. In the US–China trade war, the CCP sought to sow conflict between the United States and Europe with the aim of using the latter as part of another united front against the United States.

Local politicians are also targets of the CCP's united-front work. These include community leaders, city council members, mayors, state senators, and others. The usual approach is to donate to local politicians through Chinese organizations or merchants, who are invited to visit China, where they receive bribes. Their family businesses get special treatment in China.

Cases of sexual entrapment, known as "honey traps," often involve blackmail and the CCP often uses this tactic.

Chen Yonglin, a former officer at the Chinese Consulate in Sydney, Australia, who defected in 2005, told *The Epoch Times* that the UFWD had infiltrated the Australian government and had corrupted officials. Chen said: "The amount of private bribery for the officials far surpassed political donations. Especially those higher-ranking officials; the bribes were huge. ... Another aspect of bribery is the all-expenses-paid trips to China, where officials are treated as kings. This includes prostitution paid for by Chinese companies. Many officials changed their stances after returning from China." [137]

With its strong financial backing, the CCP has paid communist and leftist politicians around the world to become its agents in those nations in order to further spread communist ideology.

The CCP uses the same tactics on those in the financial sector and a number of other industries. Business people and entrepreneurs are treated as kings and given business incentives. In return, they become the CCP's voice for lobbying their governments and influencing their countries' financial and economic policies. In the US–China trade war, the CCP had frequent contact with Wall Street tycoons. Many top financial companies and international corporations do business in China. To help expand their business there, these companies hire numerous children of high-ranking Chinese officials, called "princelings." In turn, these princelings act as the Party's eyes, ears, and voice in those companies.

Academic Circles and Think Tanks

Many think tanks in the West directly shape their country's policies and strategy toward China; therefore, the CCP pays them special attention. The CCP exerts control over think tanks via financial sponsorship. It has bribed, controlled, or influenced almost all think tanks related to China. [138] The Chinese tech giant Huawei has provided financial support to think tanks in Washington, who then write positive reports about Huawei, according to a 2018 *Washington Post* report. [139]

Huawei sponsors more than twenty universities in the UK, including Cambridge and Oxford universities. Historian Anthony Glees, a British expert in national security, said: "This is about the electronic agenda being driven by the injection of Chinese money into British universities. That is a national security issue." [140] Huawei, through its Seeds for the Future program, attracted a large number of young talented engineers — a classic communist subversion tactic.

The CCP buys off overseas scholars, especially China observers, with money, status, and fame. Some such scholars then closely follow the CCP's rhetorical line, publishing books and articles to explain the CCP's "peaceful rise," the concepts of the "China dream" or the "China model." The viewpoints of these scholars then influence the China policies of Western governments to accommodate the CCP as it goes about hijacking the international order.

To make things worse, over the past several decades, Western humanities scholars and sociologists have been heavily influenced by strains of communist ideology. With a small amount of CCP influence, they can go from merely supporting leftist ideology to embracing the Party's rule.

Overseas Chinese Leaders, Businessmen, and Students

The CCP has successfully exploited the patriotism of overseas Chinese students to create sympathy for CCP policies and ideology. To gain the support of overseas Chinese, the CCP provides them with financial support. It frequently uses the phrase "the love for one's homeland, the friendship of kin" as part of its deliberate conflation of China and the CCP in order to deceive overseas Chinese. The Party also uses an extensive overseas network of organizations, supporters, and spies to marginalize and attack its opponents.

The CCP uses various pretexts to invite overseas Chinese to do business with and invest in mainland China. It gives overseas Chinese leaders special treatment when visiting the country, arranging for them to meet with high-ranking officials and invites them to attend PRC national-day celebrations.

Zach Dorfman, a senior fellow at Carnegie Council for Ethics in International Affairs, published an investigative report in *Politico* revealing Chinese and Russian espionage activities in Silicon Valley, with a particular focus on Chinese actors. The report examined Rose Pak, the San Francisco Chinese powerbroker, as an example. It noted that the CCP used Pak to have the Chinese Chamber of Commerce in San Francisco marginalize Falun Gong, Tibetan, pro-Taiwan, and Uyghur groups, preventing them from participating in the Chinese New Year parade. [141]

The USCC report also detailed how Chinese Students and Scholars Associations (CSSA) are controlled by the CCP. On their websites, some CSSA branches directly state that they were established by the local Chinese consulate or are its subsidiaries, while in other cases, the control is carried out clandestinely. These organizations receive orders from the PRC consulates, preventing any dissonant views from being aired. Consulate officials harass, intimidate, and monitor students who dissent from the Communist Party line.

CSSAs and those affiliated with them sometimes even conduct industrial and economic espionage. In 2005, France's *Le Monde* reported that the CSSA at the University of Leuven in Belgium was the CCP's front-line spy group in the country. Sometimes such spy networks consist of several hundred agents working in various companies in Europe. [142]

The Film and Entertainment Industries

In recent years, the CCP has increased efforts at infiltrating the US entertainment industry. In 2012, the mainland Chinese Wanda Group spent $2.6 billion to acquire AMC, the second-largest movie theater chain in the United States. Since then, it has acquired Legendary Entertainment for $3.5 billion, and Carmike Cinemas, the fourth-largest movie theater chain in the United States, for $1.1 billion. [143] In 2016, Ali Pictures acquired a stake in Steven Spielberg's Amblin Partners, and placed a representative on Amblin's board of directors to participate in major decision-making. [144]

One of the CCP's main goals in infiltrating the entertainment industry is to have the world follow the CCP's script — painting a positive image of the CCP and China's so-called peaceful rise — to conceal the regime's tyrannical ambitions. At the same time, this image covers up how the exportation of Party culture has corrupted the world. From 1997 to 2013, China invested in only twelve out of the top one hundred highest-grossing Hollywood movies. But in the ensuing five years, China co-financed forty-one of Hollywood's most popular movies. [145]

Hollywood covets China's rapidly growing movie market, and executives are well-aware that they'll be excluded from it if they fail to toe the Party line. Thus, they set about ensuring they are in compliance with Chinese censorship. [146] American movie stars who've taken a stand against CCP oppression are blocked from entering the country, or their films are excluded from the Chinese market. Hollywood star Richard Gere's clear support for Tibet, for example, led to his being denied access to China, thus limiting his career in the United States as film producers sought to avoid offending or provoking the CCP. [147] Other movie stars have been blacklisted for such "transgressions" as well.

Marginalizing Overseas Experts and Dissidents

The CCP has used intimidation and incentives to influence Western China scholars and marginalize the experts who are critical of the regime. This has led many to willingly self-censor. Intimidation includes refusal to issue visas, which has the greatest impact on young scholars. For the sake of professional advancement, many voluntarily avoid discussing human rights, Tibet, and other sensitive topics that might attract the Party's ire.

Perry Link, a professor of East Asian Studies, was black-listed by the CCP for his scholarship on the Tiananmen Square massacre. His treatment by the regime became a "lesson" for young scholars as to what not to do. [148]

In October 2017, Benedict Rogers, deputy chairman of the British Conservative Party's Human Rights Commission and supporter of the Hong Kong democracy movement, went to Hong Kong on a private visit to see friends, including democracy activists, but was refused entry and repatriated at the Hong Kong airport. [149]

The 2018 report by the USCC also said that PRC intelligence agents attempt to recruit people from ethnic minorities, including Uyghurs living abroad, to act as spies. Refusal may lead to persecution of their family members in China. Uyghurs who have been threatened state that the purpose of such threats is not only to collect information about the Uyghur diaspora, but also to create discord and prevent them from effectively opposing the CCP. [150]

C. ECONOMIC WARFARE: THE CCP'S HEAVY WEAPONRY

If external foreign propaganda, perception-management, and united-front work are the CCP's forms of soft power, then its high-tech industry must be the Party's hard power. In the 1950s, the CCP's slogan was to "surpass the United Kingdom and catch up with the United States." Today, that strategy has become a legitimate threat.

Since the 1980s, the PRC has implemented a series of strategic plans in science and technology, including the 863 Program (also known as the State High Technology Research and Development Program), which helped facilitate the theft of technology from other countries; the Torch Program, which helped build high-tech commercial industries; the 973 Program, for scientific research; and the 211 Project, which helped "reform" universities. [151][152] The Made in China 2025 plan aims to transform China from a manufacturing country to a manufacturing power by 2025, taking the lead in big data, 5G, and the like. The strategy includes ambitious plans for artificial intelligence, in which China aims to be a world leader by 2030. The purpose is to upgrade the PRC's status as the world factory to that of an advanced manufacturing giant, thereby attaining global supremacy. [153]

Under normal circumstances, it is normal for a country to mobilize state resources for the benefit of industrial development, or to invest in the research of key technologies. But the CCP's high-tech development strategy poses a fundamental threat to the free world. The PRC is not a normal country, and does not respect the norms that govern international relations. The purpose of the CCP's technological development is not so it can join the ranks of the world's other high-tech countries or compete on equal footing with them, but to eliminate opponents and take down Western economies — especially that of the United States — and thus be one step closer to world domination.

Technological innovation is the fruit of individual liberty, which is in natural conflict with the totalitarian rule of communism. Researchers in mainland China are deprived of the freedom to use foreign search engines, let alone express their freedom in other ways. Thus it is indeed difficult to make real breakthroughs in scientific and technological innovation given the CCP's restrictions on thought and access to information.

To make up for this, the Party has used various underhanded means to steal Western technology and win over cutting-edge talent, and has also used unfair and extraordinary measures to undermine Western industry. The PRC has adopted an all-of-state approach, including government bodies and firms, the military, private business, and individuals to steal technologies the West spent decades and vast sums of money to develop. After assimilating and improving upon the stolen intellectual property, mainland Chinese companies mass-produce high-tech goods at low costs and dump them in international markets, squeezing out foreign enterprises, which are privately owned and cannot flout regulations as is done in the PRC. This economic strategy forms an important component in the CCP's use of "unrestricted warfare" against the West.

The Trap of Trading Technology for Market Access

In recent years, China's high-speed rail network has become almost like an advertisement for the country's high-end manufacturing prowess, and the concept of "high-speed rail diplomacy" has arisen. Chinese state media has called China's work in this area "legendary," given its rapid development in only ten years. But to Western companies, China's high-speed rail buildup has been a nightmare of technological theft, entrapment, and what ultimately became huge losses in exchange for only small gains.

Work on the high-speed rail project began in the early 1990s. By the end of 2005, the CCP abandoned the idea of developing the technology independently and turned to Western technology. The CCP's goal was clear from the beginning: It planned to first acquire the technology, then manufacture the same technology and sell it for cheaper prices on the global market.

The Chinese side requires that foreign manufacturers sign a technology-transfer contract with a Chinese domestic firm before bidding on construction contracts. The Chinese regime also established formal internal assessments called "technology-transfer-implementation evaluations," which focus not on how well foreign businesses teach their systems, but rather on how well domestic companies learn them. If domestic enterprises don't completely master the technology, China doesn't pay. The authorities also require that by the last batch of orders, local companies must produce 70 percent of the orders. [154]

Because foreign companies felt that accessing China's market was an opportunity not to be missed, such terms didn't stop them from signing contracts. Japan's Kawasaki, France's Alstom, Germany's Siemens, and Canada's Bombardier all submitted bids. Still, no Western company was willing to transfer its core, most-valued technology. The CCP thus continued to play games with several of the companies in the hope that at least one would relent and give up something of real value for the benefit of short-term interests. Sure enough, when it appeared that one company would get a chunk of the Chinese market in exchange for technology, the others began to fear being left out. Thus, several of them fell into the CCP's trap, with the result that China was able to extract key technology from the above four companies.

The PRC has invested huge sums in the rail project, acting regardless of cost, and Chinese firms built out the world's most extensive high-speed rail system by mileage. In a few years, China rapidly assimilated Western technology, which was then turned into "independent intellectual property rights." What really shocked Western companies was when the PRC then began applying for high-speed rail patents abroad, with Chinese firms becoming fierce competitors against their former teachers on the international market. Because Chinese companies have accumulated a great deal of practical experience in this realm, and are afforded all the industrial advantages brought by large-scale production capacity and massive state financial backing, China's high-speed rail industry possesses a competitive advantage against peers. It has become a key element of the Party's One Belt, One Road project.

While foreign companies once dreamed of getting their share of the huge market for high-speed rail in China, they found instead that not only were they squeezed out of that market, but they also had created a tough international competitor. Yoshiyuki Kasai, an honorary chairman of the Central Japan Railway Company, said: "The Shinkansen [Japanese bullet train] is the jewel of Japan. The technology transfer to China was a huge mistake." [155]

The CCP itself acknowledges that China's success in high-speed rail was achieved by standing on the shoulders of giants. Indeed, its purpose from the beginning was to become a giant so as to slay all the others. The CCP has an explicit dual purpose: Its short-term goal is to use economic achievements to prove the legitimacy of its regime and to make economic and technological progress to maintain and excite nationalist sentiment and propaganda. But its long-term purpose is to prove that its communist system is superior to the capitalist system, so it unscrupulously steals technology and uses the power of the entire country to compete with capitalist free enterprise.

The CCP's tactics — promising market access in exchange for technology, coercing tech transfers, absorbing and improving foreign technology, having mainland Chinese firms practice in the domestic market before advancing to the world, and dumping products globally to undercut competitors — have led Western companies, and job markets, to suffer immensely.

In 2015, the CCP proposed the ten-year Made in China 2025 project, envisioning that by 2025, China would have transformed from a big manufacturing country to a manufacturing power, and that by 2035, the country's manufacturing industry would surpass that of industrially advanced countries like Germany and Japan. The PRC hopes it will lead innovation in key manufacturing sectors by 2049. Using such lofty rhetoric, the CCP has raised the status of its manufacturing sector to "the foundation of the nation" and "the instrument for rejuvenating the country."

A Manufacturing Superpower Built on Theft

How did the CCP boost Chinese manufacturing and innovative potential in such a short period of time? It used the same old tricks: It coerced companies to transfer their technologies, as in the case of high-speed rail and demanded that foreign companies form joint ventures with Chinese firms so they could acquire the foreign companies' technologies. In addition, the regime encouraged domestic firms to make acquisitions of overseas high-tech companies, directly investing in startups with key technologies, and establishing overseas research-and-development centers. It induced leading foreign tech and scientific research institutes to set up R&D centers in China, and it used targeted policies to bring in foreign technology experts.

Many startups in Silicon Valley need capital. The CCP uses taxpayer money to invest in them in order to get its hands on new technologies, including rocket engines, sensors for autonomous navy ships, and 3D printers that manufacture flexible screens that could be used in fighter-plane cockpits. Ken Wilcox, chairman emeritus of Silicon Valley Bank, said in 2017 that within a six-month period, he was approached by three different Chinese state-owned enterprises about buying technology on their behalf. He said: "In all three cases, they said they had a mandate from Beijing, and they had no idea what they wanted to buy. It was just any and all tech." [156] A 2018 investigative report by the Office of the United States Trade Representative said that Digital Horizon Capital (formerly Danhua Capital) uses China's venture capital to help the CCP gain top technologies and intellectual property in the United States. [157]

The PRC's aptitude for industrial espionage far exceeds the scope of commercial spies in the past. In order to steal technology and secrets from the West, the regime mobilizes all available personnel and tactics — including espionage, hackers, international students, visiting scholars, mainland Chinese and Taiwanese immigrants working in Western companies, and Westerners lured by monetary interests.

The CCP has always coveted the US F-35 stealth fighter jet. In 2016, a Canadian permanent citizen from China, Su Bin, was sentenced to forty-six months in prison for helping steal plans for the F-35 and other US military aircraft. Su worked with two hackers from the Chinese military to penetrate the computer systems of the manufacturer Lockheed Martin and steal the trade secrets. Investigators found that Su's group had also stolen information about Lockheed's F-22 stealth fighter and Boeing's C-17 strategic transport aircraft, as well as 630,000 files from Boeing's system, totaling some 65 gigabytes of data. [158] The PLA's own J-20 stealth fighter exhibited in recent years is now very similar to the American F-22, and the smaller Chinese FC-31 is an imitation of the F-35.

David Smith, an expert on metamaterials at Duke University, invented a kind of "invisibility cloak" with the potential to one day protect US forces. The US military invested millions in support of his research. In 2006, Chinese student Ruopeng Liu came to the United States with the express purpose of studying at Smith's lab, becoming the scientist's protégé. An FBI counterintelligence official believes Liu had a specific mission: to obtain Smith's research. In 2007, Liu brought two former colleagues, traveling at the Chinese regime's expense, to visit Smith's lab, and they worked on the invisibility cloak for a period of time. Later, the equipment used to make the cloak was duplicated at Liu's old lab in China. [159]

On December 20, 2018, the Department of Justice sued two Chinese citizens from the Chinese hacker organization APT 10, which has close ties with the CCP. According to the indictment, from 2006 to 2018, APT 10 carried out extensive hacking attacks, stealing massive amounts of information from more than forty-five organizations, including NASA and the Department of Energy. The documents stolen included information on medicines, biotechnology, finance, manufacturing, petroleum, and natural gas. FBI Director Christopher Wray said: "China's goal, simply put, is to replace the US as the world's leading superpower, and they're using illegal methods to get there. They're using an expanding set of non-traditional and illegal methods." [160]

PRC theft of technology and patents is hard to combat and prevent. Kathleen Puckett, a former US counterintelligence officer in San Francisco, said that the CCP puts all its efforts into espionage and gets everything for free. [161]

The CCP has launched a "war against everyone" to loot advanced technology from the West, using patriotism, racial sentiments, money, and prestige to drive its unprecedented stealing spree.

Some have defended Chinese intellectual property theft by arguing that such activity can't amount to much, because Chinese firms don't get the full picture of how technology is deployed and scaled. But it's very dangerous to look at the PRC's industrial espionage this way. Espionage in the electronic age is completely different from that in decades past, in which spies might take some photos. CCP spies now steal entire databases of research, and in many cases, scoop up not only the technology, but also the experts. With the power of the world factory that the PRC has developed for decades and the R&D potential it has accumulated, the regime is truly willing and able to build a manufacturing superpower based on theft — and it is on course to do so.

The Thousand Talents Program: Espionage and Talent Attraction

From when mainland China opened up in the 1970s until today, millions of Chinese students have studied overseas, and many have become accomplished in various fields. The CCP seeks to recruit and use these talented individuals, invested in and trained by the West, to directly bring back to China the technology and economic information they've acquired so as to support the Party's campaign for global dominance. Until its recent disappearance, multiple PRC government departments ran the Thousand Talents Program. Started in 2008, the Thousand Talents Program was ostensibly about recruiting top Chinese talent overseas to return to China for full-time or short-term positions. But the real goal was for state industry to get its hands on new technology and intellectual property from the West. In 2020, following mounting pressure from the West, information about the Program has been scrubbed from public view.

The FBI declassified a document about the talent programs in September 2015. It concludes that recruiting target individuals allows China to profit in three ways: gaining access to research and expertise in cutting-edge technology, benefiting from years of scientific research conducted in the United States and supported by US government grants and private funding, and severely impacting the US economy. [162]

The US National Institutes of Health (NIH) noted in a 2018 report that foreign nationals had transferred US intellectual property to their native countries while on the US government payroll. Their actions have unfairly impacted all US academic institutions. [163] M. Roy Wilson, a report co-author and co-chair of the advisory committee to the NIH director, said that a key qualification of becoming part of the Thousand Talents Program is having access to valuable intellectual property. He said that the problem was significant, not random, and that the severity of the intellectual property losses was impossible to ignore. [164]

Peter Harrell, adjunct senior fellow in the energy, economics, and security program at the Center for a New American Security, said: "China is pursuing a whole-of-society approach to its technological capabilities. That includes purchasing innovative companies through overseas investments, requiring Western companies to transfer cutting-edge technologies to China as a condition of market access, providing vast state resources to finance domestic technological development, financing training for top Chinese students and researchers overseas, and paying a hefty premium to attract talent back to China." [165]

The Thousand Talents Program included as its targets almost all Chinese students who have come to the United

States since the 1980s and who find themselves with access to useful information for the regime's industrial, technological, and economic development — potentially tens of thousands of individuals. The CCP is mobilizing the capacity of the entire country and population to conduct unrestricted warfare in its recruitment of talent and accumulation of intellectual property.

A Sinister, 'Whole-of-Government' Effort

In addition to outright stealing, PRC state support and subsidies are also an important means for the CCP to fulfill its ambitions. State support means that the regime can use huge sums of money to support key industries. Effectively, this is about using China's national power to exert pressure on private businesses in the West. This poses an enormous, unique challenge to countries where leaders are democratically elected and leave business decisions to businesses themselves. Chinese subsidies — ultimately taken out of the pocket of the unconsenting taxpayer — mean that Chinese manufacturers can ignore the real costs of doing business, making them unstoppable predators in international markets.

The solar cell industry is a classic example of the CCP regime's subsidies. In the early 2000s, no Chinese companies existed among the top ten solar-panel manufacturers, but by 2017 there were six, including the top two. The green energy industry was heavily promoted during US President Barack Obama's first term, but before long, dozens of solar-panel makers were filing for bankruptcy or had to cut back their businesses in the face of unrelenting competition from China, which ultimately undermined enthusiasm in the clean energy industry. [166] The damage was wrought by China's dumping of products on the international market, enabled by the regime's subsidies for its domestic solar industry.

In Western countries, states also fund key projects, including those on the cutting edge of technological development.

The prototype of the internet, for instance, was first developed by the US Department of Defense. However, in the West, government participation at the national level is limited. Once a technology is commercialized, private companies are free to act as they will. For example, NASA disseminated its advanced research results to industry through its Technology Transfer Program. Many of its software projects simply put their source code on the Web as open source. In contrast, the CCP directly uses the power of the state to commercialize high-tech, which is equivalent to using a "China Inc." to compete against individual Western firms.

The Made in China 2025 project is, of course, inseparable from state subsidies and state industrial planning. If the CCP continues on its current track, the story of the solar panel companies will play out in other industries, and Chinese products will become global job-killers. Through unrestricted economic and technological warfare, the CCP has successfully led many Western companies, including multinational corporations, into a trap. They handed over capital and advanced technology, but weren't able to compete fairly in the Chinese market, and instead helped create their own state-backed competitors. The CCP used them as pawns to achieve its ambitions.

D. USING THE MASSES FOR ESPIONAGE

The CCP regards information as simply another weapon in its arsenal. Regardless of the field, whether pertaining to the state, private enterprise, or individual endeavors, all forms of information are seen as fair game for the fulfillment of the regime's strategic ambitions.

The CCP also has used legislation to force all Chinese people to participate in its unrestricted warfare. The National Intelligence Law of the People's Republic of China, passed by the Standing Committee of the National People's Congress, states that "national intelligence agencies may require relevant agencies, organizations, and citizens to provide necessary support, assistance, and cooperation." [167] This means that any Chinese citizen can be coerced by the CCP to collect intelligence and become a spy.

On December 12, 2018, the US Senate Judiciary Committee held a hearing about the CCP's non-traditional espionage activities. Bill Priestap, assistant director of the FBI counterintelligence division, outlined the CCP's approach: The Party plays by the rules when it's advantageous, while at other times, it bends or breaks the rules to achieve its goals. When possible, the Party also tries to rewrite the rules and reshape the world according to its own requirements. [168]

John Demers, assistant attorney general of the National Security Division of the US Department of Justice, testified that the CCP's Made in China 2025 plan is essentially a handbook for what to steal. He disclosed that from 2011 to 2018, more than 90 percent of the cases of economic espionage allegedly involving or benefiting a country, and more than two-thirds of the trade-secret theft cases were related to the PRC. [169]

The CCP's espionage is far from limited to intellectual property. The CCP controls all major private companies in China and uses them for international intelligence gathering. US Senator Ted Cruz called Huawei a "Communist Party spy agency thinly veiled as a telecom company," in a Twitter post in 2018. "Its surveillance networks span the globe and its clients are rogue regimes such as Iran, Syria, North Korea, and Cuba. The arrest of Huawei's CFO Wanzhou Meng in Canada is both an opportunity and a challenge," Cruz wrote. [170]

An investigation published in January 2018 by the French newspaper *Le Monde*, revealed that confidential information from the African Union (AU) headquarters in Ethiopia had been sent to Shanghai every night for five years, starting in January 2012. The CCP was accused of being behind the hack. A report released by the Australian Strategic Policy Institute six months later revealed that Huawei was the key provider of the information and communications technology infrastructure at the AU headquarters building. [171]

André Ken Jakobsson, a postdoctoral fellow at the Center for Military Studies in Copenhagen, said: "What is worrying is that the CCP can get very critical and sensitive information. They can enter a system that controls our entire society. Everything will be connected to the 5G network in the future. We are worried that the country that provides such equipment — China — controls the switch." [172]

For at least two decades, the CCP has used hackers on a large scale to obtain critical information from other countries. As early as 1999, CCP hackers disguised as a Falun Gong overseas website attacked the US Department of Transportation. The department contacted the website to investigate the attack and traced it back to a hacker from a Party-run intelligence agency. [173]

In June 2015, CCP hackers attacked the US Office of Personnel Management, stealing the data and security information of more than 21.5 million Americans. Those affected included 19.7 million government employees and 1.8 million of their family members.

In November 2018, Marriott International announced that private information, including passport details, of up to 500 million guests had been stolen by hackers, dating back to 2014. US Secretary of State Michael Pompeo confirmed on December 12 that the hacking was carried out by the CCP. Marriott is the largest hotel supplier to the US government and military.

E. THE MANY FORMS OF UNRESTRICTED WARFARE

The CCP utilizes other methods of unrestricted warfare. A few major areas are listed below.

Diplomatic Warfare

The CCP's typical diplomatic method is to divide and conquer. When the world criticizes the CCP for its human rights abuses, regime officials invite each country to discuss human rights separately and in private; consequently, such criticism can have no restraining effect. Moreover, the CCP has virtually disintegrated the international norms that safeguard human rights.

The CCP used this method to escape condemnation and sanctions right before being admitted to the World Trade Organization. Once admitted, the CCP immediately began using economic means to tempt various countries, and again used divide-and-conquer to achieve large-scale breakthroughs in various areas.

The CCP also uses rogue tactics of hostage diplomacy to arrest and threaten both Chinese and non-Chinese until its demands are met. Before the PRC was granted permanent normal trade relations status by the United States in 2002, regime authorities arrested dissidents before almost every negotiation session, then used the release of the dissidents as a bargaining chip during the negotiations. The Communist Party disregards the lives of its own people, but it knows that Western societies care about basic human rights. Therefore, it uses its own citizens as hostages, puts a knife to the neck of the Chinese people, and uses them to threaten the enemy — the United States.

With the rapid development of the Chinese economy, the CCP has become bolder, even taking foreign hostages. Six weeks after the aforementioned Su Bin was arrested in Canada for hacking into a US military database, Canadian couple Kevin and Julia Garratt were arrested in China and accused by the CCP of espionage. [174]

After the arrest of Huawei's vice president and chief financial officer, Meng Wanzhou, in Vancouver on December 1, 2018, the Chinese Ministry of Foreign Affairs incited a series of protests, with the Chinese Embassy in Canada mobilizing a large number of pro-communist overseas Chinese for the action. In addition, the PRC arrested two Canadian citizens in retaliation. [175] This was both to put direct pressure on Canada and to drive a wedge between Canada and the United States.

Lawlessness is the CCP's modus operandi. Any foreigner in China may become a hostage at any time and be used as a bargaining chip for political, economic, and diplomatic purposes. Additionally, when the CCP threatens overseas Chinese, especially dissidents, it often uses their relatives in China as hostages.

Military Warfare

The CCP has developed asymmetric weapons, such as anti-ship missiles and anti-aircraft carrier missiles. In terms of conventional weapons, the CCP has attempted to surpass the technological supremacy of the United States by having a larger quantity of matériel targeting high-value assets. The CCP has grown economically and technically, giving it greater operational space to implement cyberwarfare, outer-space warfare, and other unconventional high-tech attack vectors against the United States, as addressed in the last section.

The PLA publicly declares that the conduct of the kind of war it wishes for would "appear in a manner that is cross-national, cross-domain, and utilizes any means necessary." In the PLA's ideal war, "tangible national boundaries, intangible cyberspace, international law, national law, codes of conduct, and ethics are not binding on them [PLA forces]. ... They don't take responsibility for anyone, and are not restricted by any rules. Anyone can be a target, and any means can be used." The authors of *Unrestricted Warfare* declare to their readers: "Have [you] considered combining the battlefield with the non-battlefield, war with non-war, military with non-military — specifically, combining stealth aircraft, cruise missiles and network killers, nuclear war, financial warfare, and terrorist attacks? Or, simply put, Schwarzkopf [then-commander-in-chief of US Central Command] + Soros [leftist billionaire] + Morris [creator of the Morris Worm computer virus] + bin Laden? This is our true card." [176]

Internet Warfare

Through the efforts of Huawei and ZTE to seize the 5G technology market, the CCP is striving to gain a dominant position in 5G standards, and wants to play a leading global role in the new technology. The former head of the Federal Reserve of Dallas said, "If China were to win the race, they would establish the protocols for the internet, just as English replaced German as the language of science and became the language of all crucial activity on a global scale." [177]

At present, with the impending rollout of 5G technology, the internet faces a new round of evolution. With the combination of 5G and artificial intelligence, the internet's control over the physical world is dramatically expanding, and the rules of the entire world are being rewritten. If the CCP dominates 5G, it will be able to act unimpeded.

In addition, once the CCP's external propaganda operations are successfully integrated with a China-controlled 5G, its efforts at indoctrinating foreign audiences will greatly exceed their current scale and impact.

Narcotics Warfare

At a US Cabinet meeting held on August 16, 2018, President Donald Trump said that the proliferation of opioids, particularly the synthetic drug fentanyl from China, is "almost a form of warfare." [178] In 2017, more than seventy thousand people died of a drug overdose in the United States, of which more than 40 percent were related to synthetic opioids (mainly fentanyl and its analogues). These drugs are primarily produced in China and then enter the United States through the US Postal Service or are smuggled in via the US–Mexico border. [179]

Markos Kounalakis, a senior researcher at the Central European University and a visiting scholar at the Hoover Institution of Stanford University, in November 2017, wrote that fentanyl was "being used as a weapon in China's 21st Century Opium War against America." Kounalakis cited fentanyl trafficking as an example of CCP strategy: The CCP sees the real value of this chemical as a "profitable opiate export that also destroys American communities and roils the US political landscape." [180]

Mass Mobilization Warfare

In September 2018, a Chinese family traveling in Sweden claimed they were mistreated by police after they were removed from a hotel for attempting to sleep in the lobby. A video of the melodramatic family being removed was then exaggerated by the Chinese Embassy and media, and Chinese people began boycotting Swedish companies Ikea and H&M. [181] The Swedish TV station SVT aired a satirical segment about the incident on its comedy show, which further exacerbated the situation. Tens of thousands of Chinese internet users flooded the websites of the Swedish Embassy, segment host Jesper Rönndahl, and the TV station's Facebook page. [182]

After sixty years of destruction of traditional culture and its replacement with Communist Party culture, the CCP is able to coerce millions of Chinese people and turn them into a mass army. Before the ninetieth anniversary of the People's Liberation Army in 2017, the CCP came up with software that can add PLA uniforms to an individual in an uploaded image. In just several days, the app received over one billion visits.

The CCP is able to use nationalism to control the public because it has suppressed information about the Party's true history, leaving the people ignorant of its crimes. In particular, people don't know the CCP's history of killing. Thus, generations of Chinese people who grew up in the Party culture carry the Party culture with them. When they travel abroad to make a living, they export Party culture overseas and become part of the regime's massive overseas army. This has strengthened the CCP's ability to control this army in the free world and use it for subversion.

Cultural Warfare

The CCP has been peddling Party culture and its values under the banner of Chinese traditional culture and customs for many years. People all over the world have a strong interest in China's long history and rich culture, yet their understanding is very limited. The CCP knows this well and takes full advantage of it. By adopting some of the superficial forms of traditional culture, the CCP has disguised itself as the guardian and true representative of Chinese culture, making it extremely difficult for people in other countries to see through the deceit.

Financial Warfare

The CCP has begun promoting its own financial payment system and use of the renminbi through "economic assistance" and private enterprises, in an attempt to build a global infrastructure. It intends to use the renminbi to replace the US dollar's dominance in international currency circulation. According to the CCP's unrestricted financial-warfare strategy, the regime can achieve its goals simply by printing massive amounts of money, thus destroying the financial system when necessary. CCP think tanks have advocated the weaponization of foreign exchange reserves.

Other Forms of Unrestricted Warfare

During the 1989 student democracy movement, the CCP ordered soldiers and police to disguise themselves as Beijing civilians and create riots so that the military could use them as an excuse for its mass killing, which it called "suppressing riots." During the early years of the persecution campaign against Falun Gong, the CCP fabricated the "self-immolation" incident to justify the ensuing escalation of the persecution. During Hong Kong's Occupy Central With Love and Peace movement, the CCP transported people from Shenzhen to incite violence in Hong Kong, effectively forcing police action to escalate toward violence.

In the eyes of the CCP, murder and assassination are commonplace methods, and in the future, the Party may well use any means — poisoning, assassination, explosions, the sabotage of power grids or transportation facilities, and so on — to create chaos and conflict in the West.

The core of unrestricted warfare is about mobilizing evil people to destroy mankind step by step. The CCP is highly skilled at tempting people to go against morality and their own conscience, and those who do so often end up as either passive in the face of the CCP's abuses, or active participants. Therefore, for influential figures in the political, economic, military, media, cultural, technological, educational, and other fields, the CCP uses all means to discover their weaknesses — whether vested interests or desires — and uses them to make people willingly collaborate with the Party. When this doesn't work, the CCP uses threats and intimidation to exploit their fears or mistakes, effectively blackmailing them into assisting the Party. In some cases, the CCP has even provided transplant organs obtained by killing to buy off influential figures in need of a transplant.

The resources the CCP is able to bring to bear to infiltrate other countries defy the imagination, and the facts uncovered at present are only the tip of the iceberg. People in all walks of life, especially in politics and business, have become the CCP's pawns in its unrestricted warfare campaign. Almost all countries in the world have begun to feel the CCP's global ambitions and its evil, unrestricted means.

4. The Communist 'China Model'

The CCP's nature means that it will always set itself against traditional culture, morality, and universal values. Today's CCP is the world's axis of evil and the enemy of humankind. The world must wake up and take action.

China has a vast territory and the largest population of any country on earth. It has become the world's second-largest economy and, from 2010, the second-largest military power. No tyrannical force in history has had such economic and military power. The Party has absorbed the most sinister and deformed elements of modern totalitarian regimes and ancient Chinese tactics, and therefore, it never plays by the rules. Its strategies are both deep and ruthless, often beyond the imagination and understanding of leaders and strategists in other countries. By hijacking 1.3 billion Chinese people, the CCP has presented a huge and greatly coveted market to the world, attracting foreign capital, business people, and politicians. It has them turn a blind eye to the CCP's human rights abuses and evil, and in some cases, even gets them to cooperate with the CCP in its crimes.

The CCP has killed eighty million Chinese people. In recent times, it has committed countless crimes against Falun Gong practitioners, underground Christians, Tibetans, Uyghurs, dissidents, and those at the lower end of society. Once the regime collapses, it will be brought to justice and punished for all its crimes. To avoid this fate, the CCP will not hesitate to commit more horrific crimes to protect itself.

The Chinese Communist Party is the communist specter's main agent in the human realm. Fated for elimination, its existence has always been accompanied by a strong sense of crisis and fear. Driven by this sense of constant crisis, the CCP resorts to any means necessary at critical moments, taking extreme measures to keep itself going. It has built itself up in an attempt to replace the United States and dominate the world and is preparing for the final battle with the United States with determination and nonstop effort. At the same time, it has used a range of means to export the CCP's model and the Communist Party's ideology, poisoning the world.

If the orthodox morality that has helped humankind survive for thousands of years is ever truly destroyed, the result will be the destruction of the entire human race. Therefore, in addition to its military, economic, scientific, and technological endeavors, the CCP is also bent on imposing its ideology of atheism and warped views of good and evil on other countries.

All the CCP's ambitions — which it pursues through soft power, hard power, and sharp power — are based on a total disregard for morality and are aimed at serving its larger ambition of destroying traditional morality and universal values. The CCP's goal is to establish itself as an evil empire and world ruler. It aims to bring totalitarian oppression to the world — a global police state characterized by brainwashing, mind control, mass surveillance, the elimination of private ownership, official atheism, the elimination of religion and traditional culture, unrestrained carnal desires, corruption, and moral degeneration. Its aim is to drag the world into poverty and turmoil, turning men into beasts and sending humankind into an abyss of moral degradation. All this is the path arranged by the communist specter in its attempt to destroy mankind.

5. Lessons Learned and the Way Out

A. THE POLICY OF APPEASEMENT: A GRAVE MISTAKE

Ambitious and eager to assert its global hegemony, the CCP poses a serious threat to the world. Sadly, to this day, many countries, governments, and political figures still wish to befriend the CCP, oblivious of the danger. The relationship is illustrated by a Chinese saying, "If you raise a tiger cub, eventually it'll grow up to devour you."

Without the aid of the developed Western countries and the support of so many multinational corporations, high-tech giants, and large financial institutions, the CCP could not have developed from a weak economy with a regime on the verge of collapse to an indomitable axis of evil over the short span of just a few decades.

Pillsbury, the national security expert, has argued that the West all along has held unrealistic expectations of the CCP, such as believing that China would inevitably become more democratic, that it longed for an American-style capitalist society, that it would inevitably integrate into the international social order, that US–China exchanges would bring about full cooperation, or that the hawkish elements in the CCP were weak, and so forth. In his 2015 book, he strongly urged the US government to quickly face reality and adopt counter-measures against the CCP, lest it allow the CCP to win. [183]

A March 2018 article in *The Economist* reflected on the policy that Western countries adopted toward China — specifically their gamble that China would head toward democracy and the free market economy. It conceded that the West's gamble has failed; China under the CCP isn't a market economy and, on its present course, will never be one. On the contrary, the CCP treats business and trade as extensions of state power and controls them as such. It uses its monopoly on power to shape the global economy, uses money to manipulate trading partners, and punishes individuals and groups it does not agree with. [184]

B. WHY THE WEST GOT CHINA WRONG

The West got China wrong for many reasons: the communist specter's complex arrangements mentioned earlier, the duplicity and chameleon-like nature of the CCP, and the difficulty that free societies have in differentiating the CCP from China. In addition, the West got China wrong because of the pursuit of short-term gains, whether by individuals, companies, or entire nations. This provided yet another opportunity for the CCP to exploit.

The morally corrupt CCP targets gaps in the morality of people in free societies, people whose pursuit of short-term profits allows the CCP to infiltrate and corrupt the very foundations of these societies. Policies adopted by the United States regarding the CCP, are largely based on considerations of short-term gain instead of the most fundamental, long-term interests of America — such as the spirit upon which the country was founded.

Humankind's glory and authority come from the divine and are determined by humankind's moral level. The prosperity and strength bestowed on an ethnic group or nation also depend on its level of morality. Using ordinary means, humans are incapable of negating the arrangements made by the communist specter. Following this logic, where the West has gone wrong becomes clear — whatever the human methods applied, ultimately these cannot succeed in overcoming the forces of evil.

Many governments, large companies, and business people may, for a period of time, ostensibly obtain benefits from the CCP in exchange for the sacrifice of their moral principles. But in the end, they'll lose more than they gain. Such ill-gained, superficial benefits are all poisonous.

The CCP is not a political party or regime in the normal sense. It does not represent the Chinese people. It represents the communist specter. To associate with the CCP is to associate with the devil. To be friendly with the CCP is to appease the devil, aid it, and play a role in pushing humanity toward destruction. Conversely, to push back against the CCP is to engage in the battle between good and evil. This is not a simple matter of countries fighting over national interests. It is a battle for the future of humanity.

C. THE WAY OUT

Today, China and the world are at a crossroads. For the Chinese people, the Chinese Communist Party, which owes countless debts of blood, cannot be expected to make any real reforms. China will be free only when the Communist Party is consigned to history.

For people around the world, China is known as the land of an ancient civilization characterized by courtesy and righteousness. Free of the Communist Party, China will once again be a normal member of the civilized world — a nation whose human and natural resources, diverse ancient traditions, and cultural heritage will be part of the wealth of humanity.

Moving forward during times of great difficulty, more and more Chinese people are coming to realize the evil nature of the CCP. With the publication of *Nine Commentaries on the Communist Party* in November 2004, a growing number of people began to regain their moral courage and made the decision to separate themselves from the communist specter. More than 350 million Chinese have renounced the CCP and its affiliated organizations. If the free world can support the trend of renouncing the CCP and sever all ties with the specter, the CCP will not be able to continue to act as it does.

The seemingly indomitable Soviet Union dissolved overnight. Though the CCP is baring its fangs globally, its dissolution could occur just as rapidly once the world recognizes its evil nature and makes the righteous choice.

The rise of the CCP resulted mostly from moral corruption and from people's being blinded by the pursuit of vested interests. To escape this fate, we need to summon up our moral courage, revive traditional values, and firmly believe in the divine.

To defeat the CCP, simply depending on ordinary secular means will never be enough. The communist specter has greater power than humans, and this is the underlying cause of the CCP's continuous expansion. However, evil can never rival the divine. As long as humans can stand by the divine and abide by divine will, they will be blessed and overcome the specter's infernal arrangements.

The CCP is the enemy of all humanity, having established the bloodiest yet most powerful tyranny history has ever seen. All nations and peoples must resist its global ambitions if they are to secure their future and that of all civilization. The evil CCP is destined for elimination; thus, to reject the CCP is to avoid sharing in its fate.

How the Specter
of Communism Is Ruling
Our World

Conclusion

IN THE LONG COURSE OF HISTORY, mankind has seen eras of splendor and glory, but has also endured countless episodes of tragedy and disaster. Looking back, we find that moral rectitude ushers in clean governance, economic prosperity, cultural brilliance, and national strength, whereas moral degeneracy signals the fall of nations and the extinction of entire civilizations.

Today, mankind has reached a zenith in material wealth, yet it faces unprecedented challenges caused by the havoc of communism. The ultimate goal of communism is not to establish a heaven on earth, but to destroy mankind. The nature of communism is that of an evil specter forged by hate, degeneracy, and other elemental forces in the universe. Out of hate, it slaughtered more than 100 million people, trampled several thousand years of exquisite civilization, and corrupted human morality.

The communist specter made arrangements to corrupt both the East and the West, adopting different strategies in different countries. In the East, it committed ruthless slaughter and forced people to accept atheism. In the West, communism took an alternate route: It infiltrated society in covert form, coaxing people into abandoning their traditional faiths and moral values.

Using communist regimes and organizations, fellow travelers, accomplices, and other agents, communism rallied negative elements in the human world to amass formidable power. With this power, it subverted and established control in all social spheres, including politics, economics, law, education, media, arts, and culture. Today's mankind is in dire straits.

In hindsight, the reasons for communism's triumph over the past two centuries are clear. When people indulge in the material pleasures brought by technological advancement and allow atheism to spread, they reject divine mercy and turn themselves over to evil. Having strayed from the traditions established by the divine, much of humanity is easily deceived by communism and its myriad ideological permutations, such as socialism, liberalism, and progressivism.

Traditional culture shows the path for humans to maintain their morality and gain salvation in the final epoch. But with traditional culture under attack and basic moral truths cast aside, the link between man and the divine has been severed. Man can no longer understand divine instruction, and evil reigns supreme, wreaking havoc in the human realm. When human morality drops below the basic standards required of human beings, the divine must reluctantly abandon humankind, as the devil leads man into the abyss of damnation.

But having reached an extreme, the circumstances are bound

to reverse. It is an eternal principle in the human realm that evil can never defeat righteousness. Communism's momentary victory is a temporary phenomenon, brought about by the devil, which has intimidated people with its illusory might and treacherous temptations. Man, while imperfect, innately carries kindness, virtue, and moral courage, which have been nurtured and passed down for millennia. In this, we find hope.

Global events are developing at an incredible pace. Righteous elements are growing stronger, and the world's people are awakening.

In China, millions of people have peacefully resisted the Chinese Communist Party's tyrannical rule by remaining steadfast in their faith and morality. Inspired by the editorial series *Nine Commentaries on the Communist Party,* more than 350 million Chinese have bravely renounced their ties with the CCP and its affiliated organizations, through the act of "tui dang," or "quitting the Party." More and more individuals are making a heartfelt decision to free themselves from the shackles of communism. The disintegration of the Communist Party is already well underway.

The end of the Communist Party is a matter of divine arrangement. Should China's leaders take steps to dismantle the Party, they will be provided with all the conditions required for a clean transition. In the future, they stand to gain true authority — that which is granted by the divine. Should they stubbornly refuse to make this break, they will take the Party's fate as their own, joining in the calamities of its final downfall.

The world is experiencing a revival of traditional culture and morality in alignment with the universal values of truthfulness, compassion, and tolerance. At the fore of this renaissance is Shen Yun Performing Arts, which tours five continents every year. In its display of classical Chinese dance, Shen Yun brings universal values to audiences around the world.

The West has begun to recognize the communist infiltration and its subversion of traditional culture that has taken place over the past century. Society has begun to be cleansed of communist elements and deviated modern culture in many spheres, from law and education, to government administration and international relations. Governments are becoming more vigilant against communist regimes and their enablers, which is greatly reducing communism's influence on the global scene.

Communism is not an enemy that can be defeated by military force. To free the world from its grasp, we must start by purifying ourselves from the inside. Li Hongzhi, the founder of Falun Gong, wrote in his article "Pacify the External by Cultivating the Internal":

> *If people do not value virtue, the world will be in great chaos and out of control; everyone will become enemies of one another and live without happiness. Living without happiness, they will not fear death. Lao Zi said, "If the populace doesn't fear death, what good will it do to threaten them with death?" This is a great, imminent danger. A peaceful world is what people hope for. If at this point an excessive number of laws and decrees are created to secure stability, it will end up having the opposite effect. In order to solve this problem, virtue has to be cultivated around the world — only this way can the problem be fundamentally resolved. If officials are unselfish, the state will not be corrupt. If the population values self-cultivation and the nurturing of virtues, and if both officials and civilians alike exercise self-restraint in their minds, the whole nation will be stable and supported by the people. Being solid and stable, the nation will naturally intimidate foreign enemies and peace will thus reign under heaven. This is the work of a sage.* [1]

The merciful Creator has always been watching over mankind. Disasters occur when man turns against the divine, and humanity can be saved only by returning to our divinely bestowed heritage. As long as we stay unmoved by the devil's facades, maintain true compassion, follow divine standards for being human, revive traditional values, and return to traditional culture, the divine will deliver mankind from evil. Today, whether or not humanity will walk this path is the choice that we all face.

Notes

Chapter Fifteen: The Communist Roots of Terrorism

1. BRIAN WHITAKER,
    "The Definition of Terrorism,"
    The Guardian, May 7, 2001,
    https://www.theguardian.
    com/world/2001/may/07/
    terrorism.

2. KARL KAUTSKY, *Terrorism
    and Communism:
    A Contribution to the Natural
    History of Revolution,* trans.
    W. H. Kerridge (Manchester,
    United Kingdom: The
    National Labour Press Ltd.,
    1919), Marxists Internet
    Archive, accessed on May 5,
    2020, https://www.marxists.
    org/archive/kautsky/1919/
    terrcomm/index.htm.

3. FELIX DZERZHINSKY,
    as quoted in Michael Foley,
    *Russian Civil War: Red Terror,
    White Terror, 1917–1922*
    (United Kingdom: Pen &
    Sword Books, 2018).

4. SERGEI MELGUNOV,
    The Red Terror in Russia
    (United Kingdom: Hyperion
    Press, 1975), chap. 3.

5. DEBORAH SEWARD,
    "Statue of Soviet Intelligence
    Chief Pulled Down,"
    The Associated Press, August 22,
    1991, https://apnews.com/863f5
    1d5087d19bee14a280626730385.

6. STANISLAV LUNEV,
    *Through the Eyes of the Enemy:
    The Autobiography of Stanislav
    Lunev* (Washington, DC:
    Regnery Publishing, Inc.,
    1998), 80.

7. ION MIHAI PACEPA, "Russian
    Footprints," *National Review*,
    August 24, 2006, https://www.
    nationalreview.com/2006/08/
    russian-footprints-ion-mihai-
    pacepa.

8. ION MIHAI PACEPA
    AND RONALD RYCHLAK,
    *Disinformation: Former
    Spy Chief Reveals Secret
    Strategies for Undermining
    Freedom, Attacking Religion,
    and Promoting Terrorism*
    (Washington, DC: WND
    Books, 2013), 259–266.

9. PAUL BERMAN,
    "The Philosopher of Islamic
    Terror," *New York Times
    Magazine*, March 23, 2003,
    https://www.nytimes.
    com/2003/03/23/magazine/
    the-philosopher-of-islamic-
    terror.html.

10. RAYMOND IBRAHIM,
    "Ayman Zawahiri and Egypt:

A Trip Through Time," The Investigative Project on Terrorism, November 30, 2012, https://www.investigativeproject.org/3831/ayman-zawahiri-and-egypt-a-trip-through-time.

11. ROBERT R. REILLY, *The Roots of Islamist Ideology,* Centre for Research Into Post-Communist Economies, February 2006, 4.

12. BERMAN, "The Philosopher."

13. ANDREW MCGREGOR, "Al-Qaeda's Egyptian Prophet: Sayyid Qutb and the War on Jahiliya," *Terrorism Monitor* 1, no. 3 (May 4, 2005), https://jamestown.org/program/al-qaedas-egyptian-prophet-sayyid-qutb-and-the-war-on-jahiliya.

14. A. E. STAHL, "'Offensive Jihad' in Sayyid Qutb's Ideology," International Institute for Counter-Terrorism, March 24, 2011, https://www.ict.org.il/Article/1097/Offensive-Jihad-in-Sayyid-Qutbs-Ideology#gsc.tab=0.

15. MCGREGOR, "Al-Qaeda's Egyptian Prophet."

16. STAHL, "'Offensive Jihad.'"

17. MCGREGOR, "Al-Qaeda's Egyptian Prophet."

18. DALE EIKMEIER, "Qutbism: An Ideology of Islamic-Fascism," *Parameters*, vol. 37, issue 1, http://www.dtic.mil/docs/citations/ADA485995.

19. WILLIAM MCCANTS, "Problems With the Arabic Name Game," Combating Terrorism Center, May, 22, 2006.

20. HASSAN HASSAN, *The Sectarianism of the Islamic State: Ideological Roots and Political Context* (Washington DC: Carnegie Endowment for International Peace, June 2016), 26, https://carnegieendowment.org/files/CP_253_Hassan_Islamic_State.pdf.

21. ROXANNE L. EUBEN, "Mapping Modernities, 'Islamic' and '"Western,"'" in *Border Crossings: Toward a Comparative Political Theory,* ed. Fred Dallmayr (Lanham, MD: Lexington Books, 1999), 20.

22. VLADIMIR LENIN, "What Is to Be Done?" in *Lenin's Selected Works*, trans. Joe Fineberg and George Hanna (Moscow: Foreign Languages Publishing House, 1961), vol. 1, 119–271, Marxists Internet Archive, accessed on May 5, 2020, https://www.marxists.org/archive/lenin/works/1901/witbd.

23. GLENN E. ROBINSON, "Jihadi Information Strategy: Sources, Opportunities, and Vulnerabilities," in John Arquilla and Douglas A. Borer, eds., *Information Strategy and Warfare: A Guide to Theory and Practice* (London: Routledge, 2007), 92.

24. MCGREGOR, "Al-Qaeda's Egyptian Prophet."

25. ABDALLAH AL-QUTBI, as quoted in "Impaling Leninist Qutbi Doubts: Shaykh Ibn Jibreen Makes Takfir Upon (Declares as Kufr) the Saying of Sayyid Qutb That Islam Is a Mixture of Communism and Christianity," TheMadKhalis.com, January 2, 2010, http://www.themadkhalis.com/md/articles/bguiq-shaykh-ibn-jibreen-making-takfir-upon-the-saying-of-sayyid-qutb-that-islam-is-a-mixture-of-communism-and-christianity.cfm.

26. DAMON LINKER, "The Marxist Roots of Islamic Extremism," *The Week*, March 25, 2016, http://theweek.com/articles/614207/marxist-roots-islamic-extremism.

27. CHARLES MOSCOWITZ, *Islamo-Communism: The Communist Connection to Islamic Terrorism* (Boston: City Metro Enterprises, 2013).

28. ANTERO LEITZINGER, "The Roots of Islamic Terrorism," *The Eurasian Politician*, no. 5 (March 2002), http://users.jyu.fi/~aphamala/pe/issue5/roots.htm.

29. LAWRENCE WRIGHT, *The Looming Tower: Al-Qaeda and the Road to 9/11* (New York: Knopf Publishing Group, 2006), 42.

30. DAWN PERLMUTTER, *Investigating Religious Terrorism and Ritualistic Crimes* (New York: CRC Press, 2003), 104.

31. NATIONAL COMMISSION ON TERRORIST ATTACKS UPON THE UNITED STATES, *The 9/11 Commission Report* (Washington DC: National Commission on Terrorist Attacks Upon the United States, 2004), 55, https://www.9-11commission.gov/report/911Report.pdf.

32. WRIGHT, *The Looming Tower,* 36–37.

33. LAWRENCE WRIGHT, "The Man Behind Bin Laden: How an Egyptian Doctor Became a Master of Terror," *New Yorker,* September 16, 2002, https://www.newyorker.com/magazine/2002/09/16/the-mn-behind-bin-laden.

34. GLENN E. ROBINSON, "The Four Waves of Global Jihad, 1979–2017," *Middle East Policy* 24, no. 3 (Fall 2017): 70, accessed via Research Gate on May 5, 2020, https://www.researchgate.net/publication/319160351_The_Four_Waves_of_Global_Jihad_1979-2017.

35. ROBINSON, "Jihadi Information Strategy," 88.

36. ROBINSON, "The Four Waves of Global Jihad," 85.

37. ANTHONY BUBALO AND GREG FEALY, "Between the Global and the Local: Islamism, the Middle East, and Indonesia," *The Brookings Project on US Policy Towards the Islamic World,* no. 9 (October 2005): 7, https://www.brookings.edu/

wp-content/uploads/2016/06/
20051101bubalo_fealy.pdf.

38. SETH G. JONES, *A Persistent Threat: The Evolution of al Qa'ida and Other Salafi Jihadists* (Santa Monica, CA: RAND Corporation, 2014), 64–65, https://www.rand. org/content/dam/rand/pubs/ research_reports/RR600/ RR637/RAND_RR637.pdf.

39. ROBERT MANNE, "Sayyid Qutb: Father of Salafi Jihadism, Forerunner of the Islamic State," Australian Broadcasting Corporation, November 7, 2016, http:// www.abc.net.au/religion/ articles/2016/11/07/4570251.htm.

40. ANTHONY CORDESMAN, "Islam and the Patterns in Terrorism and Violent Extremism," Center for Strategic and International Studies, October 17, 2017, https://www.csis.org/analysis/ islam-and-patterns-terrorism- and-violent-extremism.

41. BUREAU OF COUNTERTERRORISM AND COUNTERING VIOLENT EXTREMISM, *Country Reports on Terrorism 2018* (Washington, DC: Department of State, 2019), https://www. state.gov/reports/country- reports-on-terrorism-2018.

42. ALEX NOWRASTEH, "Terrorists by Immigration Status and Nationality: A Risk Analysis, 1975–2017," Cato Institute, May 7, 2019, https://www.cato.org/ publications/policy-analysis/ terrorists-immigration-

status-nationality-risk- analysis-1975-2017.

43. SHI YANCHUN 時延春, "Zhou Enlai yu Zhongdong" 周恩來 與中東 ["Zhou Enlai and the Middle East"], *Party History in Review,* issue 1 (2006), 7–8, http://waas.cssn.cn/webpic/ web/waas/upload/2011/06/ d20110602193952375.pdf. [In Chinese]

44. STEFAN M. AUBREY, *The New Dimension of International Terrorism* (Zürich: vdf Hochschulverlag AG an der ETH, 2004), 34–36.

45. "911 kongbufenzi xiji shijian zhi hou: guonei yanlun zhaideng" 911恐怖分子袭击事件之后 : 国内言论摘登 ["A Sampling of Chinese Public Opinion Following the 9/11 Terrorist Attacks"], *Modern China Studies,* issue 4 (2001), http:// www.modernchinastudies. org/us/issues/past-issues/75- mcs-2001-issue-4/596-911.html. [In Chinese]

46. YITZHAK SHICHOR, "The Great Wall of Steel: Military and Strategy," in S. Frederick Starr, ed Z., *Xinjiang: China's Muslim Borderland* (London: Routledge, 2004), 149.

47. JOHN HOOPER, "Claims That China Paid Bin Laden to See Cruise Missiles," *The Guardian,* October 19, 2001, https://www. theguardian.com/world/2001/ oct/20/china.afghanistan.

48. "Chinese Firms Helping Put Phone System in Kabul," *The Washington Times,*

September 28, 2001, https://
www.washingtontimes.com/
news/2001/sep/28/20010928-
025638-7645r.

49. SHICHOR, "The Great Wall of
Steel," 158.

50. QIAO LIANG 乔良 AND WANG
XIANGSUI 王湘穗, *Chao xian
zhan* 超限战 [*Unrestricted
Warfare*], (Beijing: Zhongguo
shehui chubanshe, 2005), chap.
2. [In Chinese]

51. D. J. MCGUIRE, "How
Communist China Supports
Anti-US Terrorists,"
Association for Asian
Research, September 15, 2005,
https://web.archive.org/
web/20110914053923/http://
www.asianresearch.org/
articles/2733.html.

52. DANIEL FLYNN, *Why the Left
Hates America: Exposing the
Lies That Have Obscured Our
Nation's Greatness* (United
States: Crown Publishing
Group, 2004).

53. "Ward Churchill" [profile],
Discover the Networks,
accessed on May 5, 2020, http://
www.discoverthenetworks.
org/individualProfile.
asp?indid=1835.

54. Transcript of Osama bin
Laden tape, BBC, February 12,
2003, accessed on June 9, 2020,
http://news.bbc.co.uk/2/hi/
middle_east/2751019.stm.

55. JAMIE GLAZOV, *United in
Hate: The Left's Romance
With Tyranny and Terror* (Los
Angeles: WND Books, 2009),
164–165.

56. DAVID HOROWITZ, *Unholy
Alliance: Radical Islam and the
American Left* (Washington
DC: Regnery Publishing, Inc.,
2004), 37.

57. GLAZOV, *United in Hate*,
159–176.

58. "Nicholas De Genova" [profile],
Discover the Networks,
accessed on May 5, 2020, http://
www.discoverthenetworks.
org/individualProfile.
asp?indid=2189.

59. "Lynne Stewart" [profile],
Discover the Networks,
accessed May 5, 2020, http://
www.discoverthenetworks.
org/individualProfile.
asp?indid=861.

Chapter Sixteen:
The Communism Behind
Environmentalism

1. DONG ZHONGSHU 董仲舒,
Chunqiu fan lu, di shisi 春秋
繁露 [*Luxuriant Dew of the
Spring and Autumn Annals*],
fu zhi xiang 服制象 ["Images
for the Regulation of Dress"],
14, https://ctext.org/chun-qiu-
fan-lu/fu-zhi-xiang/zh. The
line in question appears both
as "天之生物也，以养人" and "
天地之生萬物也以養人." [In
Chinese]

2. CONFUCIUS, *The Universal
Order or Conduct of Life, a
Confucian Catechism (Being a
Translation of One of the Four
Confucian Books, Hitherto
Known as the Doctrine of the
Mean)*, (Shanghai: Shanghai

Evening Post & Mercury Limited, 1906), 68, https://bit.ly/2T74Dsb.

3. YI ZHOU SHU 逸周書 [*Lost Book of Zhou*], "Da Jujie" 大聚解, https://ctext.org/lost-book-of-zhou/da-ju/zh. [In Chinese]

4. ZENGZI, as quoted in *Li Ji* 禮記 [*The Classic of Rights*], "Zhai Yi" 祭儀 , https://ctext.org/text.pl?node=61379&if=gb&show=parallel. [In Chinese]

5. WES VERNON, "The Marxist Roots of the Global Warming Scare," Renew America, June 16, 2008, https://web.archive.org/web/20100724052619/http://www.renewamerica.com:80/columns/vernon/080616.

6. FRIEDRICH ENGELS, "Notes and Fragments," in *Dialectics of Nature,* trans. Clemens Dutt (Moscow: Progress Publishers, 1883), 295–311, accessed via Marxists Internet Archive on April 30, 2020, https://www.marxists.org/archive/marx/works/1883/don/ch07g.htm.

7. BRIAN SUSSMAN, *Eco-Tyranny: How the Left's Green Agenda Will Dismantle America* (Washington, DC: WND Books, 2012), 8–9.

8. KARL MARX, as quoted in Sussman, *Eco-Tyranny,* 10.

9. Ibid., 11–15.

10. MAURICE STRONG, as quoted in Grace Baumgarten, *Cannot Be Silenced* (Grand Rapids, MI: WestBow Press, 2016).

11. SUSSMAN, *Eco-Tyranny,* 35.

12. NATALIE GRANT WRAGA, as quoted in Vernon, "The Marxist Roots."

13. JOHN BELLAMY FOSTER, "Marx's Ecology in Historical Perspective," *International Socialism Journal* 96 (Winter 2002), http://pubs.socialistreviewindex.org.uk/isj96/foster.htm.

14. RAY LANKESTER, as quoted in Lewis S. Feuer, "The Friendship of Edwin Ray Lankester and Karl Marx: The Last Episode in Marx's Intellectual Evolution," *Journal of the History of Ideas* 40, no. 4: 633–648.

15. JAMES O'CONNOR, *Natural Causes: Essays in Ecological Marxism* (New York: The Guilford Press, 1997).

16. JOEL KOVEL AND MICHAEL LÖWY, "The First Ecosocialist Manifesto," September 2001, accessed April 30, 2020, http://green.left.sweb.cz/frame/Manifesto.html.

17. BOB BROWN AND PETER SINGER, *The Greens* (Melbourne: Text Publishing Company, 1996), 55.

18. MIKHAIL GORBACHEV, "We Have a Real Emergency," *The New York Times,* December 9, 2009, http://www.nytimes.com/2009/12/10/opinion/10iht-edgorbachev.html.

19. "Jack Mundey," Sydney's Aldermen, accessed April 30, 2020, http://www.

sydneyaldermen.com.au/
alderman/jack-mundey.

20. SAUL ALINSKY, "Tactics," in
*Rules for Radicals: A Practical
Primer for Realistic Radicals*
(New York: Vintage Books,
1971).

21. ZOMBIE, "Climate Movement
Drops Mask, Admits
Communist Agenda," PJ
Media, September 23, 2014,
https://pjmedia.com/
zombie/2014/9/23/climate-
movement-drops-mask-
admits-communist-agenda.

22. DAN BARRY AND AL BAKER,
"For 'Eco-Terrorism' Group, a
Hidden Structure and Public
Messages," *The New York
Times*, January 8, 2001, https://
www.nytimes.com/2001/01/08/
nyregion/for-eco-terrorism-
group-a-hidden-structure-
and-public-messages.html.

23. NOEL MOAND, "A Spark That
Ignited a Flame: The Evolution
of the Earth Liberation Front,"
in *Igniting a Revolution: Voices
in Defense of the Earth,* eds.
Steven Best and Anthony J.
Nocella, II (Oakland, CA: AK
Press, 2006), 47.

24. PAUL WATSON, as quoted in
Leslie Spencer, Jan Bollwerk,
and Richard C. Morais, "The
Not So Peaceful World
of Greenpeace," *Forbes*,
November 1991, accessed
via the Heartland Institute,
https://www.heartland.
org/_template-assets/
documents/publications/the_
not_so_peaceful_world_of_
greenpeace.pdf.

25. TED THORNHILL, "Humans
Are Not to Blame for Global
Warming, Says Greenpeace
Co-founder, as He Insists
There Is 'No Scientific Proof'
Climate Change Is Manmade,"
Daily Mail, February 27, 2014,
http://www.dailymail.co.uk/
sciencetech/article-2569215/
Humans-not-blame-glo-
bal-warming-says-Greenpe-
ace-founder-Patrick-Moore.
html#ixzz2vg02btWJ.

26. JOHN VIDAL, "Not Guilty:
The Greenpeace Activists
Who Used Climate Change
as a Legal Defence,"
The Guardian, Sept 10, 2008,
https://www.theguardian.com/
environment/2008/sep/11/acti-
vists.kingsnorthclimatecamp.

27. RICHARD LINDZEN,
"The Climate Science Isn't Settled," *The Wall Street Journal*,
last updated November 30,
2009, https://www.wsj.com/
articles/SB10001424052748703
939404574567423917025400.

28. STEVEN E. KOONIN, "Climate
Science Is Not Settled," *The
Wall Street Journal*, September 19, 2014, https://www.wsj.
com/articles/climate-scien-
ce-is-not-settled-1411143565.

29. STEVEN E. KOONIN,
"A 'Red Team' Exercise Would
Strengthen Climate Science,"
The Wall Street Journal, April
20, 2017, https://www.wsj.com/
articles/a-red-team-exercise-
would-strengthen-climate-
science-1492728579.

30. MICHAEL GRIFFIN, "NASA
Chief Questions Urgency

of Global Warming," interview by Steve Inskeep, National Public Radio, May 31, 2007, https://www.npr.org/templates/story/story.php?storyId=10571499.

31. ALICIA CHANG, "NASA Chief Regrets Remarks on Global Warming," NBC News, June 5, 2007, http://www.nbcnews.com/id/19058588/ns/us_news-environment/t/nasa-chief-regrets-remarks-global-warming.

32. MICHAEL GRIFFIN, as quoted in Rebecca Wright, Sandra Johnson, and Steven J. Dick, eds., *NASA at 50: Interviews With NASA's Senior Leadership* (Washington, DC: National Aeronautics and Space Administration, 2009), 18, https://www.nasa.gov/sites/default/files/716218main_nasa_at_50-ebook.pdf.

33. LENNART BENGTSSON, as quoted in "Lennart Bengtsson Resigns: GWPF Voices Shock and Concern at the Extent of Intolerance Within the Climate Science Community," The Global Warming Policy Foundation, May 5, 2014, http://www.thegwpf.org/lennart-bengtsson-resigns-gwpf-voices-shock-and-concern-at-the-extent-of-intolerance-within-the-climate-science-community.

34. US CONGRESS, HOUSE, Committee on Science, Space and Technology of the United States House of Representatives, *Hearing on Climate Science: Assumptions,* *Policy Implications and the Scientific Method*, 115th Cong., 1st sess., March 29, 2017, https://docs.house.gov/meetings/SY/SY00/20170329/105796/HHRG-115-SY00-Wstate-CurryJ-20170329.pdf.

35. Ibid.

36. FREDERICK SEITZ, "Major Deception on Global Warming," *The Wall Street Journal*, June 12, 1996, https://www.wsj.com/articles/SB834512411338954000.

37. Ibid.

38. TIM HIGHAM, as quoted in Larry Bell, "The New York Times' Global Warming Hysteria Ignores 17 Years of Flat Global Temperatures," *Forbes*, August 21, 2013, https://www.forbes.com/sites/larrybell/2013/08/21/the-new-york-times-global-warming-hysteria-ignores-17-years-of-flat-global-temperatures.

39. PAUL REITER, as quoted in Christopher C. Horner, *Red Hot Lies: How Global Warming Alarmists Use Threats, Fraud, and Deception to Keep You Misinformed* (Washington, DC: Regnery Publishing, 2008), 319.

40. US CONGRESS, SENATE, Committee on Commerce, Science, and Transportation, *Projected and Past Effects of Climate Change: A Focus on Marine and Terrestrial Systems*, 109th Cong., 2nd sess., April 26, 2006.

41. BLOOMBERG, as quoted in James Taylor, "Mosquitoes Ignore Global Warming Predictions," *Forbes*, October 5, 2011, https://www.forbes.com/sites/jamestaylor/2011/10/05/mosquitoes-ignore-global-warming-predictions/#20938da66c1b.

42. LEONARD J. BRUCE-CHWATT, "Malaria Research and Eradication in the USSR," World Health Organization Bulletin, 1959, accessed via National Institutes of Health on April 30, 2020, https://www.ncbi.nlm.nih.gov/pmc/articles/PMC2537933/pdf/bullwho00505-0074.pdf.

43. ZOË CORBYN, "Global Warming Wilts Malaria," *Nature*, December 21, 2011, https://www.nature.com/news/global-warming-wilts-malaria-1.9695.

44. CHRISTOPHER LANDSEA, as quoted in James Taylor, "Climate Scientist Quits IPCC, Blasts Politicized 'Preconceived Agendas,'" The Heartland Institute, April 1, 2005, https://www.heartland.org/news-opinion/news/climate-scientist-quits-ipcc-blasts-politicized-preconceived-agendas?source=policybot.

45. US CONGRESS, SENATE, Committee on Environment and Public Works, *Full Committee Hearing on Climate Change and the Media*, 109th Cong., 2nd sess., December 6, 2006, https://www.epw.senate.gov/public/index.cfm/hearings?ID=BFE4D91D-802A-23AD-4306-B4121BF7ECED.

46. JONATHAN LEAKE, "Wildlife Groups Axe Bellamy as Global Warming 'Heretic,'" *Sunday Times Online*, May 15, 2005, https://web.archive.org/web/20080906161240/http://www.timesonline.co.uk/tol/news/uk/article522744.ece.

47. HORNER, *Red Hot Lies*, 78–79.

48. Ibid., 73–74.

49. PATRICK J. MICHAELS AND ROBERT C. BALLING JR., *Climate of Extremes: Global Warming Science They Don't Want You to Know* (Washington, DC: Cato Institute, 2009), x–xiii.

50. JAMES TAYLOR, "Associate State Climatologist Fired for Exposing Warming Myths," The Heartland Institute, June 1, 2007, https://www.heartland.org/news-opinion/news/associate-state-climatologist-fired-for-exposing-warming-myths.

51. HILARY LAWSON, dir., *The Greenhouse Conspiracy* (UK: Channel 4 Television, 1990), posted on YouTube by ZilogBob on February 16, 2015, https://www.youtube.com/watch?v=lvpwAwvDxUU.

52. MARC MORANO, "Climate Skeptics Reveal 'Horror Stories' of Scientific Suppression," US Senate Committee on Environment and Public Works, March 6, 2008, https://www.epw.senate.gov/public/

index.cfm/press-releases-
all?ID=865dbe39-802a-23ad-
4949-ee9098538277.

53. US CONGRESS, SENATE,
Subcommittee on Space,
Science and Competitiveness,
"Data or Dogma? Promoting
Open Inquiry in the Debate
Over the Magnitude of
Human Impact on Climate
Change," 114th Cong., 2nd
sess., December 8, 2015, https://
curryja.files.wordpress.
com/2015/12/curry-senate-
testimony-2015.pdf.

54. SCOTT WALDMAN, "Judith
Curry Retires, Citing
'Craziness' of Climate Science,"
E&E News, January 4, 2017,
https://www.eenews.net/
stories/1060047798.

55. ROGER PIELKE JR., as quoted
in Waldman, "Judith Curry
Retires."

56. RICH LOWRY, "A Shameful
Climate Witch Hunt,"
National Review, February
27, 2015, https://www.
nationalreview.com/2015/02/
shameful-climate-witch-hunt-
rich-lowry/.

57. US CONGRESS, SENATE,
Committee on Environment
and Public Works, US Senate
Minority Report: More Than
650 International Scientists
Dissent Over Man-Made
Global Warming Claims.
Scientists Continue to Debunk
'Consensus' in 2008, S. Rep.,
December 11, 2008, https://
www.epw.senate.gov/public/_
cache/files/8/3/83947f5d-
d84a-4a84-ad5d-6e2d71d

b52d9/01AFD79733D77F
24A71FEF9DAFCCB056.
senateminorityreport2.pdf.

58. ROY SPENCER, The Great
Global Warming Blunder:
How Mother Nature Fooled the
World's Top Climate Scientists
(New York: Encounter Books,
2010), 31.

59. BRENDAN O'NEILL,
"A Climate of Censorship,"
The Guardian, November
22, 2006, https://www.
theguardian.com/
commentisfree/2006/nov/22/
aclimateofcensorship.

60. HORNER, Red Hot Lies, 107.

61. HANS VON SPAKOVSKY AND
NICOLAS LORIS, "The Climate
Change Inquisition: An Abuse
of Power That Offends the First
Amendment and Threatens
Informed Debate," The
Heritage Foundation, October
24, 2016, https://www.heritage.
org/report/the-climate-
change-inquisition-abuse-
power-offends-the-first-
amendment-and-threatens.

62. O'NEILL, "A Climate of
Censorship."

63. JOHN FUND, "Rollback
Obama's CAFE Power Grab,
Give Car Consumers Freedom,"
National Review, May 23, 2018,
https://www.nationalreview.
com/corner/fuel-standards-
cafe-epa-rolls-back.

64. REN BINGYAN, as quoted in
Ariana Eunjung Cha, "Solar
Energy Firms Leave Waste
Behind in China," The
Washington Post, March 9,

2008, http://www.washing-tonpost.com/wp-dyn/content/article/2008/03/08/AR2008030802595.html?refer-rer=emailarticle&noredirec-t=on.

65. "The Paris Agreement on Climate Change," Natural Resources Defense Council (NRDC), December 2015, issue brief: 15-11-Y, https://www.nrdc.org/sites/default/files/paris-climate-agreement-IB.pdf.

66. US PRESIDENT DONALD J. TRUMP, "Statement by President Trump on the Paris Climate Accord," The White House, June 1, 2017, https://www.whitehouse.gov/briefings-statements/statement-president-trump-paris-climate-accord.

67. MICHAEL CRICHTON, "Environmentalism Is a Religion: Remarks to the Commonwealth Club," Hawaii Free Press, September 15, 2003, http://www.hawaiifreepress.com/ArticlesMain/tabid/56/ID/2818/Crichton-Environmentalism-is-a-religion.aspx.

68. ROBERT H. NELSON, "New Religion of Environmentalism," Independent Institute, April 22, 2010, http://www.independent.org/news/article.asp?id=5081.

69. FREEMAN DYSON, "The Question of Global Warming," The New York Review of Books, June 2008, https://www.nybooks.com/articles/2008/06/12/the-question-of-global-warming.

70. DAMIAN CARRINGTON, "IPCC Chair Rajendra Pachauri Resigns," The Guardian, February 24, 2015, https://www.theguardian.com/environment/2015/feb/24/ipcc-chair-rajendra-pachauri-resigns.

71. VÁCLAV KLAUS, "An Anti-Human Ideology," Financial Post, October 20, 2010, https://business.financialpost.com/opinion/vaclav-klaus-an-anti-human-ideology.

72. MARK STEYN, "Children? Not If You Love the Planet," The Orange County Register, December 14, 2007, https://www.ocregister.com/2007/12/14/mark-steyn-children-not-if-you-love-the-planet.

73. EMMA BRINDAL, as quoted in Horner, Red Hot Lies, 214.

74. Ibid., 211–215.

75. Ibid., 227.

76. DAVID SHEARMAN AND JOSEPH WAYNE SMITH, The Climate Change Challenge and the Failure of Democracy (Westport, CT: Praeger, 2007).

77. JANET BIEHL, as quoted in Horner, Red Hot Lies, 219–220.

78. PAUL EHRLICH, as quoted in Václav Klaus, Blue Planet in Green Shackles: What Is Endangered: Climate or

Freedom? (Washington, DC: Competitive Enterprise Institute, 2008), 14.

79. ALISTER DOYLE, "China Says One-Child Policy Helps Protect Climate," *Reuters*, August 30, 2007, https://www.reuters.com/article/environment-climate-population-dc-idUSKUA07724020070831.

80. JOHN BACHTELL, "China Builds an 'Ecological Civilization' While the World Burns," *People's World*, August 21, 2018, https://www.peoplesworld.org/article/china-builds-an-ecological-civilization-while-the-world-burns.

81. KLAUS, *Blue Planet*, 4.

82. Ibid., 7–8.

Chapter Seventeen: Globalization and Communism

1. KARL MARX AND FRIEDRICH ENGELS, "The German Ideology," in *Marx-Engels Collected Works*, vol. 5 (1932), accessed via Marxists Internet Archive on May 4, 2020, https://www.marxists.org/archive/marx/works/1845/german-ideology/index.htm.

2. VLADIMIR LENIN, "The Third Communist International," in *Lenin's Collected Works*, 4th English edition, vol. 29 (Moscow: Progress Publishers,

1972), 240–241, Marxists Internet Archive, accessed on May 4, 2020, https://www.marxists.org/archive/lenin/works/1919/mar/x04.htm.

3. G. EDWARD GRIFFIN, *Fearful Master: A Second Look at the United Nations* (Appleton, WI: Western Islands, 1964), chap. 7.

4. WILLIAM Z. FOSTER, *Toward Soviet America* (New York: Coward-McCann, 1932), chap. 5, Marxists Internet Archive, accessed on May 4, 2020, https://www.marxists.org/archive/foster/1932/toward/06.htm.

5. JAMES BOVARD, "The World Bank vs. the World's Poor," Cato Institute Policy Analysis, no. 92, September 28, 1987, https://object.cato.org/sites/cato.org/files/pubs/pdf/pa092.pdf.

6. DANI RODRIK, *The Globalization Paradox: Why Global Markets, States, and Democracy Can't Coexist* (New York: Oxford University Press, 2011), 19.

7. ROBERT ATKINSON, "Why the 2000s Were a Lost Decade for American Manufacturing," *IndustryWeek*, March 14, 2013, https://www.industryweek.com/the-economy/article/22006840/why-the-2000s-were-a-lost-decade-for-american-manufacturing.

8. US BUREAU OF LABOR STATISTICS, "A Profile of the Working Poor, 2016," *BLS Reports*, July 2018, https://www.

bls.gov/opub/reports/working-poor/2016/home.htm.

9. WILLIAM F. JASPER, *Global Tyranny ... Step by Step: The United Nations and the Emerging New World Order* (Appleton, WI: Western Islands Publishers, 1992), chap. 4.

10. J. EDGAR HOOVER, as quoted in Griffin, *Fearful Master*, 48.

11. AMITY SHLAES, "Communism Becomes Cronyism at the UN," *The Wall Street Journal*, October 24, 1991.

12. COLUM LYNCH, "China Enlists UN to Promote Its Belt and Road Project," *Foreign Policy*, May 10, 2018, https://foreignpolicy.com/2018/05/10/china-enlists-u-n-to-promote-its-belt-and-road-project.

13. DORE GOLD, *Tower of Babble: How the United Nations Has Fueled Global Chaos* (New York: Crown Forum, 2004), 1–24.

14. DORE GOLD, as quoted in Robert Chandler, *Shadow World: Resurgent Russia, The Global New Left, and Radical Islam* (Washington, DC: Regnery Publishing, 2008), 403.

15. GRIFFIN, *Fearful Master*, chap. 11.

16. NORMAN COUSINS, as quoted in Gary Benoit, "'Earth Day' — The Greatest Sham on Earth," *The New American*, April 21, 2016, https://www.thenewamerican.com/tech/environment/item/23011-earth-day-the-greatest-sham-on-earth.

17. AMERICAN HUMANIST ASSOCIATION, "Humanist Manifesto II" (Washington, DC: American Humanist Association, 1973), https://americanhumanist.org/what-is-humanism/manifesto2.

18. HILARY F. FRENCH, et al., "After the Earth Summit: The Future of Environmental Governance," Worldwatch Institute 107, March 1992.

19. JASPER, *Global Tyranny*, chap. 4.

20. CHANDLER, *Shadow World*, 401–403.

21. W. CLEON SKOUSEN, *The Naked Communist* (Salt Lake City: Izzard Ink Publishing, 1958), chap. 12.

22. WILLI MÜNZENBERG, as quoted in Bernard Connolly, *The Rotten Heart of Europe: Dirty War for Europe's Money* (London: Faber & Faber, 2013).

23. "Sign the Boycott Target Pledge!" American Family Association, April 2016, https://www.afa.net/target.

24. UNITED NATIONS OFFICE OF THE HIGH COMMISSIONER FOR HUMAN RIGHTS, "Convention on the Rights of the Child" (Geneva: United Nations, 1989), https://www.ohchr.org/en/professionalinterest/pages/crc.aspx.

25. GRACE CARR, "Ontario Makes Disapproval of Kid's

Gender Choice Potential Child Abuse," Daily Caller, June 5, 2017, https://dailycaller.com/2017/06/05/ontario-makes-disapproval-of-kids-gender-choice-child-abuse.

Chapter Eighteen:
The Chinese Communist Party's Global Ambitions

1. ZHAO KEJIN 趙可金, "Heping fazhan daolu: moshi de tupo" 和平發道路：模式的突破 ["The Road of Peaceful Development: A Paradigmatic Breakthrough"], *People.cn*, November 11, 2009, http://theory.people.com.cn/GB/10355796.html. [In Chinese]

2. MICHAEL PILLSBURY, *The Hundred-Year Marathon: China's Secret Strategy to Replace America as the Global Superpower* (New York: Henry Holt and Co., 2015), chap. 5.

3. US CONGRESS, SENATE, Committee on Foreign Relations: Subcommittee on East Asian and Pacific Affairs, *US–China Relations: Status of Reforms in China*, 108th Cong., 1st sess., April 22, 2004, https://www.foreign.senate.gov/imo/media/doc/WaldronTestimony040422.pdf.

4. CHRIS GILES, "China Poised to Pass US as World's Leading Economic Power This Year," *Financial Times*, April 29, 2014, https://www.ft.com/content/d79ffff8-cfb7-11e3-9b2b-00144feabdc0.

5. "CMHI and CMA CGM Complete the Terminal Link Transaction," CMA-CGM and CMHI, June 11, 2013, https://www.cma-cgm.com/static/News/Attachments/CMHI%20and%20CMA%20CGM%20complete%20the%20Terminal%20Link%20transaction.pdf.

6. DEREK WATKINS, K. K. REBECCA LAI, AND KEITH BRADSHER, "The World, Built by China," *The New York Times*, November 18, 2018, https://www.nytimes.com/interactive/2018/11/18/world/asia/world-built-by-china.html.

7. ANDREW SHENG, "A Civilizational Clash With China Comes Closer," Asia Global Institute: The University of Hong Kong, January 16, 2018, https://www.asiaglobalinstitute.hku.hk/news-post/a-civilizational-clash-with-china-comes-closer.

8. WU XINBO 吳心伯, "Dui zhoubian waijiao yanjiu de yixie sikao" 對周邊外交研究的一些思考 ["Reflections on the Study of Periphery Diplomacy"], *World Affairs*, issue 2 (2015), http://www.cas.fudan.edu.cn/picture/2328.pdf. [In Chinese]

9. NICK MCKENZIE AND SARAH FERGUSON, *Power and Influence: The Hard Edge of China's Soft Power*, Australian Broadcasting Corporation,

June 5, 2017, video, https://www.abc.net.au/4corners/power-and-influence-promo/8579844.

10. "Sam Dastyari Resignation: How We Got Here," Australian Broadcasting Corporation, December 11, 2017, https://www.abc.net.au/news/2017-12-12/sam-dastyari-resignation-how-did-we-get-here/9249380.

11. CHRIS UHLMANN AND ANDREW GREENE, "Chinese Donors to Australian Political Parties: Who Gave How Much?" Australian Broadcasting Corporation, June 7, 2017, https://www.abc.net.au/news/2016-08-21/china-australia-political-donations/7766654?nw=0.

12. JOHN FITZGERALD, "China in Xi's 'New Era,'" *Journal of Democracy,* no. 29, April 2018, https://muse.jhu.edu/article/690074.

13. TARA FRANCIS CHAN, "Rejected Three Times Due to Fear of Beijing, Controversial Book on China's Secret Influence Will Finally Be Published," Business Insider, February 5, 2018, https://www.businessinsider.com/australian-book-on-chinas-influence-gets-publisher-2018-2.

14. JONATHAN PEARLMAN, "US Alarm Over Aussie Port Deal With China Firm," *The Straits Times,* November 19, 2015, https://www.straitstimes.com/asia/australianz/us-alarm-over-aussie-port-deal-with-china-firm.

15. CHRISTOPHER WALKER AND JESSICA LUDWIG, "From 'Soft Power' to 'Sharp Power': Rising Authoritarian Influence in the Democratic World," in *Sharp Power: Rising Authoritarian Influence* (Washington, DC: National Endowment for Democracy, 2017), 20, https://www.ned.org/wp-content/uploads/2017/12/Sharp-Power-Rising-Authoritarian-Influence-Full-Report.pdf.

16. "2017 Foreign Policy White Paper," Australian government, November 23, 2017, https://www.fpwhitepaper.gov.au/foreign-policy-white-paper/overview.

17. CAITLYN GRIBBIN, "Malcolm Turnbull Declares He Will 'Stand Up' for Australia in Response to China's Criticism," Australian Broadcasting Corporation, December 8, 2017, https://www.abc.net.au/news/2017-12-09/malcolm-turnbull-says-he-will-stand-up-for-australia/9243274.

18. IRENE LUO, "Former Chinese Diplomat on China's Infiltration of Australia," *The Epoch Times,* July 5, 2017, https://www.theepochtimes.com/former-chinese-diplomat-on-chinas-infiltration-of-australia_2264745.html.

19. CLIVE HAMILTON, *Silent Invasion: China's Influence in Australia* (Melbourne: Hardie Grant, 2018), chap. 1.

20. Ibid.

21. Ibid.

22. Ibid.

23. Ibid., chap. 3.

24. ANNE-MARIE BRADY, "Magic Weapons: China's Political Influence Activities Under Xi Jinping," Wilson Center, September 16, 2017, https://www.wilsoncenter.org/sites/default/files/media/documents/article/magic_weapons.pdf.

25. ELEANOR AINGE ROY, "'I'm Being Watched': Anne Marie Brady, the China Critic Living in Fear for Beijing," The Guardian, January 22, 2019, https://www.theguardian.com/world/2019/jan/23/im-being-watched-anne-marie-brady-the-china-critic-living-in-fear-of-beijing.

26. BRADY, "Magic Weapons."

27. LIN TINGHUI 林廷輝, "Long zai mosheng de haiyu: Zhongguo dui Taipingyang daoguo waijiao zhi kunjing" 龍在陌生海域：中國對太平洋島國外交之困境 ["The Dragon in Strange Waters: China's Diplomatic Quagmire in the Pacific Islands"], Journal on International Relations, issue 30, p. 58, https://diplomacy.nccu.edu.tw/download.php?filename=451_b9915791.pdf&dir=archive&title=File. [In Chinese]

28. BEN BOHANE, "The US Is Losing the Pacific to China," The Wall Street Journal, June 7, 2017, https://www.wsj.com/articles/the-u-s-is-losing-the-pacific-to-china-1496853380.

29. JOSH ROGIN, "Inside China's 'Tantrum Diplomacy' at APEC," The Washington Post, November 20, 2018, https://www.washingtonpost.com/news/josh-rogin/wp/2018/11/20/inside-chinas-tantrum-diplomacy-at-apec.

30. INTERNATIONAL CRISIS GROUP, "China's Central Asia Problem," report, no. 244, February 27, 2013, https://www.crisisgroup.org/europe-central-asia/central-asia/china-s-central-asia-problem.

31. WU JIAO AND ZHANG YUNBI, "Xi Proposes a 'New Silk Road' With Central Asia," China Daily, September 8, 2013, http://www.chinadaily.com.cn/sunday/2013-09/08/content_16952160.htm.

32. RAFFAELLO PANTUCCI AND SARAH LAIN, "China's Eurasian Pivot: The Silk Road Economic Belt," Whitehall Papers 88, no. 1 (May 16, 2017): 1–6, https://www.tandfonline.com/doi/full/10.1080/02681307.2016.1274603.

33. INTERNATIONAL CRISIS GROUP, "China's Central Asia Problem."

34. KONG QUAN 孔泉, "Zhongguo zhichi Wuzibiekesitan wei guojia anquan suo zuo nuli" 中國支持烏茲別克斯坦為國家安全所做努力 ["China Supports Uzbekistan's Efforts for National Security"],

People.cn, May 17, 2005, http://world.people.com.cn/GB/8212/14450/46162/3395401.htm. [In Chinese]

35. BENNO ZOGG, "Turkmenistan Reaches Its Limits With Economic and Security Challenges," IPI Global Observatory, July 31, 2018, https://theglobalobservatory.org/2018/07/turkmenistan-limits-economic-security-challenges.

36. JAKUB JAKÓBOWSKI AND MARIUSZ MARSZEWSKI, "Crisis in Turkmenistan: A Test for China's Policy in the Region," Centre for Eastern Studies, August 31, 2018, https://www.osw.waw.pl/en/publikacje/osw-commentary/2018-08-31/crisis-turkmenistan-a-test-chinas-policy-region-0.

37. EIJI FURUKAWA, "Belt and Road Debt Trap Spreads to Central Asia," *Nikkei Asian Review*, August 29, 2018, https://asia.nikkei.com/Spotlight/Belt-and-Road/Belt-and-Road-debt-trap-spreads-to-Central-Asia.

38. "Tajikistan: Chinese Company Gets Gold Mine in Return for Power Plant," Eurasianet, April 11, 2018, https://eurasianet.org/tajikistan-chinese-company-gets-gold-mine-in-return-for-power-plant.

39. DANNY ANDERSON, "Risky Business: A Case Study of PRC Investment in Tajikistan and Kyrgyzstan," The Jamestown Foundation, *China Brief*, 18, no. 14, August 10, 2018, https://jamestown.org/program/risky-business-a-case-study-of-prc-investment-in-tajikistan-and-kyrgyzstan.

40. JUAN PABLO CARDENAL AND HERIBERTO ARAÚJO, *China's Silent Army: The Pioneers, Traders, Fixers and Workers Who Are Remaking the World in Beijing's Image*, trans. Catherine Mansfield (New York: Crown Publishing Group, 2013), chap. 2.

41. LINDSEY KENNEDY AND NATHAN PAUL SOUTHERN, "China Created a New Terrorist Threat by Repressing Secessionist Fervor in Its Western Frontier," Quartz, May 31, 2017, https://qz.com/993601/china-uyghur-terrorism.

42. XU JIN 徐進 et al., "Dazao Zhongguo zhoubian anquan de 'zhanlue zhidian' guojia" 打造中國周邊安全的「戰略支點」國家 ["Making 'Strategic Pivots' for China's Border Security"], *World Affairs 2014,* no. 15 (2014): 14–23, http://cssn.cn/jjx/xk/jjx_lljjx/sjjjygjjjx/201411/W020141128513034121053.pdf. [In Chinese]

43. THERESE DELPECH, *Iran and the Bomb: The Abdication of International Responsibility* (New York: Columbia University Press, 2007), 49.

44. CARDENAL AND ARAÚJO, *China's Silent Army*, epilogue.

45. SEYED REZA MIRASKARI et al., "An Analysis of International

Outsourcing in Iran–China Trade Relations," *Journal of Money and Economy,* vol. 8, No. 1 (Winter 2013): 110–39, http://jme.mbri.ac.ir/files/site1/user_files_10c681/admin_t-A-10-25-59-c2da06b.pdf.

46. SCOTT HAROLD AND ALIREZA NADER, *China and Iran: Economic, Political, and Military Relations* (Washington, DC: RAND Corporation, 2012), 7, https://www.rand.org/content/dam/rand/pubs/occasional_papers/2012/RAND_OP351.pdf.

47. "Raoguo 'Maliujia kunju' de shangye jichu — ruhe baozheng Zhong Mian youqi guandao youxiao yunying" 繞過「馬六甲困局」的商業基礎——如何保證中緬油氣管道有效運營 ["The Commercial Foundation to Bypass the 'Malacca Dilemma': How to Ensure the Effective Operation of the China–Myanmar Oil and Gas Pipelines"], *The First Finance Daily,* July 22, 2013, https://www.yicai.com/news/2877768.html. [In Chinese]

48. BERTIL LINTNER, "Burma and Its Neighbors," Asia Pacific Media Services, February 1992, http://www.asiapacificms.com/papers/pdf/burma_india_china.pdf.

49. "Xianzhi liangnian hou, Zhong Mian yuanyou guandao zhongyu tongkai" 閒置兩年後 中緬原油管道終於開通 ["After Two Years of Inactivity, the China–Myanmar Crude Oil Pipeline Is Finally Opened"], BBC Chinese, April 10, 2017, https://www.bbc.com/zhongwen/simp/chinese-news-39559135. [In Chinese]

50. ZHUANG BEINING 莊北甯 AND CHE HONGLIANG 車宏亮, "Zhong Mian qianshu Jiaopiao shenshuigang zhuan'an kuangjia xieding" 中緬簽署皎漂深水港專案框架協定 ["China–Myanmar Signs the Framework Agreement for the Kyaukpyu Deep-Water Port Project"], *Xinhuanet.com*, November 8, 2018, http://www.xinhuanet.com/2018-11/08/c_1123686146.htm. [In Chinese]

51. LU CHENG 鹿鋮, "Zhong Mian Jingji zoulang: Miandian fabiao de xinxing tujing" 中緬經濟走廊：緬甸發展的新興途徑 ["China–Myanmar Economic Corridor: An Emerging Approach to Myanmar's Development"], *Guangming Net,* September 17, 2018, http://news.gmw.cn/2018-09/17/content_31210352.htm. [In Chinese]

52. LIN PING 林坪, "Jiemi Zhongguo rui liliang (shiyi): Ouzhou zhengjie" 揭祕中國銳實力（十一）欧洲政界 ["Disclosing China's Sharp Power (Part XI) European Politics"], Radio Free Asia, November 5, 2018, https://www.rfa.org/mandarin/ytbdzhuantixilie/zhongguochujiao shenxiangshijie/yl-11052018102634.html. [In Chinese]

53. JASON HOROWITZ AND LIZ ALDERMAN, "Chastised by EU, a Resentful Greece Embraces China's Cash and Interests," *The New York Times,* August 26, 2017, https://www.nytimes.com/2017/08/26/world/europe/greece-china-piraeus-alexis-tsipras.html.

54. JAN VELINGER, "President's Spokesman Lashes Out at Culture Minister for Meeting With Dalai Lama," Radio Prague International, October 18, 2016, https://www.radio.cz/en/section/curraffrs/presidents-spokesman-lashes-out-at-culture-minister-for-meeting-with-dalai-lama.

55. LIN PING, "Disclosing China's Sharp Power."

56. "Deguo lanpishu: Zhongguo zai Deguo feijinrong zhijie touzi dafu zengzhang" 德國藍皮書：中國在德國非金融直接投資大幅增長 ["German Blue Book: China's Non-Financial Direct Investment in Germany Has Grown Substantially"], Sina.com.cn, July 9, 2017, http://mil.news.sina.com.cn/dgby/2018-07-09/doc-ihezpzwt8827910.shtml. [In Chinese]

57. HOOVER INSTITUTION, *Chinese Influence and American Interests: Promoting Constructive Vigilance* (Stanford, CA: Hoover Institution Press, 2018), 163, https://www.hoover.org/sites/default/files/research/docs/chineseinfluence_americaninterests_fullreport_web.pdf.

58. PHILIP OLTERMANN, "Germany's 'China City': How Duisburg Became Xi Jinping's Gateway to Europe," *The Guardian*, August 1, 2018, https://www.theguardian.com/cities/2018/aug/01/germanys-china-city-duisburg-became-xi-jinping-gateway-europe.

59. "Xilake: Re'ai Zhongguo de ren" 希拉克：熱愛中國的人 ["Chirac: A Man Who Loved China"], *China Net*, March 20, 2007, http://www.china.com.cn/international/txt/2007-03/20/content_18421202.htm. [In Chinese]

60. VARIOUS, *Di jiu zhang: Tan zhan (shang)* 第九章：貪戰（上）["Chapter 9: The War of Greed (Part I)"], in *Zhenshi de Jiang Zemin* 真實的江澤民 [*The Real Jiang Zemin*], *The Epoch Times*, June 18, 2012, http://www.epochtimes.com/b5/12/6/18/n3615092.htm. [In Chinese]

61. HOLLY WATT, "Hinkley Point: The 'Dreadful Deal' Behind the World's Most Expensive Power Plant," *The Guardian*, December 21, 2017, https://www.theguardian.com/news/2017/dec/21/hinkley-point-c-dreadful-deal-behind-worlds-most-expensive-power-plant.

62. NICK TIMOTHY, "The Government Is Selling Our National Security to China," Conservative Home, October 20, 2015, http://www.conservativehome.com/thecolumnists/2015/10/nick-timothy-the-

government-is-selling-our-national-security-to-china.html.

63. LIN PING 林坪, "Jiemi Zhongguo rui liliang (shi'er): zai Ouzhou de jingji shentou" 揭祕中國銳實力（十二）在歐洲的經濟滲透 ["Disclosing China's Sharp Power (Part XII) Economic Infiltration in Europe"], Radio Free Asia, November 12, 2018, https://www.rfa.org/mandarin/zhuanlan/zhuantixilie/zhongguochujia oshenxiangshijie/yl-11082018122750.html; "Jiemi Zhongguo rui liliang (shisan): Ouzhou xueshu, yanlun ziyou" 揭祕中國銳實力（十三）歐洲學術、言論自由 ["Disclosing China's Sharp Power (Part XIII) Encroachment on Academic Freedom and Freedom of Speech in Europe"], Radio Free Asia, November 12, 2018 [自由亞洲電台], https://www.rfa.org/mandarin/zhuanlan/zhuantixilie/zhongguochujiaosh enxiangshijie/MCIEU-11122018165706.html. [In Chinese]

64. JACK HAZLEWOOD, "China Spends Big on Propaganda in Britain ... but Returns Are Low," Hong Kong Free Press, April 3, 2016, https://www.hongkongfp.com/2016/04/03/china-spends-big-on-propaganda-in-britain-but-returns-are-low.

65. THORSTEN BENNER et al., "Authoritarian Advance: Responding to China's Growing Political Influence in Europe," Global Public Policy Institute, February 2018, https://www.gppi.net/media/Benner_MERICS_2018_Authoritarian_Advance.pdf.

66. CHRISTOPHE CORNEVIN AND JEAN CHICHIZOLA, "The Revelations of Le Figaro on the Chinese Spy Program That Targets France," Le Figaro, October 22, 2018 ["Les révélations du Figaro sur le programme d'espionnage chinois qui vise la France"], http://www.lefigaro.fr/actualite-france/2018/10/22/01016-20181022ARTFIG00246-les-revelations-du-figaro-sur-le-programme-d-espionnage-chinois-qui-vise-la-france.php. [In French]

67. "German Spy Agency Warns of Chinese LinkedIn Espionage," BBC News, December 10, 2017, https://www.bbc.com/news/world-europe-42304297.

68. SERGE MICHEL AND MICHEL BEURET, China Safari: On the Trail of Beijing's Expansion in Africa (New York: Nation Books, 2010), 162.

69. "China Is the Single Largest Investor in Africa," CGTN, May 7, 2017, https://africa.cgtn.com/2017/05/07/china-is-the-single-largest-investor-in-africa.

70. "Not as Bad as They Say," The Economist, October 1, 2011, https://www.economist.com/middle-east-and-africa/2011/10/01/not-as-bad-as-they-say.

71. JOSEPH HAMMOND, "Sudan: China's Original Foothold in Africa," *The Diplomat*, June 14, 2017, https://thediplomat.com/2017/06/sudan-chinas-original-foothold-in-africa.

72. "Beijing shengqing kuandai zao tongji de Sudan zongtong Baxier" 北京盛情款待遭通緝的蘇丹總統巴希爾 ["Beijing Shows Hospitality to the Wanted Sudanese President Bashir"], Radio France Internationale (RFI), June 29, 2011, http://cn.rfi.fr/中國/20110629-北京盛情款待遭通緝的蘇丹總統巴希爾. [In Chinese]

73. "Zhongguo de heping fazhan daolu" 中国的和平发展道路 ["China's Path of Peaceful Development"], Information Office of the State Council, http://www.scio.gov.cn/zfbps/ndhf/2005/Document/307900/307900.htm. [In Chinese]

74. PAN XIAOTAO 潘小濤, "Zhongguoren, qing zhunbei zai dasa bi" 中國人，請準備再大撒幣 ["Chinese, Get Ready to Give Out More Money"], *Apple Daily*, August 31, 2018, https://hk.news.appledaily.com/local/daily/article/20180831/20488504. [In Chinese]

75. CHEN HAIFENG 陈海峰, ed., "Shangwubu: Feizhou 33 ge zui bu fada guojia 97% de chanpin xiangshou ling guanshui" 商務部：非洲33個最不發達國家97%的產品享受零關稅 ["Ministry of Commerce: 97 Percent of Products in 33 Least-Developed Countries in Africa Enjoy Zero Tariffs"], China News, August 28, 2018, http://www.chinanews.com/gn/2018/08-28/8612256.shtml. [In Chinese]

76. JIA AO 家傲, "Zhongguo zai xiang Feizhou dasa bi, Meiguo jingjue" 中國再向非洲大撒幣美國警覺 ["China Gives Africa Big Bucks Again and America Gets Alert"], Radio Free Asia, September 3, 2018, https://www.rfa.org/mandarin/yataibaodao/junshiwaijiao/hc-09032018110327.html. [In Chinese]

77. CAI LINZHE 蔡臨哲, "Aisai'ebiya xuexi 'Zhongguo moshi'" 埃塞俄比亞學習「中國模式」["Ethiopia Is Learning the 'Chinese Model'"], Phoenix Weekly, May 15, 2013, http://www.ifengweekly.com/detil.php?id=403. [In Chinese]

78. ANDREW HARDING, "Jizhe laihong: Feizhou chu le ge 'Xin Zhongguo'" 記者來鴻：非洲出了個「新中國」["Correspondence From Our Reporters: 'A New China' in Africa"], BBC Chinese, July 27, 2015, https://www.bbc.com/ukchina/simp/fooc/2015/07/150727_fooc_ethiopia_development. [In Chinese]

79. SI YANG 斯洋, "Zhengduo huayuquan, shuchu Zhongguo moshi, Zhongguo yingxiang OuMei he YaFei fangshi da butong" 爭奪話語權，輸出中國模式，中國影響歐美和亞非方式大不同 ["To Seize

Discursive Power and Export the 'Chinese Model,' China Resorts to Different Means in Europe-America and Asia-Africa"], Voice of America, December 7, 2018, https://www.voachinese.com/a/4420434.html. [In Chinese]

80. QUAN YE 泉野, "Duihua Wang Wen: cong cheqian lun dao 'xin zhimin zhuyi' wuqu beihou de zhen wenti" 對話王文：從撒錢論到「新殖民主義」誤區背後的真問題 ["A Dialogue With Wang Wen: From the Theory of Spending Money to the Real Problem Behind the Misconstrued New Colonialism"], Duowei News, September 2, 2018, http://news.dwnews.com/china/news/2018-09-02/60081911_all.html. [In Chinese]

81. TED PICCONE, "The Geopolitics of China's Rise in Latin America," Brookings Institution, *Geoeconomics and Global Issues* 2 (November 2016), 4, https://www.brookings.edu/wp-content/uploads/2016/11/the-geopolitics-of-chinas-rise-in-latin-america_ted-piccone.pdf.

82. MEGHA RAJAGOPALAN, "China's Xi Woos Latin America With $250 Billion Investments," *Reuters,* January 7, 2015, https://www.reuters.com/article/us-china-latam-idUSKBN0KH06Q20150108.

83. ALFONSO SERRANO, "China Fills Trump's Empty Seat at Latin America Summit," *The New York Times*, April 17, 2018, https://www.nytimes.com/2018/04/13/opinion/china-trump-pence-summit-lima-latin-america.html.

84. JORDAN WILSON, "China's Military Agreements with Argentina: A Potential New Phase in China–Latin America Defense Relations," *US–China Economic and Security Review Commission: Staff Research Report*, November 5, 2015, https://www.uscc.gov/sites/default/files/Research/China%27s%20Military%20Agreements%20with%20Argentina.pdf.

85. JIN YUSEN 金雨森, "Zhonggong jinqian waijiao kong chengwei zuihou yi gen daocao" 中共金錢外交恐成為最後一根稻草 ["The CCP's Dollar Diplomacy May Be the Last Straw"], *watchinese.com*, July 5, 2017, https://www.watchinese.com/article/2017/23053. [In Chinese]

86. "Zhonggojng ju'e jinyuan qiang Saerwaduo, yin Meiguo youlü" 中共巨額金援搶薩爾瓦多 引美國憂慮 ["The CCP's Huge Amount of Financial Aid to El Salvador Causes Anxiety for America"], NTD Television, August 22, 2018, http://www.ntdtv.com/xtr/gb/2018/08/23/a1388573.html. [In Chinese]

87. HUANG XIAOXIAO 黃瀟瀟, "La Mei he Jialebi diqu Kongzi Xueyuan da 39 suo" 拉美和加勒比地區孔子學院達39所 ["Number of Confucius Institutes in Latin America

and the Caribbeans Increases to 39"], *People.cn*, January 26, 2018, http://world.people.com.cn/n1/2018/0126/c1002-29788625.htm. [In Chinese]

88. "Pentagon Says Chinese Vessels Harassed US Ship," CNN, March 9, 2009, http://www.cnn.com/2009/POLITICS/03/09/us.navy.china/index.html.

89. BARBARA STARR, "Chinese Boats Harassed US Ship, Officials Say," CNN, May 5, 2009, http://edition.cnn.com/2009/WORLD/asiapcf/05/05/china.maritime.harassment/index.html.

90. BARBARA STARR, RYAN BROWNE, AND BRAD LENDON, "Chinese Warship in 'Unsafe' Encounter With US Destroyer, Amid Rising US-China Tensions," CNN, October 1, 2018, https://www.cnn.com/2018/10/01/politics/china-us-warship-unsafe-encounter/index.html.

91. MILITARY STRATEGY RESEARCH DEPARTMENT OF THE ACADEMY OF MILITARY SCIENCE, *Zhanlue xue* 戰略學 [*Strategic Studies*], (Beijing: Military Science Publishing House, 2013), 47. [In Chinese]

92. OFFICE OF THE SECRETARY OF DEFENSE, *Annual Report to Congress: Military and Security Developments Involving the People's Republic of China 2018* (Washington DC: US Department of Defense, May 16, 2018), 46–47, https://media.defense.gov/2018/Aug/16/2001955282/-1/-1/1/2018-china-military-power-report.pdf.

93. LAWRENCE SELLIN, "The US Needs a New Plan to Address Chinese Power in Southern Asia," The Daily Caller, June 5, 2018, https://dailycaller.com/2018/06/05/afghanistan-pakistan-america-china/.

94. PANOS MOURDOUKOUTAS, "China Will Lose The South China Sea Game," *Forbes*, July 1, 2018, https://www.forbes.com/sites/panosmourdoukoutas/2018/07/01/china-will-lose-the-south-china-sea-game/#5783cad73575.

95. MICHAEL LELYVELD, "China's Oil Import Dependence Climbs as Output Falls," Radio Free Asia, December 4, 2017, https://www.rfa.org/english/commentaries/energy_watch/chinas-oil-import-dependence-climbs-as-output-falls-12042017102429.html.

96. M. TAYLOR FRAVEL, "Why Does China Care So Much About the South China Sea? Here Are 5 Reasons," *The Washington Post*, July 13, 2016, https://www.washingtonpost.com/news/monkey-cage/wp/2016/07/13/why-does-china-care-so-much-about-the-south-china-sea-here-are-5-reasons.

97. BRAHMA CHELLANEY, "Why the South China Sea Is Critical to Security," *The Japan Times*, March 26, 2018,

https://www.japantimes.
co.jp/opinion/2018/03/26/
commentary/world-
commentary/south-china-
sea-critical-security/#.
XAnOBBNKiF1.

98. SCOTT MONTGOMERY, "Oil,
History, and the South
China Sea: A Dangerous
Mix," *Global Policy*, August
7, 2018, https://www.
globalpolicyjournal.com/
blog/07/08/2018/oil-history-
and-south-china-sea-
dangerous-mix.

99. HAL BRANDS, "China's
Master Plan: A Global
Military Threat," *The
Japan Times*, June 12, 2018,
https://www.japantimes.
co.jp/opinion/2018/06/12/
commentary/world-
commentary/chinas-master-
plan-global-military-threat/#.
W9JPPBNKj5V.

100. JOEL WUTHNOW, "China's
Other Army: The People's
Armed Police in an Era of
Reform," Center for the
Study of Chinese Military
Affairs, Institute for National
Strategic Studies, *China
Strategic Perspectives* 14
(Washington DC: National
Defense University Press,
April 2019), https://inss.ndu.
edu/Portals/82/China%20
SP%2014%20Final%20
for%20Web.pdf.

101. US DEPARTMENT OF DEFENSE,
OFFICE OF THE SECRETARY
OF DEFENSE, *Annual Report
to Congress: Military and
Security Developments
Involving the People's Republic
of China 2018*, May 16, 2018,
https://media.defense.
gov/2018/Aug/16/2001955282/-
1/-1/1/2018-china-military-
power-report.pdf.

102. DAVID E. SANGER, "US Blames
China's Military Directly for
Cyberattacks," *The New York
Times*, May 6, 2013, http://
www.nytimes.com/2013/05/07/
world/asia/us-accuses-chinas-
military-in-cyberattacks.html.

103. SHARON WEINBERGER,
"China Has Already Won
the Drone Wars," *Foreign
Policy*, May 10, 2018, https://
foreignpolicy.com/2018/05/10/
china-trump-middle-east-
drone-wars/.

104. RICK JOE, "China's Air
Force on the Rise: Zhuhai
Airshow 2018," *The Diplomat*,
November 13, 2018, https://
thediplomat.com/2018/11/
chinas-air-force-on-the-rise-
zhuhai-airshow-2018/.

105. HUANG YUXIANG 黃宇翔,
"Zhongguo wurenzhanji
jingyan Zhuhai Hangzhan
liangxiang, jiaxiang di shi
Meiguo" 中國無人戰機驚
豔珠海航展亮相假想敵
是美國 ["Chinese Drones,
Whose Target Is America,
Stun the Audience at Zhuhai
Air Show"], *Asia Weekly*,
vol. 32, issue 46 (November
25, 2018), https://www.
yzzk.com/cfm/blogger3.
cfm?id=1542252826622&
author=%E9%BB%83%
E5%AE%87%E7%BF%94.
[In Chinese]

106. Ibid.

107. PETER NAVARRO, *Crouching Tiger: What China's Militarism Means for the World* (New York: Prometheus Books, 2015).

108. STEVEN LEE MYERS, "With Ships and Missiles, China Is Ready to Challenge US Navy in Pacific," *The New York Times*, August 29, 2018, https://www.nytimes.com/2018/08/29/world/asia/china-navy-aircraft-carrier-pacific.html.

109. SAN RENXING 三人行, "Ping xuexinggongsi de mori fengkuangdu" 評血腥公司的末日瘋狂賭 ["On the Bloody Company's Mad Doomsday Gambling"], *The Epoch Times*, August 1, 2005, http://www.epochtimes.com/b5/5/8/1/n1003911.htm and http://www.epochtimes.com/b5/5/8/2/n1004823.htm [In Chinese]; and Li Tianxiao, "Shen yao Zhonggong wang, bi xian shi qi kuang" 神要中共亡 必先使其狂 ["If God Wants the CCP to Die, He Will Make It Go Mad First"], *The Epoch Times*, August 17, 2005, http://www.epochtimes.com/gb/5/8/17/n1021109.htm. [In Chinese]

110. JONATHAN WATTS, "Chinese General Warns of Nuclear Risk to US," *The Guardian*, July 15 2005, https://www.theguardian.com/world/2005/jul/16/china.jonathanwatts.

111. PILLSBURY, *The Hundred-Year Marathon*, chap. 2.

112. "Commentary Two: On the Beginnings of the Chinese Communist Party," in *Nine Commentaries on the Communist Party* (New York: Broad Press Inc., 2004), http://www.ninecommentaries.com/english-2.

113. QIAO LIANG 乔良 AND WANG XIANGSUI 王湘穗, *Chao xian zhan* 超限战 [*Unrestricted Warfare*], (Beijing: People's Liberation Army Literature and Art Press, 1999), 1, 62. [In Chinese]

114. QIAO LIANG 喬良 AND WANG XIANGSUI 王湘穗, *Chao xian zhan yu Fan chao xian zhan: Zhongguoren tichu de xin zhanzhengguan Meiguoren ruhe yingdui* 超限戰與反超限戰：中國人提出的新戰爭觀美國人如何應對 [*Unrestricted Warfare and Anti-Unrestricted Warfare: How Will the Americans Counter the New Chinese Strategy?*] (Beijing: Changjiang Literature and Art Press, 2016). [In Chinese]

115. LOUISA LIM AND JULIA BERGIN, "Inside China's Audacious Global Propaganda Campaign," *The Guardian*, December 7, 2018, https://www.theguardian.com/news/2018/dec/07/china-plan-for-global-media-dominance-propaganda-xi-jinping.

116. MAO ZEDONG 毛澤東, *Mao Zedong xinwen gongzuo wenxuan* 毛澤東新聞工作文選 [*Selected Works on Journalism*], (Beijing: Xinhua Press, 1983), 182. [In Chinese]

117. "Zhong jin pulu Zhonggong Dawaixuan haiwai kuozhang" 重金鋪路中共大外宣海外擴張 ["The CCP Spends

Big Money Expanding Its Overseas Propaganda"], Radio Free Asia, November 15, 2015, https://www.rfa.org/cantonese/news/propaganda-11052015084921.html. [In Chinese]

118. ANNE-MARIE BRADY, "China's Foreign Propaganda Machine," Wilson Center, October 26, 2015, https://www.wilsoncenter.org/article/chinas-foreign-propaganda-machine.

119. "Chinese President Xi Jinping Visits With CCTV America via Video Call," CGTN, February 19, 2016, https://america.cgtn.com/2016/02/19/chinese-president-xi-jinping-visits-with-cctv-america-via-video-call.

120. KOH GUI QING AND JOHN SHIFFMAN, "Beijing's Covert Radio Network Airs China-Friendly News Across Washington, and the World," Reuters, November 2, 2015, https://www.reuters.com/investigates/special-report/china-radio.

121. LIM AND BERGIN, "Inside China's Audacious."

122. JAMES FALLOWS, "Official Chinese Propaganda: Now Online From the WaPo!" The Atlantic, February 3, 2011, https://www.theatlantic.com/international/archive/2011/02/official-chinese-propaganda-now-online-from-the-wapo/70690.

123. DONNELLE ELLER, "Chinese-Backed Newspaper Insert Tries to Undermine Iowa Farm Support for Trump, Trade War," The Des Moines Register, September 24, 2018, https://www.desmoinesregister.com/story/money/agriculture/2018/09/24/china-daily-watch-advertisement-tries-sway-iowa-farm-support-trump-trade-war-tariffs/1412954002.

124. BETHANY ALLEN-EBRAHIMIAN, "Beijing Builds Its Influence in the American Media," Foreign Policy, December 21, 2017, https://foreignpolicy.com/2017/12/21/one-of-americas-biggest-chinese-language-newspapers-toes-beijings-party-line-china-influence-united-front.

125. "Zhan zhong jiekai hongse shentou, 142 jia haiwai Dangmei shunjian baoguang" 占中揭開紅色滲透 142家海外黨媒體瞬間曝光 ["'Occupy Central' Reveals Red Infiltration, 142 of the CCP's Overseas Media Outlets Are Disclosed"], NTD Television, October 6, 2014, http://www.ntdtv.com/xtr/gb/2014/10/06/a1143788.html. [In Chinese]

126. YUAN JIRONG 苑基榮, "Zhongguo dianshiju rebo Feizhou dalu" 中國電視劇熱播非洲大陸 ["Chinese TV Series Are Trendy in Africa"], People's Daily, January 5, 2015, https://web.archive.org/web/20160206004955if_/http://paper.people.com.cn/rmrb/html/2015-01/05/nw.D110000renmrb_20150105_3-03.htm. [In Chinese]

127. JEFFREY GIL, "Why the NSW Government Is Reviewing Its Confucius Classrooms Program," The Conversation, May 17, 2018, http://theconversation.com/why-the-nsw-government-is-reviewing-its-confucius-classrooms-program-96783.

128. ALEXANDER BOWE, "China's Overseas United Front Work: Background and Implications for the United States," US–China Economic and Security Review Commission, August 24, 2018, 5–6, https://www.uscc.gov/sites/default/files/Research/China%27s%20Overseas%20United%20Front%20Work%20-%20Background%20and%20Implications%20for%20US_final_0.pdf.

129. US CONGRESS, HOUSE, *John S. McCain National Defense Authorization Act for Fiscal Year 2019*, 115th Cong., 2nd sess., https://docs.house.gov/billsthisweek/20180723/CRPT-115hrpt863.pdf.

130. "Wei fazhan he jinbu, yu Zhongguo xieshuo tongxing — Zhongguo gaige youyi jiangzhang huodezhe qunxiang" 为发展和进步，与中国携手同行——中国改革友谊奖章获得者群像 ["Marching Forward Hand in Hand With China for Development and Progress: Vignettes of Winners of 'China Reform Friendship Medal'"], *Xinhua News*, December 18, 2018, http://www.xinhuanet.com/politics/2018-12/18/c_1123872219.htm. [In Chinese]

131. BOWE, "China's Overseas," 5–6.

132. THORSTEN BENNER et al., "Authoritarian Advance: Responding to China's Growing Political Influence in Europe," Global Public Policy Institute, February 2018, https://www.gppi.net/media/Benner_MERICS_2018_Authoritarian_Advance.pdf.

133. *Chinese Influence & American Interests: Promoting Constructive Vigilance* (Stanford, CA: Hoover Institution Press, 2018), https://www.hoover.org/sites/default/files/research/docs/chineseinfluence_americaninterests_fullreport_web.pdf.

134. US DEPARTMENT OF JUSTICE, "Patrick Ho, Former Head of Organization Backed by Chinese Energy Conglomerate, Convicted of International Bribery, Money Laundering Offenses," December 5, 2018, https://www.justice.gov/usao-sdny/pr/patrick-ho-former-head-organization-backed-chinese-energy-conglomerate-convicted.

135. NICK MCKENZIE AND ANGUS GRIGG, "China's ZTE Was Built to Spy and Bribe, Court Documents Allege," *The Sydney Morning Herald*, May 31, 2018, https://www.smh.com.au/business/companies/china-s-zte-was-built-to-spy-and-bribe-court-documents-allege-20180531-p4ziqd.html.

136. ALEXANDRA STEVENSON, et al., "A Chinese Tycoon Sought Power and Influence. Washington Responded," *The New York Times*, December 12, 2018, https://www.nytimes.com/2018/12/12/business/cefc-biden-china-washington-ye-jianming.html.

137. RONA RUI 駱亞, "Zhuanfang Chen Yonglin: Zhonggong quanmian shentou Aozhou neimu" 專訪陳用林：中共全面滲透澳洲內幕 ["Exclusive Interview With Chen Yonglin: How the Chinese Communist Party Has Thoroughly Infiltrated Australia"], *The Epoch Times*, June 19, 2017, http://www.epochtimes.com.tw/n215385. [In Chinese]

138. *Chinese Influence & American Interests*, 57–78.

139. ISAAC STONE FISH, "Huawei's Surprising Ties to the Brookings Institution," *The Washington Post*, December 7, 2018, https://www.washingtonpost.com/opinions/2018/12/08/chinese-companys-surprising-ties-brookings-institution/?utm_term=.2720ba57db52.

140. MARGARET WOLLENSAK, "Canadian, UK Universities Warned by Intelligence Agencies to Be Wary of Huawei," *The Epoch Times*, December 19, 2018, https://www.theepochtimes.com/universities-warned-to-be-wary-of-research-partnerships-with-huawei_2743679.html.

141. ZACK DORFMAN, "How Silicon Valley Became a Den of Spies," *Politico*, July 27, 2018, https://www.politico.com/magazine/story/2018/07/27/silicon-valley-spies-china-russia-219071.

142. BOWE, "China's Overseas," 10–12.

143. GAO SHAN 高山, "Zhongguo Wanda: 20 yi Meiyuan maixia Meiguo liang jia dianyinggongsi" 中國萬達：20億美元買下美國兩家電影公司 ["China's Wanda Buys Two US Film Companies for 2 Billion US Dollars"], Radio Free Asia, August 23, 2016, https://www.rfa.org/mandarin/yataibaodao/jingmao/hc-08232016102649.html. [In Chinese]

144. CUI PENG 崔鵬, "Ali yingye rugu Amlin Partners, Ma Yun touzi Sipierboge" 阿里影業入股Amblin Partners 馬雲投資斯皮爾伯格 ["Ali Pictures Invests in Amblin Partners; Ma Yun Makes Investment in Spielberg"], sohu.com, October 9, 2016, http://www.sohu.com/a/115703678_115565. [In Chinese]

145. AMY QIN AND AUDREY CARLSEN, "How China Is Rewriting Its Own Script," *The New York Times*, November 18, 2018, https://www.nytimes.com/interactive/2018/11/18/world/asia/china-movies.html.

146. BEN FRITZ AND JOHN HORN, "Reel China: Hollywood Tries to Stay on China's Good

Side," *The Los Angeles Times,* March 16, 2011, http://articles. latimes.com/2011/mar/16/ entertainment/la-et-china-red-dawn-20110316.

147. LIN PING 林坪, "Jiemi Zhongguo rui liliang (wu): Meiguo dianying yule ye" 揭秘中國銳實力（五）美國電影娛樂業 ["Disclosing China's Sharp Power (Part V) American Film and Entertainment Industries"], Radio Free Asia, September 7, 2018, https://www.rfa. org/mandarin/zhuanlan/ zhuantixilie/zhongguoch ujiaoshenxiangshijie/ yl5-09072018150445.html. [In Chinese]

148. LIN PING 林坪, "Jiemi Zhongguo rui liliang (san) Meiguo xueshu jie, gaoxiao" 揭秘中國銳實力（三）美國學術界、高校 ["Disclosing China's Sharp Power (Part III) American Universities and Academia"], Radio Free Asia, September 5, 2018, https:// www.rfa.org/mandarin/ zhuanlan/zhuantixilie/ zhongguochujiaoshenxi angshijie/yl3-09052018122139. html. [In Chinese]

149. "Ying Baoshaodang ren bei ju rujing Xianggang, Yuehanxun biao guanqie" 英保守黨人被拒入境香港 約翰遜表關切 ["British Conservatives Were Denied Entry to Hong Kong; Johnson Expresses Concern"], BBC Chinese, October 12, 2017, https://www.bbc.com/

zhongwen/trad/chinese-news-41591196. [In Chinese]

150. BOWE, "China's Overseas," 7–8.

151. WILLIAM PENTLAND, "Entrepreneurial Espionage – Made in China," *Forbes,* January 22, 2011, https:// www.forbes.com/sites/ williampentland/2011/01/22/ entrepreneurial-espionage-made-in-china/#7e0175c65207.

152. JOSHUA PHILIPP, "How Hacking and Espionage Fuel China's Growth," *The Epoch Times,* September 10, 2015, https://www.theepochtimes. com/investigative-report-china-theft-incorporated_1737917.html.

153. ANNIE WU, "What Is the 'Made in China 2025' Program That Is the Target of US Tariffs?" *The Epoch Times,* April 5, 2018, https:// www.theepochtimes.com/ what-is-the-chinese-industrial-policy-made-in-china-2025-that-is-the-target-of-us-tariffs_2485482.html.

154. HIGH-SPEED RAIL NEWS, *Gaotie Fengyun lu* 高鐵風雲錄 [*A Record of the High-speed Rail Saga*], (Changsha: Hunan Literature and Art Press, 2015). See "Di wu zhang: Zhongguo gaotie sanguo sha" 第五章中國高鐵三國殺 [Chapter 5, "China's High-Speed Rail Three Kingdom Legends"]. [In Chinese]

155. SANKEI SHIMBUN, "Japan's Transfer of Bullet Train

Technology a Mistake. China, of Course, Has Copied It," *Japan Forward*, August 18, 2017, https://japan-forward.com/japans-transfer-of-bullet-train-technology-a-mistake-china-of-course-has-copied-it.

156. PAUL MOZUR AND JANE PERLEZ, "China Bets on Sensitive US Start-Ups, Worrying the Pentagon," *The New York Times*, March 22, 2017, https://www.nytimes.com/2017/03/22/technology/china-defense-start-ups.html.

157. OFFICE OF THE UNITED STATES TRADE REPRESENTATIVE, EXECUTIVE OFFICE OF THE PRESIDENT, *Update Concerning China's Acts, Policies and Practices Related to Technology Transfer, Intellectual Property, and Innovation*, November 20, 2018, https://ustr.gov/sites/default/files/enforcemen t/301Investigations/301%20 Report%20Update.pdf, 46.

158. US DEPARTMENT OF JUSTICE, "Chinese National Who Conspired to Hack Into US Defense Contractors' Systems Sentenced to 46 Months in Federal Prison," July 13, 2016, https://www.justice.gov/opa/pr/chinese-national-who-conspired-hack-us-defense-contractors-systems-sentenced-46-months.

159. CYNTHIA MCFADDEN, ALIZA NADI, AND COURTNEY MCGEE, "Education or Espionage? A Chinese Student Takes His Homework Home to China," NBC News, July 24, 2018, https://www.nbcnews.com/news/china/education-or-espionage-chinese-student-takes-his-homework-home-china-n893881.

160. FEDERAL BUREAU OF INVESTIGATION, "Chinese Hackers Indicted," December 20, 2018, https://www.fbi.gov/news/stories/chinese-hackers-indicted-122018.

161. ZACH DORFMAN, "How Silicon Valley."

162. FEDERAL BUREAU OF INVESTIGATION, "Chinese Talent Programs," Counterintelligence Strategic Partnership Intelligence Note, SPIN: 15-007, September 2015, https://info.publicintelligence.net/FBI-ChineseTalentPrograms.pdf.

163. LAWRENCE A. TABAK AND M. ROY WILSON, "Foreign Influences on Research Integrity," Presentation at the 117th Meeting of the Advisory Committee to the Director, National Institutes of Health, December 13, 2018, https://acd.od.nih.gov/documents/presentations/12132018ForeignInfluences.pdf.

164. LEV FACHER, "NIH Report Scrutinizes Role of China in Theft of US Scientific Research," STAT, December 13, 2018, https://www.statnews.com/2018/12/13/nih-report-scrutinizes-role-of-china-in-theft-of-u-s-scientific-research.

165. JENNIFER ZENG, "Communist

China Poses Greatest Threat to US and World, Senators Told," *The Epoch Times*, updated December 17, 2018, https://www.theepochtimes.com/senate-told-communist-china-poses-greatest-threat-to-us-and-the-world_2738798.html.

166. KEITH BRADSHER, "When Solar Panels Became Job Killers," *The New York Times*, April 8, 2017, https://www.nytimes.com/2017/04/08/business/china-trade-solar-panels.html?_ga=2.20981 7942.255138535.1542571491-142437734.1525387950.

167. "Zhonghua renmin gongheguo guojia qingbao fa" 中華人民共和國國家情報法 ["The National Intelligence Law of the People's Republic of China"], National People's Congress Net, June 27, 2017, http://www.npc.gov.cn/npc/xinwen/2017-06/27/content_2024529.htm. [In Chinese]

168. US CONGRESS, SENATE, Statement of Bill Priestap Before the Committee on the Judiciary, *China's Non-Traditional Espionage Against the United States: The Threat and Potential Policy Responses,* 115th Cong., 1st sess., December 12, 2018, https://www.judiciary.senate.gov/download/12-12-18-priestap-testimony.

169. US CONGRESS, SENATE, Statement of John C. Demers Before the Committee on the Judiciary, *China's Non-Traditional Espionage Against the United States: The Threat and Potential Policy Responses,* 115th Cong., 1st sess., December 12, 2018, https://www.judiciary.senate.gov/imo/media/doc/12-12-18%20Demers%20Testimony.pdf.

170. TED CRUZ (@SenTedCruz), "Huawei is a Communist Party spy agency thinly vieled [sic] as a telecom company. Its surveillance networks span the globe & its clients are rogue regimes such as Iran, Syria, North Korea & Cuba. The arrest of Huawei's CFO Wanzhou Meng in Canada is both an opportunity & a challenge," Twitter, December 6, 2018, https://twitter.com/SenTedCruz/status/1070708648865861633.

171. DANIELLE CAVE, "The African Union Headquarters Hack and Australia's 5G Network," Australian Strategic Policy Institute, July 13, 2018, https://www.aspistrategist.org.au/the-african-union-headquarters-hack-and-australias-5g-network.

172. THEIS LANGE OLSEN AND CATHRINE LAKMANN, "Huawei Now on the Danish Mark: 'The Chinese Can Access Systems That Govern Our Society,'" Danish Broadcasting Corporation, December 7, 2018, https://www.dr.dk/nyheder/indland/huawei-nu-paa-dansk-sigtekorn-kineserne-kan-faa-adgang-til-systemer-der-styrer-vores. [In Danish]

173. TANG MING 唐銘, "Zhonggong haike weizhuang Falun Gong wangzhan, Mei yu Zhong zunshou guoji guize" 中共駭客偽裝法輪功網站 美籲中遵守國際規則 ["CCP Hackers Feigned Falun Gong Websites; America Calls on China to Observe International Rules"], *The Epoch Times*, March 16, 2013 [大紀元新聞網], http://www.epochtimes.com/gb/13/3/16/n3824225.htm. [In Chinese]

174. DAN LEVIN, "Couple Held in China Are Free, but 'Even Now We Live Under a Cloud'," *The New York Times*, January 1, 2017, https://www.nytimes.com/2017/01/01/world/canada/canadian-couple-china-detention.html.

175. "Peter Navarro on China's National Security Risks to US," Fox Business, December 13, 2018, https://video.foxbusiness.com/v/5979037938001/?#sp=show-clips.

176. QIAO LIANG 乔良 AND WANG XIANGSUI 王湘穗, *Unrestricted Warfare*, 61. [In Chinese]

177. ERI SUGIURA, "China's 5G a Bigger Threat Than Trade War, Says Ex-Dallas Fed Chief," Nikkei Asian Review, September 24, 2018, https://asia.nikkei.com/Economy/China-s-5G-a-bigger-threat-than-trade-war-says-ex-Dallas-Fed-chief.

178. GREGG RE, "Trump Declares Opioids From Mexico, China 'Almost a Form of Warfare,' Tells Sessions to Sue Drug Makers," Fox News, August 16, 2018, https://www.foxnews.com/politics/trump-declares-opioids-from-mexico-china-almost-a-form-of-warfare-tells-sessions-to-sue-drug-makers.

179. KIRSTEN D. MADISON, "Stopping the Poison Pills: Combating the Trafficking of Illegal Fentanyl from China," prepared statement before the Senate Caucus on International Narcotics Control, October 2, 2018, https://www.drugcaucus.senate.gov/sites/default/files/Final%20INL%20Written%20Statement%20for%20Senate%20Drug%20Caucus%20Hearing%20on%20Chinese%20Fe.._.pdf.

180. MARKOS KOUNALAKIS, "China Is Using Fentanyl in a Chemical War Against America," *McClatchy*, November 2, 2017, https://www.mcclatchydc.com/opinion/article182139386.html.

181. ANNA FIFIELD, "China's Row With Sweden Over a 'Racist' TV Skit Has Citizens Urging Boycotts of Ikea and H&M," *The Washington Post*, September 26, 2018, https://www.washingtonpost.com/world/2018/09/26/chinas-row-with-sweden-over-racist-tv-skit-has-citizens-urging-boycott-ikea-hm/?noredirect=on&utm_term=.15e1b22bc530.

182. XINMEI SHEN, "How China's Army of Online Trolls Turned on Sweden," Abacus News,

September 26, 2018, https://
www.abacusnews.com/
digital-life/how-chinas-army-
online-trolls-turned-sweden/
article/2165747.

183. PILLSBURY, *The Hundred-Year
Marathon*, introduction.

184. "How the West Got China
Wrong," *The Economist*, March
1, 2018, https://www.economist.
com/leaders/2018/03/01/
how-the-west-got-china-
wrong.

Conclusion

1. LI HONGZHI, "Pacify the
External by Cultivating the
Internal," in *Essentials for
Further Advancement*, January
5, 1996, https://www.falundafa.
org/eng/eng/jjyz24.htm.